Chasing Change
in Camden

John Shjarback

Chasing Change in Camden

Police Reform in One of America's Most Violent Cities

Foreword by J. Scott Thomson

TEMPLE UNIVERSITY PRESS
Philadelphia • Rome • Tokyo

TEMPLE UNIVERSITY PRESS
Philadelphia, Pennsylvania 19122
tupress.temple.edu

Copyright © 2025 by Temple University—Of The Commonwealth System
   of Higher Education
All rights reserved
Published 2025

Library of Congress Cataloging-in-Publication Data

Names: Shjarback, John, 1988– author | Thomson, J. Scott writer of foreword
Title: Chasing change in Camden : police reform in one of america's most
   violent cities / John Shjarback ; foreword by J. Scott Thomson.
Description: Philadelphia, Pennsylvania : Temple University Press, 2025. |
   Includes bibliographical references and index. | Summary: "The city
   stakeholders of Camden, New Jersey, dissolved the Camden Police
   Department and chartered the Camden County Police Department under new
   leadership, which embraced new reforms, technology, strategies, and
   training. This book tells the story and examines the consequences of
   this transition for Camden's police-resident relations and safety"—
   Provided by publisher.
Identifiers: LCCN 2025012695 (print) | LCCN 2025012696 (ebook) | ISBN
   9781439922767 (cloth) | ISBN 9781439922774 (paperback) | ISBN 9781439922781
   (pdf)
Subjects: LCSH: Police—New Jersey | Camden (N.J.). Police Department |
   Camden County (N.J.). Police Department | Police misconduct—New
   Jersey—Prevention | Police administration—New Jersey
Classification: LCC HV7571.N5 S48 2025 (print) | LCC HV7571.N5 (ebook)
LC record available at https://lccn.loc.gov/2025012695
LC ebook record available at https://lccn.loc.gov/2025012696

The manufacturer's authorized representative in the EU for product safety is
Temple University Rome, Via di San Sebastianello, 16, 00187 Rome RM, Italy
(https://rome.temple.edu/).
tempress@temple.edu

9 8 7 6 5 4 3 2 1

For my mother, Jane. My first teacher who set the foundation for a lifelong journey of learning and curiosity. I miss and love her beyond belief.

Contents

	Foreword	ix
	Acknowledgments	xiii
1.	Introduction	1
2.	A City Transformed	12
3.	Reform Efforts and the Decision to Dissolve and Rebuild	26
4.	The Newly Formed CCPD	44
5.	CCPD's Impact	60
6.	CCPD's Course Correction	78
7.	Did the Changes Take?	97
8.	Next Frontiers and Broader Police Reform Efforts	107
9.	Expanding the Narrow Focus on Public Safety and Economic Revitalization Efforts	120
10.	Conclusion	131
	References	137
	Index	161

Foreword

Camden, New Jersey, is a city like no other—rich in history and resilient in spirit. It has been home to iconic institutions like Campbell's Soup, RCA, and the New York Shipyard. Today, Camden is home to the NBA's 76ers, Subaru, and a vanguard of global clean energy production Holtec International. My connection to this city runs deep, stretching back over a century. It is here that I began my career as a street cop, patrolling neighborhoods in what was once known as the nation's most dangerous city. Over the years, I rose through the ranks, eventually becoming the youngest police chief in the Camden Police Department's 141-year history at just thirty-six years old.

I had the unique opportunity to lead two different police departments within the same city. When the Camden Police Department was dismantled, a new force, the Camden County Police Department (CCPD), was formed in 2013—the first of its kind in modern American history. My career spanned over twenty-five years, with many of those years spent in leadership roles, including eleven as chief. I dedicated my adult life to Camden's people, striving to provide them with the basic level of safety and security that so many other communities take for granted but had been absent in Camden for nearly five decades. Throughout this journey, like many city cops, I encountered the depths of human suffering and the heights of human resilience. The heart-wrenching wails of a mother discovering the loss of her child continue to haunt me to this day but often remind me of the importance of the work that needed to be done.

Policing in Camden presented extreme challenges. The deep economic disadvantages faced by its residents led to complex social issues that demanded a nuanced approach to law enforcement. High crime rates, poverty, and systemic inequality were just a few of the seemingly intractable problems that had become normalized over the years. However, despite these challenges and the reluctance of many to embrace change, Camden's community members displayed a resilience and determination that inspired those of us who served them. My tenure as chief included overseeing the transition from the Camden Police Department to the Camden County Police Department—a period marked not only by uncertainty and change but also by hope and the opportunity for reform. Although I retired in 2019, my commitment to this city remains unwavering.

Beginning in the summer of 2015, after the deaths of Michael Brown in Ferguson, Missouri, and Eric Garner in New York City, and the subsequent unrest and antipathy toward the police, Camden gained national and international attention. The city's steady reduction in crime, coupled with images of community policing—cops interacting with kids by ice cream trucks—provided a moment of pause to reconsider how to secure challenged neighborhoods and marginalized communities. In 2015, President Obama visited the Camden County Police Department's operations center to witness these "secret sauce ingredients" firsthand. He spoke with high schoolers and then addressed the nation, holding Camden up as a model for progress and a beacon that was featured in the President's Task Force on 21st Century Policing.

The CCPD's progress in reducing murders and violent crime and improving community policing was ongoing, with each year surpassing the previous fifty-year record low in crime. In 2020, the tragic murder of George Floyd by a uniformed police officer in Minneapolis once again thrust policing into the national spotlight. Camden was looked to as a model for what police reform could look like, given our efforts to dissolve and rebuild the department. Yet, despite varying degrees of coverage, much of what was written failed to capture the full story of Camden's transformation. The media's narrative often missed the complexities and nuances of what truly happened during that period. The story of Camden's policing transformation—the when, what, how, and why—remained incomplete for those eager to understand the true nature of our efforts.

This is where this book separates itself from the others. It fills in the gaps and addresses the limitations in the coverage of Camden's transition from the Camden Police Department to the Camden County Police Department, offering a comprehensive and insightful account of the events that unfolded. As I read the manuscript, I am reminded of both the successes and the shortcomings along the way. Every good leader should seek to leave things better than they found them and be honest in their assessment. This book provides a thorough analysis of Camden's history, the challenges we faced, and the innovative solutions we implemented to address them. Dr. Shjarback skillfully synthesizes complex information and conveys it with a rare clarity. His grasp of twenty-first-century policing and public safety is exceptional.

Dr. Shjarback's work is both accurate and comprehensive, covering not only the transition and early struggles—such as issues with tickets, citations, and excessive force complaints—but also the broader context of Camden's history and the challenges of modern policing. His ability to delve into the intricacies of our city's transformation, including innovative training and stricter policies, provides readers with a holistic view of Camden's evolution.

The insights offered in this book are not just for those interested in policing or public safety; they are for anyone who cares about the future of our communities and the role that law enforcement plays in shaping them. This book is a testament to the resilience of Camden and its people, as well as to the dedication and hard work of those who have served the city over the years. It is a story of hope, transformation, and the power of collaboration between law enforcement and the community.

As you read this book, I hope you gain a deeper understanding of Camden's journey and the lessons learned along the way. The challenges we faced were immense, but the progress we made is a testament to what is possible when people come together with a shared vision for a better future. Most important to me, fewer mothers are burying their sons and that should be celebrated. Camden is a city with a rich past and a promising future, and this book captures the essence of what makes it so unique.

In conclusion, I encourage you to read this book with an open mind and a willingness to learn. Dr. Shjarback has provided us with an invaluable resource, and I am grateful for his dedication to telling Camden's story with accuracy and depth. I am confident that you will find this book both enlightening and inspiring, and I am honored to have had the opportunity to be a part of Camden's history. Together, we can continue to build a safer and more prosperous future for all who call Camden home.

J. Scott Thomson

Acknowledgments

It is nearly impossible to fully articulate the impact that others have on your perspective and work. So much of a finished product is due to a multitude of different factors and individuals. I start by thanking the folks at Temple University Press: Gary Kramer, Will Forrest, and my editor, Ryan Mulligan. Ryan entrusted me with the idea behind this book, and he gave me the time and space to work through the writing and revision process. The School of Criminology and Criminal Justice at Arizona State University changed my life. The knowledge on the fifth floor of the UCENT Building is inspiring and unmatched to any other group of scholars that I have interacted with. I will forever be indebted to mentors like Mike White and Scott Decker.

I have been fortunate to collaborate with a number of colleagues and friends—Jeff Rojek, Scott Wolfe, David Pyrooz, Natalie Todak, Justin Nix, Ed Maguire, Sam Vickovic, and Weston Morrow—who have all taught me about research and writing. I am also lucky to have great former and current colleagues at the University of Texas at El Paso and in the Department of Law and Justice Studies at Rowan University, respectively.

Howard Gillette provided me with a crash course on Camden as one of the city's foremost historians. He was generous with his time and offered feedback on drafts of the first two chapters. Howard has forgotten more than most of us will ever learn about Camden and its people.

Scott Thomson kindly agreed to read this book and write its foreword. He is a true leader and was the right person to continue serving as chief for the newly created Camden County Police Department in 2013. American policing would be in better hands if more law enforcement executives, mid-level managers, and supervisors thought like Scott.

Given that much of my secondary analysis was retrospective, I am grateful to all of the local journalists and their papers for reporting on the city of Camden and its police department. Writers for the *Philadelphia Inquirer*, *Courier-Post*, and *Star-Ledger*/NJ.com, among others, closely followed the key developments and decisions during the 2011–2013 period of the planning and transition to and the early years of the Camden County Police Department. This book would not have been possible without local reporting.

Relatedly, New Jersey's Open Public Records Act (OPRA), which was passed and signed into law in 2002, provided access to information, measures, and data on both the Camden City and the Camden County Police Departments. OPRA helped to facilitate police reform efforts by shedding light on the extreme ticketing practices, problematic levels of use of force and excessive force complaints, and high rates of vehicle and pedestrian stops by officers during the early years of the new agency. Journalists, MuckRock, the Stanford Open Police Project, the American Civil Liberties Union of New Jersey, NJ Advance Media, and I all used OPRA to gather public records about policing in Camden. NJ Advance Media, in particular, spent sixteen months filing 506 public records requests in order to collect 72,677 use of force reports from every municipal police department and the state police. Their *Force Report*, which I used and relied on, covered police use of force measures throughout New Jersey from 2012 to 2016. I thank Sadaf Hashimi for providing and assisting with the raw data from *The Force Report*. The book could not have been written in this way without OPRA. Unfortunately, the state legislature amended and overhauled OPRA in 2024 in what many experts believe will limit access to government records—thus, potentially threatening accountability and transparency.

I thank the people of Camden and the community members, activists, nonprofits, and volunteers in the city. They fight for input, feedback, equality, and opportunity and are coproducers of public safety. Similarly, I extend my appreciation to those in law enforcement who earnestly strive to protect the individuals and communities that are most marginalized.

I must acknowledge that it is a privilege to study issues of violence and its correlates rather than to experience them firsthand. Likewise, it is a privilege to analyze and commentate on policing compared to actually doing it. It is often a thankless and almost-impossible job. I am fortunate to know and interact with a number of police "pracademics" who straddle both the profession and academia with skill. Steve Bishopp, Bill Walsh, Ivonne Roman, Obed Magny, Renee Mitchell, to name a few, have all provided me with much needed perspective that I would not possess otherwise.

Thank you to all my friends and extended family who have supported me along the way.

My mom and dad afforded me every conceivable opportunity to succeed throughout life. Several lifetimes are needed to repay the debt that I owe them. My mom tragically passed away during the revisions process before this book was officially accepted and published. As one of my biggest champions, she would have loved to read it. I also thank my sister Kim.

To my daughters, Selina and Viviana. May you grow up in and inherit a society that is less violent and far more equal. All of what I do is for the both of you.

And, to my wife, best friend, and life partner, Stefania, I would be nothing professionally or personally without your support and companionship. I love you.

JOHN SHJARBACK

Chasing Change in Camden

1

Introduction

American policing experienced an inflection point in 2020. Despite the national attention placed on the profession in the summer of 2014 following several deadly force incidents—such as those against Michael Brown in Ferguson, Missouri, and Eric Garner in New York—the events from the spring and summer of 2020 reignited calls for police accountability and reform. They awakened the national consciousness on issues of race and policing like few other times in our country's history—rivaling the civil rights movement in the 1960s and the fallout from the beating of Rodney King in the 1990s. Although movements inspired by police killings were gathering momentum even before that point, particularly the fatal shooting of Breonna Taylor by officers in Kentucky's Louisville Metro Police Department during a botched search warrant in March of that year, the spark that lit the flame occurred over Memorial Day weekend in Minneapolis, Minnesota.

Officers were dispatched to Cups Foods regarding a customer trying to use a counterfeit $20 bill on May 25 (BBC News, 2020). Two Minneapolis Police Department officers—Thomas Lane and J. Alexander Kueng—arrived to find the suspect of the alleged forgery, George Floyd, in the driver seat of a vehicle. After being ordered out of the car, Floyd was arrested and handcuffed for attempting to pass the counterfeit bill but resisted being placed in the police squad car. Two additional officers—Derek Chauvin and Tou Thao—joined shortly thereafter. Following a continued struggle to force Floyd into the car, Chauvin brought him to the ground and bystanders began videotaping the incident on their cell phones. Officer Derek Chauvin can be seen kneeling on Floyd's neck for almost nine minutes while Floyd was face down on his stomach, still handcuffed, and repeatedly yelling, "I can't breathe." Chauvin continued to kneel on Floyd's neck for several minutes after Floyd became unresponsive; the other three officers failed to intervene even though they had a professional and moral duty to do so. George Floyd was later pronounced dead at the hospital. The Hennepin County Medical Examiner ruled his death a homicide, and all four officers were fired, criminally charged, and, ultimately, convicted.

The cell phone video shows arguably one of the most disturbing and egregious deaths in police custody ever recorded. Disturbing and egregious because there is little-to-no defensible training or policy argument to justify the officers' actions or lack thereof. The incident set off a summerlong series of protests and demonstrations across the United States and the globe. From May 26, the day after Floyd was killed and when the video was disseminated on traditional and social media, through the end of August, more than 7,750 Black Lives Matter–associated demonstrations took place across more than 2,440 locations in all fifty states and Washington, DC (U.S. Crisis Monitor, 2020; see also Crowd Counting Consortium, 2020). Violence, specifically police-citizen clashes, looting, and the destruction of property, occurred in more than 200 of these locations including Minneapolis, New York City, Atlanta, Dallas, Louisville, Seattle, Philadelphia, and Washington, DC. The scale of the unrest and disorder matched, if not exceeded, the tumultuous times in the 1960s during the civil rights movement (National Advisory Commission on Civil Disorders, 1968).

Juxtaposed against the confrontations between police and protesters in those two hundred–plus cities, Camden, New Jersey, stood out and received an overwhelming amount of attention and praise. Not only did the citizens and police of Camden manage to keep protests and demonstrations peaceful following the death of George Floyd; an iconic image surfaced of Chief Joe Wysocki of the Camden County Police Department (CCPD), among other officers, marching alongside and holding a banner that read "Standing in Solidarity" with Black Lives Matter community activists. The event was organized by Yolanda Deaver, a city resident and salon owner (Landergan, 2020). During the protest and march, Chief Wysocki sought out Deaver and asked for permission to join her. She obliged, creating the photo opportunity that would later go viral. Many pondered how Camden—a deeply impoverished minority-majority city with, historically, some of the country's highest rates of violent crime and past police-community tension—was able to achieve such peace when so many others places, including Philadelphia, which sits right across the Delaware River, exploded with violent police-citizen clashes, looting, tear gas, and the destruction of property (Gammage, Rushing, & Graham, 2020).

The events of the summer of 2020 had a tremendous impact on the public perception of law enforcement, and they created momentum for an unprecedented amount of reform talks and proposed legislation to promote police accountability. Americans' confidence in the institution of policing was at a twenty-seven-year record low (Brenan, 2020), while the racial gap between white and Black Americans' confidence in police had never been wider (Jones, 2020). A total of 736 total bills, resolutions, and executive orders related to policing were introduced in forty states and Washington, DC, from May 25 through the end of 2020 (National Conference of State Legislatures, 2020), illustrating how many jurisdictions answered the protesters' calls for fundamental changes to be made in policing. The range of proposed legislation was broad in scope and addressed topics such as increasing the transparency of police records, improving commitments to data tracking, overhauling police policies and tactics, and prioritizing community-based solutions to public safety.

The most drastic reform discussions involved calls to "defund" or even "abolish" police departments. The Minneapolis City Council began talks of abolishing its police department shortly after George Floyd was killed. On June 26, the council voted unanimously to eliminate the Minneapolis Police Department in a move to establish a new vision of public safety (Romo, 2020). The ballot measure also set the foundation to create a Department of Community Safety and Violence Prevention composed of individuals with "non-law enforcement experience in community safety services, including but not limited to public health and/or restorative justice approaches" (Romo, 2020). Many in political, public policy, and academic circles contemplated whether it was possible for Minneapolis to abolish its current police department and start anew. Camden, yet again, was frequently and consistently cited since they dissolved their old police department and rebuilt a new one from ground up seven years prior. Could this city hold the key?

Camden, New Jersey

Camden is no stranger to violent crime, police reform, or the national spotlight regarding both its public safety failures and its successes. Facing bankruptcy, a drastic reduction of sworn officers, and problems with organizational inefficiency, the city dissolved its force—the Camden Police Department (CPD)—on April 30, 2013. A new department was officially created on May 1, 2013, at the county level (the CCPD), although its jurisdiction would only include Camden city proper for the first eleven years; CCPD began providing coverage to Woodlynne—an adjacent borough with less than three thousand residents and less than a quarter-square-mile large patrolled by three full-time officers—in September 2024 (Hartman, 2024). All CPD officers were let go and needed to reapply for their positions with the CCPD by filling out a fifty-page questionnaire along with completing psychological and physical examinations. The hiring process concluded with applicants being required to pass an interview process that was created with input from the community at large (Thomson, 2020). Most, but not all, of the previous officers were rehired in the new department. The newly formed CCPD refocused their priorities and officer performance standards to align with community engagement and building trust. Officers were retrained with a focus on de-escalation, and the department created new administrative policies governing the use of force. The new training and policies stressed restraint and patience as well as the preservation of life, which Chief Scott Thomson called the Hippocratic oath of policing: "First, do no harm." The CCPD's transition was already hailed as a success just two years in when Camden received a visit from the sitting U.S. president, who highlighted the progress the city and its new police department had made. On May 18, 2015, after touring the department's facilities, President Obama (2015; see also YouTube, 2015a) made a speech at the Salvation Army Ray and Joan Kroc Corps Community Center. He began his remarks by stating:

> So I've come here to Camden to do something that might have been unthinkable just a few years ago—and that's to hold you up as a symbol of promise for the nation. . . . But just a few years ago, this city was written off as dangerous beyond redemption—a city trapped in a downward spiral. Parents were afraid to let their children play outside. Drug dealers operated in broad daylight. There weren't enough cops to patrol the streets.

President Obama was referring to what the city and its old department experienced prior to the police reform efforts. He continued:

> So two years ago, the police department was overhauled to implement a new model of community policing. They doubled the size of the force—while keeping it unionized. They cut desk jobs in favor of getting more officers out into the streets. Not just to walk the beat, but to actually get to know the residents—to set up basketball games, to volunteer in schools, to participate in reading programs, to get to know the small businesses in the area.

Crime and disorder as well as organizational performance seemed to be positively influenced by the changes made. Obama mentioned some of the comparative statistics (see Figure 1.1):

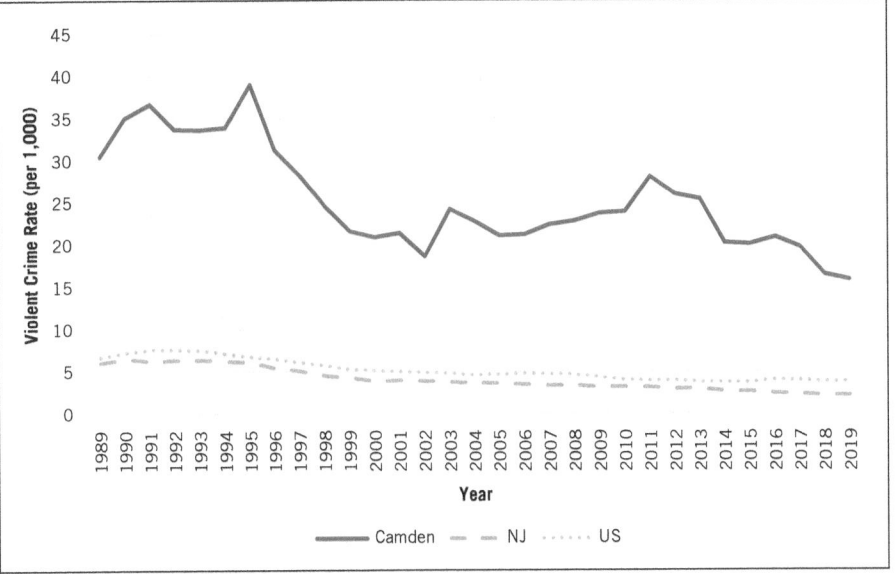

Figure 1.1 Camden, New Jersey's violent crime rate (per 1,000) over time (1989–2019). (*Note: Graph created by author using data from the FBI and NJ State Police's Uniform Crime Reporting system archive.*)

> Violent crime in Camden is down 24 percent. Murder is down 47 percent. Open-air drug markets have been cut by 65 percent. The response time for 911 calls is down from one hour to just five minutes. And when I was in the center, it was 1.3 minutes, right when I was there. And perhaps most significant is that the police and residents are building trust.

Obama concluded with the sentiment:

> But this city is on to something. You've made real progress in just two years. And that's why I'm here today—because I want to focus on the fact that other cities across America can make similar progress.

That same sentiment of praise and acclaim for the CCPD was not felt uniformly. On the same day that President Obama visited the city and made his speech, the American Civil Liberties Union of New Jersey (ACLU-NJ) issued a press release saying that policing had improved since the new department was created but concerns still remained. While agreeing with the president on a number of issues—namely, improved community policing and better relationship building, increased use of foot patrols, and a drastic reduction in response times—the ACLU-NJ (2015) also cited data that highlighted sharp increases in arrests and summonses for low-level offenses since the new police force took over. The increases included tickets for riding a bicycle without a bell, failure to adequately maintain lights or reflectors on a vehicle, disorderly conduct, and tinted car windows. The statement also expressed concern regarding the rise in excessive force complaints in 2014, and, perhaps more problematic, how the completed Internal Affairs investigations of CPD and CCPD officers had a 0% "sustained or upheld" rate since 2011 (see also Boren, 2015).

In addition to the ACLU-NJ's press release, Patrick Colligan, the president of the NJ State Policemen's Benevolent Association—the state's largest police union—wrote a scathing letter to President Obama, dated May 18, 2015, on behalf of the thirty-three thousand state, county, and local law enforcement officers represented by the organization. Among the highlights, Colligan (2015) stated:

> Mr. President, you have been misled by public relations spin and misreporting of crime statistics to believe that the Camden County Police is a success. This police department was created by union-busting tactics with the full collusion of Governor Christie and local leaders who, when crime spiked after massive officer layoffs, blamed the remaining officers instead of themselves.

He continued, "They [Camden] had a hard-working police department that was disbanded not because they couldn't fight crime but because they were deadlocked at the bargaining table." Beyond the accusations of the new department and city officials juking crime statistics to present a false sense of crime reduction, Colligan cited substantial officer turnover (e.g., "nearly 20 in April 2015 alone") due to poor pay and problematic working conditions; his high staff turnover claim has been supported by reporting from NJ.com/NJ Advance Media (Adomaitis, 2016) and the *Philadelphia Inquirer* (Boren & Wood, 2015). Therefore, the controversy surrounding whether the new CCPD was truly onto something and a model for reform dates back to 2015.

Those same competing narratives from the new department's early years were echoed in the summer and fall of 2020 (and beyond) following the murder of George Floyd and the debate surrounding the Minneapolis City Council's unanimous vote to abolish the current police department. Detailed articles on the topic with varying levels of analysis were featured in the *New York Times* (Goldstein & Armstrong, 2020), the *Washington Post* (Goldman, 2020), the *Los Angeles Times* (Megerian, 2020), National Public Radio (Doubek, 2020), and *Time* magazine (Bates & Vick, 2020), among other popular outlets with vast audiences. Camden even received international media attention from the *Guardian* (Rao, 2020) and *Aljazeera* (Newton, 2020). Much of this coverage regarding the reform efforts and subsequent impact was positive. A number of accomplishments were presented, many of which echoed the successes described during Obama's visit in 2015:

- Sixty-seven homicides in 2012, which dropped to twenty-five in 2019—a 63% reduction (Breslauer et al., 2020).
- The department made arrests in 55% of homicides in 2019, up from a clearance rate of just 16% in 2012 (Fussell, 2020).
- Substantial growth in the number of sworn police officers, from a low of 268 in 2012 to around 350–400 at any given time in the few years preceding the reporting (Everett, 2020a; see also the NJ State Police Uniform Crime Reporting archives).
- An average response time of 4.4 minutes compared to more than 60 minutes prior to the reform (Zernike, 2014).
- Sixty-five excessive force complaints in 2014 but only three in 2019 (Morgan, 2020).

As one long-form essay put it, Camden and the CCPD offered "an irresistible narrative for media outlets to explore during a summer of civil unrest and tension" (DiUlio, 2020). Another *New York Times* article headline, appearing in July 2020, read, "Could this city hold the key to the future of policing in America?" (Goldstein & Armstrong, 2020). It was precisely the question being asked among academics, journalists, law enforcement leaders, politicians, and policymakers alike.

Other publications, however, took a more nuanced approach to describing Camden's experiment with reform, detailing the complexity of the situation while attempting to differentiate the underlying reasons behind Camden's police force reconfiguration from the pressing issues raised in the wake of George Floyd (e.g., Fussell, 2020; Landergan, 2020; McQuade, 2020; see also Danley, 2020; Saul, 2020). For example, the city of Camden was nearing bankruptcy and struggled to pay for a department that benefited from a generous police union contract (Miltimore, 2020); the number of sworn officers had been dropping for years before reaching a near-record low of 268 in 2011–2012 (see Figure 1.2). It was not financially feasible for the city to continue on its current path. However, many stories highlighting the city's reform and accomplishments during the summer of 2020 either glossed over or entirely omitted mentioning the police union, specifically whether it impeded public safety and accountability in the years leading up to 2013 as well as how that union contract was essentially voided in order to create a new force (e.g., Andrew, 2020).

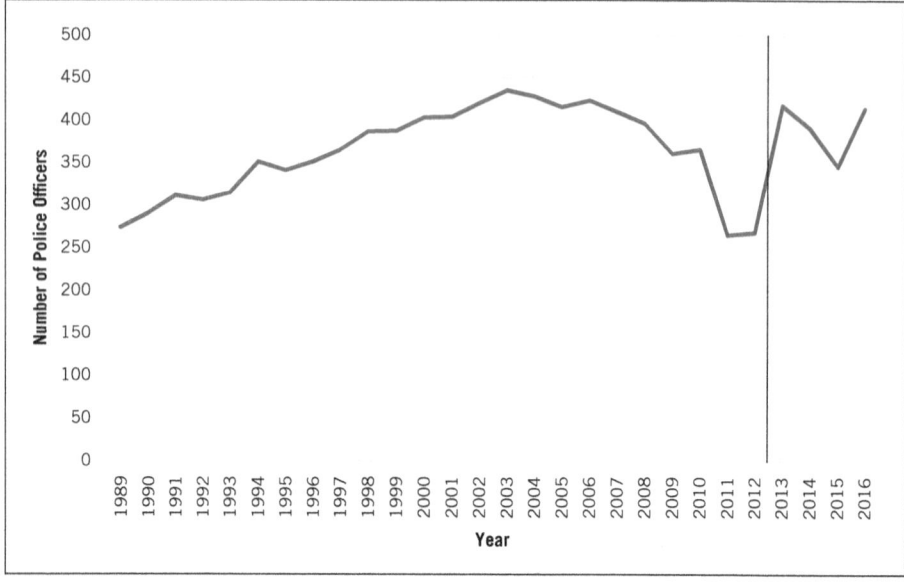

Figure 1.2 Camden, New Jersey, police officers over time (1989–2016). (*Note: Graph created by author using data from the NJ State Police's Uniform Crime Reporting system archive.*)

Much of the coverage from the summer of 2020 also ignored some of the more controversial factors that led to the crime control benefits in Camden. Some organizations and individuals, such as the representatives from the Camden County chapter of the National Association for the Advancement of Colored People (NAACP) as well as the Camden Teacher's Education Association, sounded the alarm on the concurrent rise in the excessive surveillance technology (McQuade, 2019, 2020) that accompanied the reform efforts and the role that community groups and nonprofits as well as other non–justice system actors played in crime reduction. Clearly, there are points of contention behind Camden's police reform and critical-eyed observers might fairly wonder if the successes the city experienced post-2013 can be directly attributed to its newly created department.

These alternatives and competing narratives represent the critical need for further examination since much remains unknown about Camden's experiment in police reform. There is currently an open debate as to whether true police reform was enacted and if Camden should be regarded as a model for other places to follow. It is possible that Camden is unique, and the actions taken by local politicians and community stakeholders are not applicable elsewhere—thus, limiting generalizability. By contrast, perhaps there are valuable lessons to be learned from Camden in the realm of administrative policy changes for the use of force and other areas related to discretionary officer behavior, deployment/tactical practices, training, discipline, and performance metrics signaling what is valued at the organizational level. For example, Camden collaborated with the Policing Project at New York University (NYU) School of Law to recraft the department's use of force policy by providing officers with more specificity and guidance on when and what level of force to use in response to different levels of resistance; the new use of force policy, which is eighteen pages long, was vetted and received support from both the NJ chapter of the ACLU and the new local chapter of the Fraternal Order of Police (Everett, 2019), and it articulates a number of core principles (e.g., restrictive "last resort" decisions, respecting the sanctity of life, promptly providing medical aid) and best practices from leading organizations such as the Police Executive Research Forum (PERF, 2016b). If other local jurisdictions, perhaps even state legislatures and attorney general (AG) offices, are looking toward Camden for guidance for police reform and accountability, then it is necessary to perform a rigorous empirical assessment to explore the changes (or lack thereof) that took place.

Preview of Forthcoming Chapters

As such, the purpose of this book is to conduct an in-depth case study into Camden's reform efforts, while couching it in a broader discussion of police accountability and public safety. Relying primarily on the secondary analysis of existing sources (e.g., FBI's Uniform Crime Reports; Open Public Records Act [OPRA]–requested use of force and police stops data), it provides an exploration of the substantive changes between the old and the newly created police departments as well as the CCPD's impact on crime and victimization and the Camden police's organizational performance over time. This was challenging given the lack of available data, especially when done in a retrospective manner. The broader theoretical and empirical work on restrictive administrative policies governing officer conduct, the effectiveness of an innovative police training regimen (e.g., "de-escalation"), advancements in and the diffusion of technology (e.g., acoustic gunshot detection systems [AGDS]), and evidence-based policing strategies all provide context for Camden's experience. Additionally, a number of conceptual frameworks, including the Policing Project's (2020b) "front-end versus back-end accountability" mechanisms as well as principles of democratic policing from leading accountability and professionalism scholars like Samuel Walker (1977, 1993, 2005), Lawrence Sherman (1978, 2018), Candace McCoy (2010), and the late James Fyfe (1979, 1988, 1996) help assess the reform efforts in Camden.

Chapters 2 and 3 present background information on the city of Camden and its old police department, which ended its 141-year run on April 30,

2013. More specifically, Chapter 2 provides an exhaustive overview of the study site and Camden's history. The discussion centers on deindustrialization, white flight, changing demographics, and economic shifts that led to Camden becoming one of the poorest and most dangerous cities in the country. It sets the stage for better understanding of the crucial need for police reform due to the city's functional bankruptcy and dependence on state aid to provide basic services to residents. Chapter 3 details the history of the old city department as well as its attempts and subsequent failures to reform over the years. It places a specific focus on the years 2007 through 2013 and the debates, decisions, and actions that led to the disbanding of one department and the creation of the new CCPD that officially began on May 1, 2013.

Chapters 4 through 7 detail and assess the performance of CCPD. Chapter 4, for example, examines how the new department got off the ground from a planning, financial, logistical, and operational standpoint. It explores what the new department *did* to implement change and *how* its newly adopted practices, strategies, and technologies diverged from the old city agency. Chapter 5 presents CCPD's impact on a number of different measures, including daily functions and operations (e.g., response times), crime and victimization, levels of enforcement, and citizen complaints of excessive use of force. Synthesizing and performing a secondary analysis of data, previous reports, and articles reveals that, although the CCPD made progress toward reducing rates of crime and victimization and addressing open-air drug dealing, the department and its officers also engaged in conduct that angered many in the community, which spurred activist and media attention. Chapter 6 explores CCPD's course correction—specifically, its renewed focus on de-escalation training and revising the use of force policy as well as other administrative changes—in response to the aforementioned concerns. And Chapter 7 assesses whether there was a true organizational change in the new agency—of which CCPD needed to address and reform two related aspects that were indicative of the old city agency: (1) apathy, lethargy, and an overall ineffectiveness in tackling crime, and (2) accountability.

The final three chapters look toward the future and discuss threats to the overall progress of reform and accountability efforts not only in the CCPD but in American policing more broadly. Chapter 8 outlines the CCPD's continued struggle with turnover and other workforce-related issues in the context of police officer shortages and trouble with hiring and retention nationwide. It places attention on front- versus back-end accountability mechanisms and where, specifically, law enforcement executives, policymakers, and community members and activists alike should focus their limited time and resources to maximize the greatest impact for reform and accountability.

Chapter 9 extends beyond the CCPD and policing in general to focus attention on community-based and other non–law enforcement efforts to address crime, while also describing the limitations of Camden's narrow approach toward economic revitalization. Chapter 10 provides a final synthesis and analysis, primarily weighing in on whether the dissolve and rebuild effort in the city was worth it. The chapter offers a few points of departure to hopefully serve as a springboard for future debate on issues of policing and reform as well as the best paths forward for ensuring public safety for all. If there is anything that the past five years post-Floyd has taught us, it is that the windows for addressing both police accountability and public safety are small and close quickly—especially in a hypercharged sociopolitical climate.

2

A City Transformed

> I dream'd in a dream, I saw a city invincible...
>
> —Walt Whitman, *Leaves of Grass* (1867)

"In a dream I saw a city invincible" is the official motto of Camden, NJ. It is engraved on the face of City Hill, where construction was finished in 1931, and it inspired the mural on the front cover of the book. Based on a poem by Walt Whitman—the city's most famous historical resident—the motto is as tragic as it is ironic since Camden deteriorated into one of the poorest and most violent cities in the country within a single generation. The rise and fall of Camden resembles the historic arc of many places across the country, where cities once bustling with industry and well-paying manufacturing jobs, which sustained a strong middle class, eventually fell victim to deindustrialization, outsourcing, and an exodus to the safer suburbs, beginning in the 1960s and continuing into the 1970s. This chapter serves, first, to better contextualize the city and provide a broad overview of its history to set the stage for understanding its police reform efforts of more recent years. Second, despite the familiarity of the outline of a story of postindustrial urban decline, the chapter aims to highlight how Camden's situation might have been unique from many other places that are contemplating similar reform efforts and potentially relying on the Camden model. The city was continuously unable—and still is—to meet operating budgets citywide in order to provide basic public services. Due to these issues, the State of New Jersey has subsidized Camden to make up for those tax base deficits, which includes a state takeover of the city's finances from the early 2000s through 2010—around the time when initial talks of dissolving the old police department and starting anew began.

Camden's Heyday

Camden was once one of the most productive cities in the country for its size. Howard Gillette, a professor emeritus of history at Rutgers University–Camden, best documents the growth and decline of the city. His 2005 book *Camden after the Fall: Decline and Renewal in a Post-Industrial City* is required reading for truly understanding the nuances and complexity of the city's history. Much of the information in this chapter comes from Gillette's exhaustive account and his subsequent writings about the city.

Camden's initial growth drew on its location across the Delaware River from Philadelphia—one of the leading and most influential cities during the colonial era. The city developed as an extension of Philadelphia and its ferry system that connected the two shores of the Delaware River. The late 1800s and early 1900s saw massive increases in population due to Camden's rich employment opportunities. Joseph Campbell started a canning business in the city in 1869 that was incorporated as the Campbell Soup Company in 1891 (Gillette, 2005). In 1899, the New York Ship Company opened in Camden's waterfront on the Delaware River. Tasked with building ships and other vessels for the U.S. Navy and Coast Guard, New York Ship regularly employed more than five thousand workers (Gillette, p. 18). The Victor Talking Machine Company, a recording company and phonograph manufacturer, was founded and headquartered in Camden in 1901 (Gillette, p. 18). It would later merge with the Radio Corporation of America in 1929 to become RCA Victor and continue to produce phonographs, records, radios, and other products.

But it was not just those big three that once called Camden home; a 1917 *Camden Courier* report listed a total of 365 industries located in the city, which employed fifty-one thousand people (Gillette, p. 19). The 1920 census revealed that Camden's population exceeded one hundred thousand, which placed it fifty-eighth in the country (C. Gibson, 1998). A momentous occasion in the city's history was marked in 1926 as the largest single-span suspension bridge in the world at the time—later renamed after Benjamin Franklin in 1954—opened and connected Camden to Philadelphia (Gillette, p. 19). These employment opportunities and transportation infrastructure allowed Camden to thrive as a cultural hub in the 1920s. For example, the state-of-the-art Walt Whitman Hotel opened in 1925, followed by a $1 million Stanley movie theater in 1926 and one of the nation's first Sears Department Stores in 1927 (Gillette, p. 20). It was a city on the rise that no longer stood in Philadelphia's shadow.

According to most records, Camden exhibited economic stability through the years of the Great Depression, World War II, and the 1950s. A 1937 directory of Camden enterprises suggested the city's big three companies continued to employ large segments of the population: with 5,600 working for Campbell Soup, 5,522 for New York Ship, and 13,030 for RCA Victor (Gillette, pp. 21–22). New York Ship was particularly important during the war effort when it employed more than 30,000 people at its peak and completed twenty-six major units for the Navy between December 1941 and August 1945 (Burney, 1992; New York Shipbuilding Corporation, n.d.). Camden Forge—an iron and steel company that manufactured the camshafts and propeller shafts for the engines of new sea vessels built at New York Ship—employed 1,110 workers in 1946 (Gillette, p. 22). Camden's population in the 1950 census was 124,555, and it continued its upward trajectory for another four years (Gillette, p. 42). In fact, Gillette (2005) found evidence that too much competition and business concentration in the city led to companies relocating to other places, as opposed to industries in general drying up, through the late 1950s.

Camden's population during this era, while ethnically and religiously diverse, was segregated across neighborhoods. Ethnic enclaves of Italians, Irish, Poles, Germans, Lithuanians, and Eastern European Jews clustered together in places near their various houses of worship—each with their own informal civil leaders (Gillette, p. 23). Although the Black community's presence in Camden dates back to the 1830s, the years before and during World War II saw an increased migration into the city (Gillette, p. 30). Segregation dictated much of everyday life—from schools and transportation to restaurants, recreation, and entertainment (Gillette, pp. 30–32). Steady Black employment among industrial and manufacturing jobs was generally difficult to obtain and instead was better categorized as either summer or seasonal work; those fortunate to have long-term positions usually were at the bottom of the pay scale and desirability (e.g., custodial work) (Gillette, p. 35). While Campbell Soup did have a good record of employing Black people relative to that of RCA Victor, even Campbell's segregated its restrooms by race in its new plant that opened in 1941 (Gillette, pp. 30–32). The Hispanic population, mostly Puerto Ricans, grew from 125 to approximately 6,000 during the 1950s, and they experienced a similar level of community hostility as the Black community did (Gillette, p. 56).

Gillette discusses the dichotomy between "Old Camden"—a city during a time period through the end of the 1950s when there was work and industry—and "New Camden." He summarizes the radical changes that transformed the city in the span of a generation:

> Old Camden, as it is often referred to, was never wealthy despite its considerable productivity. Its residents were overwhelmingly working people with limited access to wealth, but with considerable social capital on which to draw, enough to sustain them through difficult

times. Camden was a divided city, between different ethnic and racial groups, but its social and political institutions were sufficiently resilient to accommodate change and to assure stability. It was all the more remarkable, then, that these well-established patterns and practices could unravel in the course of only a few decades. (Gillette, 2005, p. 38)

Transition Begins in the 1960s and Continues through the 1970s

Camden's economic trajectory was solid through the 1950s and up until around 1960. The manufacturing backbone of the city held through that year. In fact, Camden reported slightly more industrial jobs in 1960 compared to 1948 (Gillette, p. 42). The tide, however, began to turn in the 1960s with the most dramatic and detrimental changes occurring in the 1970s. Broad macrosocial patterns shifted valuable resources, the tax base, and political power out of Camden City and into the surrounding suburbs—a pattern mirrored across many places in the Northeast and Midwest (see W. Wilson, 1987, 1997). A mix of suburbanization, economics, and subsequent racial strife and civil unrest combined to transform the city in a short period of time. Gillette (2005) uses historical records to detail a relatively slow post–World War II demographic shift to the suburbs compared to a boom in other places around the country. In part facilitated by the G. I. Bill, families began to move into new homes located just outside Camden in the immediate years after the war. Suburban growth was limited to those towns adjacent to the city, such as Pennsauken and Collingswood (see Figure 2.1), that had public transportation arteries in and out of Camden; Delaware Township, which was later renamed Cherry Hill, was still rural and underdeveloped with a population of only 10,538 in 1950 and did not seem to be a popular suburban destination at that time, although it grew to 31,522 by 1960 (Gillette, p. 48; Jewish Federation of Camden County, 1972).

Suburbanization grew in the 1960s, which appeared to be driven by economic factors. Camden's original big three employers in 1962—Campbell Soup, New York Ship, and RCA Victor—constituted 70% of the city's employment base (Gillette, p. 49). Unfortunately, between 1960 and 1967, twelve thousand manufacturing jobs were lost, followed by another seven thousand in the next three years—largely a result of the New York Ship Company's collapse and closure in 1967 (Gillette, p. 43). Camden's rate of jobs lost was on par with or exceeded that of other cities. Upon comparison, albeit a slightly different time period, Philadelphia lost 40% of its manufacturing jobs while Chicago, Boston, and Pittsburgh each lost more than 33% of such jobs between

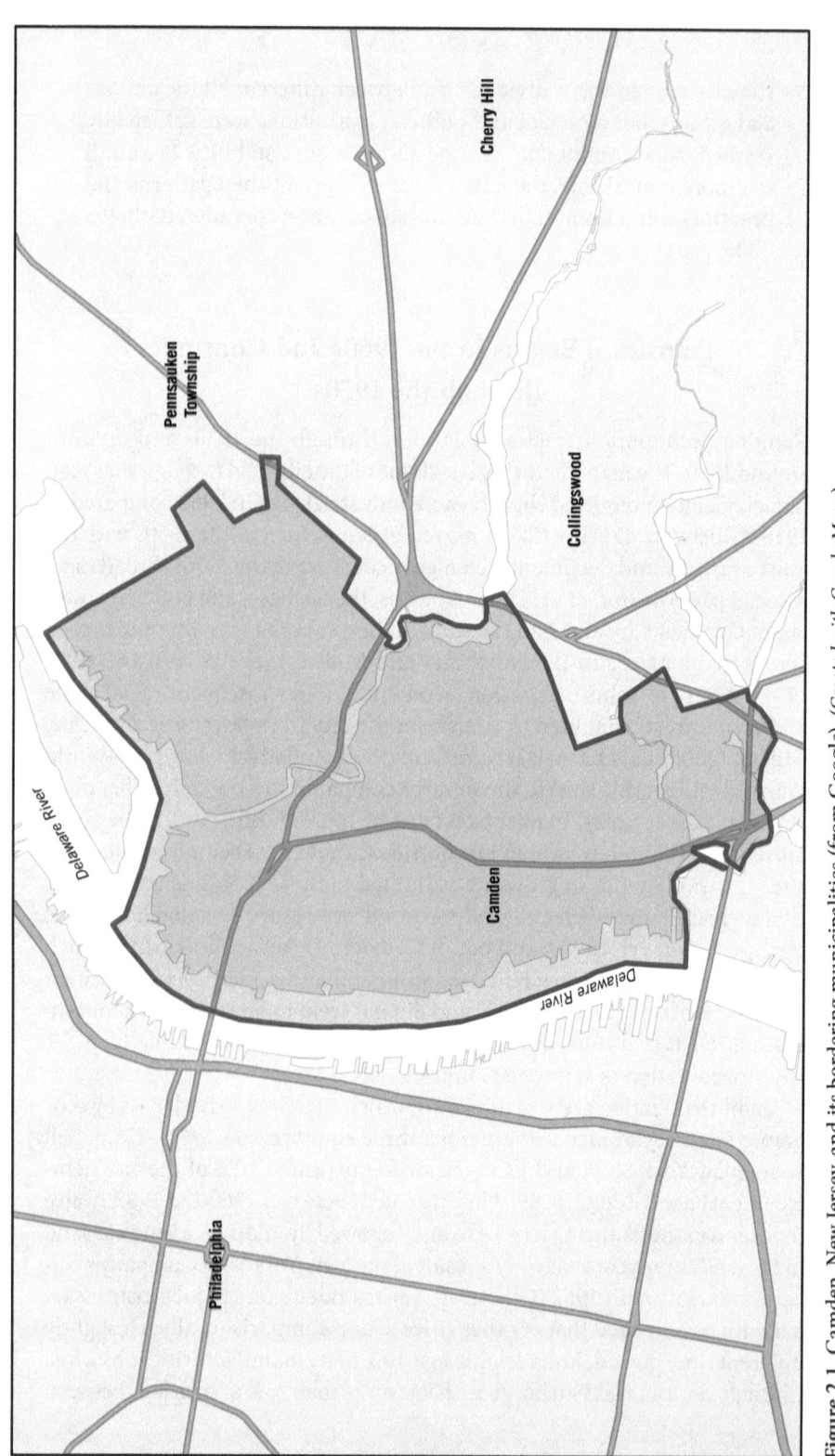

Figure 2.1 Camden, New Jersey, and its bordering municipalities (from Google). (*Created with Google Maps.*)

1967 and 1977. Deindustrialization clearly dealt Camden a debilitating misfortune: the city's manufacturing base declined by 48% in a single decade (Gillette, p. 43). An estimated twenty-eight thousand white people left the city of Camden during the 1960s (Gillette, p. 43), and, by 1970, the city was 39% Black (Gillette, p. 59).

The racial conflict and civil unrest that occurred in the city dealt a crippling blow to Old Camden. Camden was able to avoid the large-scale violent strife that affected cities across the country for most of the tumultuous 1960s. However, two separate incidents would supercharge white flight in Camden to even greater levels. While a growing civil rights movement was developing in the city with the creation of groups like the "Black People's Unity Movement" (BPUM) and "Friends of BPUM," Mayor Al Pierce and Police Chief Harold Melleby filed a lawsuit against the leader of Friends of BPUM, Sam Appel, and William Repsher, a theology student—citing that the group incited violence and conducted unlawful assemblies (Gillette, pp. 81–83). Officials managed to keep the peace until September 2, 1969—the day a grand jury indicted Appel and Repsher. While accounts differ, it is believed that police were initially attempting to arrest a man on a warrant for an assault that occurred two nights prior but were confronted by a hostile crowd of a couple hundred people in a Black neighborhood in South Camden. During the disturbance, police arrested a teenage girl after they claimed she attacked an officer with a knife, whereas the father of two teenage girls involved claimed police precipitated the violence by assaulting his daughters with blackjacks (i.e., short clubbed weapons used to strike and bludgeon). A police captain and a Black minister tried unsuccessfully to calm the crowd. Shots were fired from a rooftop, and both a twenty-two-year-old Camden police officer named Rand Chandler and an eleven-year-old Black girl were killed (Gillette, p. 83; Officer Down Memorial Page, n.d.). The shooter was never identified or apprehended.

A second event occurred in August 1971. Spawned after word of a violent arrest and hospitalization of a Puerto Rican motorist the month prior and the inaction of the police chief and mayor, three nights of fires, vandalism, and looting took place between August 19 and 21. Although the unrest consumed much of the city, the downtown commercial area along Broadway Avenue was hit particularly hard (Gillette, p. 86). Forty people were injured, and, fortunately, no one was killed. The *Courier-Post*, a newspaper based in the city at the time, reported that Camden's future never looked darker. "For sale" signs apparently sprang up all across the city. According to a grocery store owner, "You should have seen the people flying out of here. . . . There were moving trucks all over the place" (*Courier-Post*, 1971).

The 1971 riot accelerated white flight during the next decade as economic losses and racial tensions were now conflated in the public consciousness.

It sealed Camden's reputation as an undesirable place. As early as 1973, the situation was becoming dire: revenues were well short of meeting basic budgetary needs, and crime was beginning to increase (Gillette, p. 89). Mayor Angelo Errichetti described his hometown on his first day in office:

> It looked like the Vietcong bombed us to get even. The pride of Camden . . . was now a rat-infested skeleton of yesterday, a visible obscenity of urban decay. . . . The years of neglect, slumlord exploitation, tenant abuse, government bungling, indecision and short-sighted policy had transformed the city's housing, business and industrial stock into a ravaged, rat-infested cancer on a sick, old industrial city. (Gillette, p. 89; Culnan, 1979)

During the 1970s, five times as many white residents left Camden as Black people arrived—resulting in Camden becoming a majority Black city; by the end of the decade white people made up just over 30% of Camden's population. Industries fled and manufacturing jobs continued to decline. Table 2.1 presents a table depicting jobs and population in Camden for the years 1940–1982 from Gillette's book. Gillette (2005, p. 43) sums it up in his analysis, "By the end of the decade, two features stood out: Camden could no longer be considered a manufacturing center, nor was it a predominantly white working-class city." The population loss, particularly due to white flight, would have economic and political ramifications.

TABLE 2.1 JOBS AND POPULATION IN CAMDEN, 1940–1982

Year	Total jobs	Manufacturing jobs	Operatives	Total population	White	African American
1940	—	—	—	117,536	104,842	11,340
1948	57,955	38,900	—	—	—	—
1950	59,489	43,267	23,124	124,555	97,900	17,434
1954	62,564	39,500	—	—	—	—
1958	57,581	37,500	—	—	—	—
1960	58,883	39,722	18,838	117,159	89,287	27,463
1967	46,222	27,800	—	—	—	—
1970	41,588	20,671	10,324	102,305	61,303	40,132
1972	36,388	15,700	—	—	—	—
1980	27,926	—	5,983	84,910	26,003	45,009
1982	26,144	10,200	—	—	—	—

Source: U.S. census reports.
From *Camden after the Fall* by Howard Gillette Jr., Table 3, "Jobs and Population, Camden, 1940–1982," p. 42. Copyright © 2005 University of Pennsylvania Press. Reprinted with permission of the University of Pennsylvania Press.

Transfer of Power

Camden's transition during the 1960s and 1970s led to a transfer of power on a number of levels. Economically, manufacturing jobs moved from the city proper to other suburban areas in Camden County. As Camden city lost 48% of its manufacturing base in the 1960s, manufacturing jobs in the rest of the county increased by 95%; the number of such jobs in the county outside of Camden city grew from 6,184 in 1958 to 21,316 in 1970 (Gillette, p. 51; Tomlinson, 1972). In terms of regional politics, Camden experienced declining influence and found itself losing power. One-third of the county vote in 1960 came from within the city; however, it was reduced to 16% by 1980 as Cherry Hill and other towns in Camden County and South Jersey more broadly gained political strength through population growth (Gillette, p. 93). Cherry Hill's population, for one, doubled from 31,522 in 1960 to 64,390 in 1970 (Gillette, p. 48). The county's political influence over the city as well as its social and economic capital continue to this day, and they are central to the police department's reformation efforts in 2011–2013. There was also a shift toward more Black and Hispanic representation in local-level politics. Melvin "Randy" Primas became Camden's first Black mayor in 1981, following a trend of urban executives of color assuming leadership roles during an era of volatility: population decline and shrinking tax bases as well as rising crime and disorder. James Forman Jr.'s (2017) book, *Locking Up Our Own: Crime and Punishment in Black America*, details the dilemma facing many a mayor, city council, police chief, and other criminal-legal system officials who inherited challenges and societal dilemmas during this period.

FIRE SALE and Tax Failures

A declining population and shrinking tax base spelled disaster for Camden. Starting in the 1970s, the city engaged in a pattern of selling off its assets—namely its publicly owned land—and providing services for the county that other municipalities found undesirable to host in an effort to make up for huge deficits and balance the budget. At the same time, Camden continuously offered tax incentives to companies to either keep them from leaving or entice new ones to relocate to the city. Camden and, most important, its residents were generally always on the receiving end of the raw deal. Retrospectively, the city did not have much choice due to the lack of alternatives. For example, Mayor Primas, in 1982, to the dismay of many community organizations and residents, accepted an offer of $3.4 million from the state to allow the NJ Department of Corrections to build a new prison on the North Camden waterfront (Gillette, p. 103). An agreement and plans to purchase more land for a second state prison eventually fell through after successful community opposition. Still, Mayor Primas defended the second state proposal before it was, ultimately, nixed, explaining:

> I have to deal in the real world. We operate a $70 million budget and collect $11 million in property taxes. A million dollars (from both state prisons) is 38 percent of every tax dollar we collect. I have to look at that. I need revenue to run a city. I don't think a prison is as negative as people make [it] out to be. It would create jobs, create revenue and would have a positive effect on the drug problem here. It's not the solution to Camden's problems, but it's realistic. (Gillette, 2005, p. 112)

Perhaps most egregious, Camden County was looking for a location for a trash incinerator in the late 1980s. In 1989, the city sold an eighteen-acre plot of its land where the facility was to be built in exchange for $1 million (Gillette, p. 111). The funds were used to offset a $10 million budget gap during that fiscal year. Fifteen-hundred tons of garbage from the Camden County suburbs were transported each day into Camden City and turned to steam (Fedarko, 1992). Shortly after the trash incinerator became operational in March 1990, the local press reported rising cases of asthma among city children (Gillette, p. 111). The city also entered into a contract with the Camden County Municipal Utilities Authority to treat all of the suburban municipalities' waste in exchange for payment. Each day, fifty-five million gallons of raw sewage were pumped into the city while the Camden County suburbs began shutting down their own treatment plants (Fedarko, 1992).

Starting in the 1980s, the state of New Jersey began providing financial aid to Camden with stipulations for increased oversight, which gradually led to complete state takeovers of the municipal government and its functions. It began with requirements to seek state approval for all purchases over $4,500 as well as all contracts and municipal appropriations, followed by a state-appointed Financial Review Board that reviewed spending initiatives in the late 1990s (Blumgart, 2020). Such measures created an adversarial relationship between Camden and the State of New Jersey, the latter of which believed that the city never abided by the correct processes since review board members learned of spending and revenue changes from second- and thirdhand sources (Smothers, 1999). Throughout the 1990s, Camden was functionally bankrupt and relied on state aid for the vast majority—sometimes 70%—of its budget, which gradually stripped power and control away from local officials (Peterson, 2000b). Camden was unable to provide basic services for its residents. Many media reports and features exposed citizens' anger and frustration with uncollected trash, sewers backing up, and streets in complete disarray, leaving them unrepaired for years (e.g., Peterson, 2000b; *The Economist*, 2009).

A Snapshot of Social Life (1990s through the Early 2000s)

The extreme and concentrated economic disadvantage as well as the high degree of residential and racial/ethnic segregation takes a tremendous toll on the health and wellness of Camden residents. Figures from social services agencies and the U.S. Census Bureau during the 1990s and early 2000s detail a grim reality of life in Camden, particularly when compared to the neighboring suburbs and the national average on a number of metrics. In 2000, 20% of the city was unemployed with per capita income sitting at just $9,815 compared to the U.S. average of $21,587 (Gettleman, 2004). Only 51% of residents finished high school, according to the U.S. census for the year 2000 in relation to the national average of 80%, and one in twenty people in Camden (5%) had graduated from college (Gettleman, 2004; Peterson, 2000b). Nearly one-half of the city's population received public assistance, and approximately one-half of children lived in poverty through most of the 1990s and into 2000 compared to the national childhood poverty rate of 16.1% at this time (Burney, 1992; Gettleman, 2004). In 2002, 80% of children in Camden were born to single mothers, which was more than double the national average of 34% (Gettleman, 2004). And, perhaps most tragically, in the early 1990s, twenty out of every one thousand babies born in Camden did not make it to their first birthday, which was more than double the national average (Burney, 1992; Fedarko, 1992)—a figure that rose to twenty-seven per one thousand births in 1996 or three times that of the suburbs that border the city (Peterson, 2000b).

Early Reinvestment Efforts and Their Limitations

Camden's stakeholders have continuously worked to drive reinvestment in the city since the 1990s, although the majority of investment monies have been concentrated on the waterfront along the Delaware River—an area that has always been and continues to be the city's biggest asset. A new state-of-the-art aquarium opened in 1992 (now the Adventure Aquarium) with the intention of attracting visitors and improving the city's reputation. In 1995, the $40 million Sony Amphitheater (now named the Freedom Mortgage Pavilion) opened to host both outdoor concerts and indoor theatrical performances; it sits on the water with great views of the Philadelphia skyline. A particularly good year was 2001, as Campbell's Field—a six-thousand-plus seat, $25 million baseball stadium that hosted the minor league Camden Riversharks and Rutgers University–Camden teams—opened (though it was demolished in 2018), and the USS *New Jersey*, a retired navy battleship, was secured on the waterfront. Sitting in a newly constructed pier with the aid of $30 million in grant funding, the ship serves as a museum as well as host to private events like weddings, high school proms, and other group receptions.

Segments of Camden's community groups were unsupportive of the limited waterfront revitalization efforts over the past few decades, especially early on in the 1990s. For example, city residents and organizations (e.g., Concerned Citizens of North Camden) protested the opening of the aquarium, which Gillette detailed in his book. "We're paying for water that's polluted and the fish are swimming in clean water" stated Camden resident Jean Brooks. North Camden housing organizer Luis Galindez echoed that same sentiment: "The aquarium's a beautiful thing, but nobody's going to benefit from it. We got two and three families living in one house and beautiful fishes living in tanks by themselves. We could really have used that money." For context, more than seventeen hundred city homes—approximately 10% of the city's residential properties (Burney, 1992)—were vacant and abandoned at the same time that $52 million in state aid was spent on the aquarium construction (Gillette, p. 137), and, by 1996, an estimated 16% of Camden's residential properties were abandoned (Peterson, 2000b). Speaking to the *Washington Post*, Rutgers University–Camden professor emeritus of public policy and administration Michael Lang stated, "You need to do something that has a high visibility to attract people who have left the city back into the city." Lang was critical of segregating the tourist areas of Camden from the decaying residential neighborhoods: "It tends to set up an uneven development. It doesn't trickle down and filter into the lower-income neighborhoods" (Burney, 1992). City residents learned to wonder if city officials were keeping their interests in mind when those officials negotiated with outside investors—or if they saw other benefits in the deals they made on the City's behalf.

Corruption

Related to the issues of the city failing to provide basic services, three out of the five mayors of Camden were indicted on corruption-related charges from 1980 to 2000. They include Angelo Errichetti (1973–1981), Arnold Webster (1993–1997), and Milton Milan (1997–2000) (Peterson, 2000a). Milan, who was Camden's first Hispanic mayor, was convicted of fourteen corruption charges and spent nearly seven years in federal prison (Peterson, 2000c; 2001). A wave of scandals and subsequent state investigations rocked the city's public school system in the early to mid-2000s. Criminal probes focused attention on the intentional manipulation of standardized test scores and falsifying student grades as well as fraudulent spending practices in which school officials—including two principals—were indicted for stealing field trip money (Burney, 2007). While the thefts were actions of individuals, whistleblower complaints revealed a more systemic issue through the school district in which the superintendent's contract held a performance-incentive clause to earn thousands of dollars in bonuses if students' academic performance improved (Sanchez, 2006).

2002 State Takeover

The city fell under complete state control in 2002. At the time, it was the biggest city takeover in the United States since the Great Depression and the first city takeover in New Jersey state history. The state legislature passed the Municipal Rehabilitation and Economic Revitalization Act, signed by Governor Jim McGreevey, which created a chief management officer for Camden, appointed by the state, who was in charge of all city functions in exchange for facilitating a $175 million bailout plan (Gettleman, 2004). Former Camden Mayor Randy Primas served, from 2002 to 2006, as the first chief management officer. His new position granted him the power to veto the mayor and city council under the obligation of consulting with a state-selected board of local citizens and holding two public hearings each year. The state takeover relegated the positions of mayor and city council to mere figureheads—angering them—although the move was welcomed by the two major religious groups in the city: Camden Churches Organized for People and the Concerned Black Clergy (Capuzzo, 2006; Peterson, 2000b). As of December 2004, Primas already needed to take the city council to court three times for failure to carry out his directives (Gettleman, 2004). Albeit fairly comprehensive and aimed at addressing the city's concentrated poverty, the package focused heavily on tax incentives and subsidies to attract new companies and retain old ones.

Crime during This Time

From the 1990s through the early to mid-2000s, crime in Camden reached problematic levels. Figures 2.2 and 2.3 detail both the violent crime and murder rates, respectively, among the six "major urban" cities throughout New Jersey from 1990 to 2006. Camden and Newark competed for the highest violent crime rate in the state from 1990 through 1996, until 1997, when Camden retained the top spot for a decade; the city had the highest violent crime rate in the country in 2003 and 2004 among places with a population of seventy-five thousand plus (Gettleman, 2004). Camden also continued to consistently set city records for its number of murders year after year. In 1990, it was a record high of forty-four (*New York Times*, 1992), followed by fifty-one in 1992 (Nordheimer, 1995) and fifty-eight in 1995, which was nearly twice the murder rate of Newark in that year. In fact, from 1990 to 2006,

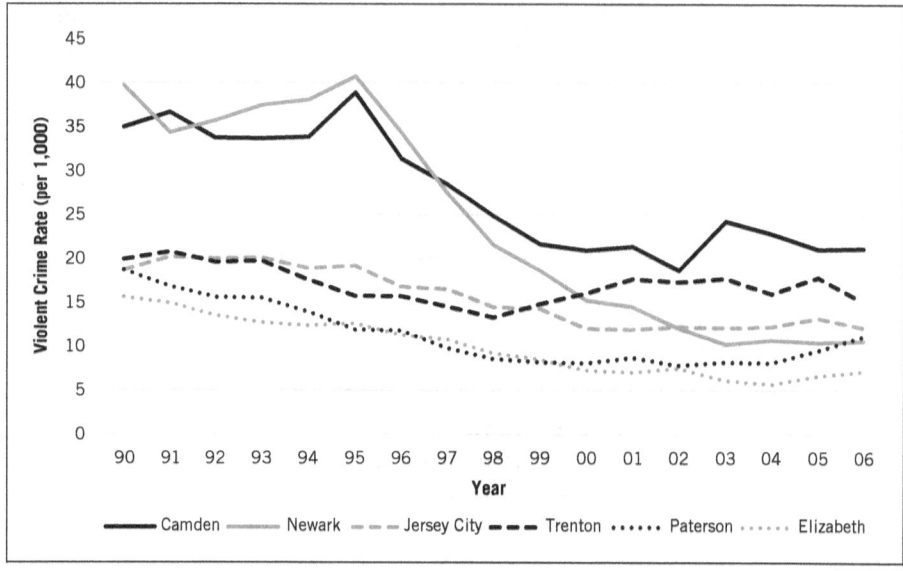

Figure 2.2 Violent crime rates (per 1,000) among New Jersey's "major urban" cities (1990–2006).

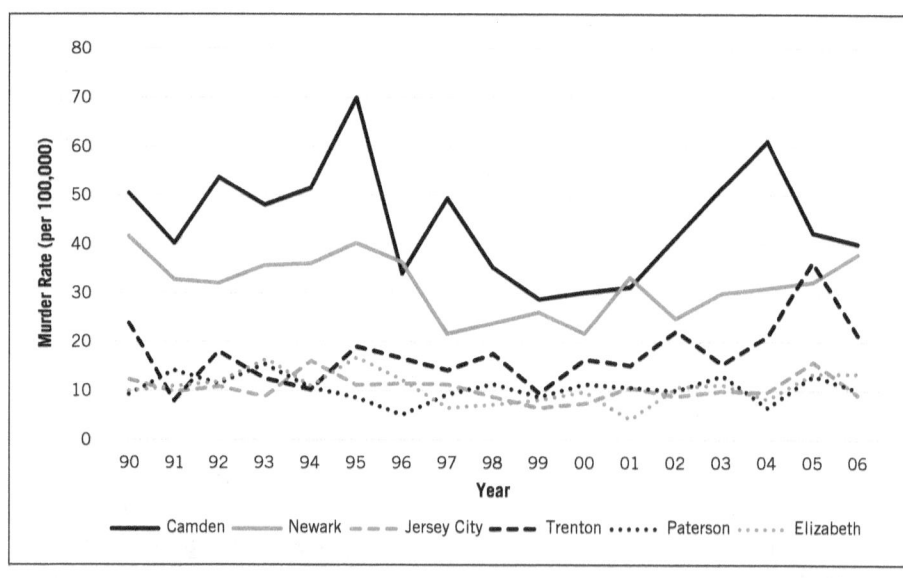

Figure 2.3 Murder rates (per 100,000) among New Jersey's "major urban" cities (1990–2006).

Camden had the highest murder rate among the six major urban cities in the state for all but two years—1996 and 2001. Police officials reported that more than two hundred open-air drug markets were located throughout the city during this era, and there were only eighty city police officers on duty at a time (Peterson, 2000b).

Setting the Stage for Police Reform

The city and its leaders were forced to make desperate financial deals—to the detriment of residents—starting in the 1980s. For decades, Camden relied heavily on state aid, to the tune of tens of millions of dollars each year, in order to balance the budget. The city struggled and largely failed to provide even basic services like trash collection and fixing potholes. Financial problems, coupled with the corruption in the Mayor's Office and the public school system, led to an unprecedented state takeover of the entire city government that began in 2002 and lasted until 2010. Such information should, hopefully, better contextualize Camden as well as the underlying conditions—including the asymmetrical power dynamics between the city, county, and state—that set the stage for the debate to disband and rebuild the city's police force between 2011 and 2013.

3

Reform Efforts and the Decision to Dissolve and Rebuild

Camden has struggled financially for decades in a postindustrial America. In addition to the city at large, the CPD also consistently experienced mismanagement dating back to the 1980s. This chapter details the history of the department and its attempts—as well as its failures—to reform over the years. It places a specific focus on 2007 through 2013, particularly the debates, decisions, and actions to disband and rebuild the department starting in 2011. The period of 2007–2010 marked a turning point: one of the most serious efforts to reform and instill accountability within the CPD. However, those efforts never quite reached their full potential due to a changing political landscape and the Great Recession but still proved crucial later. These years were virtually ignored by the vast majority of coverage and attention directed toward Camden in 2020 following the murder of George Floyd, when reformers held up the city and the CCPD as a model. Yet, the years 2007–2010 hold the key to better understanding how the CCPD came to be.

Aside from the state takeover of Camden's finances starting in 2002, the city and its police department were in a unique position due to New Jersey's state constitution and the tremendous powers afforded to the state's AG. New Jersey is one of seven states where the AG is appointed by the governor rather than elected, and the office enjoys remarkable influence over criminal justice affairs, such as all county prosecutors' offices and local policing matters. The AG's Office played a central role in Camden's police reform efforts beginning in the early 2000s.

History of Outside Intervention into Camden's Police

Both the Camden County Prosecutor's Office (CCPO) and the NJ AG's Office have regularly assisted and later intervened into CPD affairs since 1986, when then-Mayor Randy Primas voluntarily requested help (see NJ Attorney General, 2006). At that time, a review by the NJ Division of Criminal Justice within the AG's Office, primarily regarding the management and operations of the police department, yielded more than 150 recommendations to improve the quality and delivery of police services (Division of Criminal Justice, 1987). Another review of CPD's operations by the AG was conducted in 1996, which again made a slew of recommendations (Division of Criminal Justice, 1996). A subsequent AG review in 1998, to assess the progress made in implementing the 1996 recommendations, determined that the CPD had failed to meet necessary requirements. It concluded that primary response units were not properly deployed, and personnel resources were not being used effectively (Verniero, 1998). At this time, in 1998, the AG appointed the Camden County Prosecutor to serve as the "monitor" of CPD, which also followed the abrupt retirement of then-Chief William Hill after allegations of fiscal and personnel mismanagement (Capuzzo, 2006). Yet another AG review took place in 2002, which determined again that CPD had failed to make meaningful and sustainable progress in providing adequate policing services (Division of Criminal Justice, 2002). That makes four negative reviews of the department in approximately fifteen years, in addition to the county prosecutor starting to monitor it in 1998.

It was clear to the NJ AG's Office at this point that CPD was not only ineffective at addressing violence in the city but also unwilling or unable to adopt the many recommendations to basic organizational operations. In 2003, the AG took the unprecedented action of placing CPD under "supercession," which could be viewed as New Jersey's equivalent of a federal consent decree. AG Peter Harvey appointed the Camden County Prosecutor, Vincent Sarubbi, as the managing authority for CPD to oversee its operations and serve as the decision-maker for all administrative and management tasks, before the AG's Office took a more active role in the supercession (Pearce, 2003). Two years later, after Camden was named "America's most dangerous city" in 2004, Harvey created the Camden Commission on Public Safety in 2005 to "identify a strategy for moving Camden toward becoming an effective, first-class law enforcement agency" (NJ Attorney General, 2006). This commission was made up of leading regional law enforcement executives, community members, and academics, including the late Dr. George Kelling. Its final report, in 2006, offered a scathing and damning conclusion that read:

> No question remains that the Camden Police Department needs to implement major reforms if it is to become an effective, high-performing organization. . . . Without implementation of the basic reforms recommended by the Commission, the Camden Police Department will remain in a state of crisis, unable to meet the substantial policing challenges of the Camden community.

Other salient parts of the final report foreshadow the events in 2011–2013:

> The Camden Police Department is at a crossroads. It can make changes from the ground up that will impact the city and its citizens in a positive way. Or, it can stubbornly choose to remain static and thereby add to the City's ills. Of course, there can only be one choice. . . . The future, is, for the most part, in their hands.

2007–2010 with Anne Milgram and Scott Thomson

CPD's supercession continued into 2007 when Anne Milgram was officially sworn in as the NJ AG after a brief stint as the acting AG in 2006. Around that time, and following recommendations from previous reviews, the past two leaders of the CPD had been outside, civilian public safety directors. Milgram then promoted an in-house sworn police executive—Edward Hargis—to serve as interim chief: the fifth leader of the organization in five years. She has written and spoken publicly about Camden and its department (Kurlander, 2020; Milgram, 2020), describing an agency that lacked accountability due to the fact that there were no clear policies or standards; policing in the CPD was based on gut instinct and "experience" as opposed to being data driven. The CPD still incorrectly allocated a disproportionate share of resources and staffing to administrative tasks and traffic enforcement with a severe absence of officer presence in the neighborhoods where violent crime, shootings, and murder were occurring. For context, 2007 saw forty-seven homicides and 2008 was even worse with fifty-four.

Milgram detailed the difficulty of trying to implement basic reforms to the department's organizational structure and officer deployment patterns—getting more officers out on the streets at nighttime and on weekends—in 2007–2008 and meeting tremendous resistance from local politicians, the internal leadership of the department, and the police union. For example, the Traffic Unit boasted a disproportionate share of officers and resources, plus the flexibility to construct their work schedules in order to accommodate secondary employment providing uniformed security details around the city, such as the aquarium and other tourist destinations

(Kurlander, 2020). The Traffic Unit provided little, if any, support to violent crime reduction efforts, which angered the AG. Milgram confronted the chief at the time, "Chief, I can't think of any other way to say this, but you do not have a traffic problem. You have a murder problem in this city. I expect you to deploy your resources consistent with that. Are we clear?" (Kurlander, 2020). Following the failure to address the excessive resources being directed toward the Traffic Unit, Hargis eventually resigned after serving less than one year (Katz, 2008). The next interim chief that Milgram tapped to lead the CPD in 2008 would mark a turning point. Table 3.1 presents the leaders of the CPD from 2003 to 2008.

J. Scott Thomson, a deputy chief in the department at the time, was promoted to interim chief. He would become the sixth leader of the organization in five years. He was thirty-six years old with fourteen years on the job. An unlikely set of events led to Thomson even becoming named interim chief in the first place, and the preponderance of evidence suggests that Thomson—or similarly situated officers with comparable ages and years of experience—would not have gotten the job of leading the department in a normal context. Camden, like many police departments in the state of New Jersey, participates in the civil service. In addition to rigid rules that govern hiring procedures, the civil service sets the promotional practices in participating agencies. It provides the tests that officers must take if they aspire to move up in rank, which makes up a significant portion of the promotional process. Moreover, normally under civil service rules, officers must be at a certain rank to be eligible for selection in chief positions. At the time of Camden's supercession, the civil service's rules were suspended—opening the door for more freedom and flexibility in the promotional process. AG Milgram was able to bypass the regular civil service procedures and handpick her choice of interim and later official chief: Thomson.

Thomson too has written and spoken at length about his time rising through the ranks of the CPD, inheriting the job as interim chief, and the

TABLE 3.1 LEADERS OF THE CAMDEN POLICE DEPARTMENT (2003–2008)		
Name	Date of tenure	Inside or outside CPD
Robert Allenbach	1998–2004	Inside
Edwin Figueroa	2004–January 2006	Inside
Robert L. Stewart[a]	February 2006–Summer 2006	Outside[b]
Arturo Venegas Jr.[a]	Summer 2006–2007	Outside[c]
Edward Hargis	2007–2008	Inside
J. Scott Thomson	2008–on	Inside

[a] Named "supercession executives."
[b] Police captain in Washington, DC, prior to former chief of the Ormond Beach, FL, Police Department.
[c] Former chief of the Sacramento, CA, Police Department.

struggles that ensued. On a podcast in the summer of 2020 in which Milgram and Thomson recollect about 2007–2008, he explains:

> When we look at, at that point in time, the best way that I found to be able to describe the organization was that you could be the greatest cop in the world, and there were some really, really good ones, and you could also be the laziest, most corrupt cop in the world, and we certainly had them as well. Therein was the problem. There was no standard that was enforced, there were no systems of accountability to ensure that people were performing at a certain level. So the variance at which the organization operated on a daily basis was really to the individual's decision of whether they wanted to work or not when they showed up, and you would see that out on the streets as well.

Thomson continued:

> Nobody ever went over our policies and procedures. Nobody went over training. We had had five leaders in five years at that point in time. The cultural current, the flow of water, was really established by the labor union at the time, and their mindset was "Embrace the status quo. We'll circle the wagons, and we'll just outwait anyone that comes in and tries to give us direction. We'll litigate, we'll fight them and they'll be gone soon." History had shown them for that to be a successful strategy and tactic to employ. So that's what we were fighting against on that day when you put me in charge, and we turned around and tried to institute change. (Kurlander, 2020)

Thomson described an organization that was insular and did not interact much with or learn from other police departments. The CPD believed that they were experts since they dealt with some of the highest levels of violent crime and other problems plaguing economically disadvantaged urban areas. There was no frame of reference for the department to compare itself with other agencies. According to Thomson, "We didn't know what we didn't know." The department was incredibly siloed with many different specialty units that ostensibly performed similar functions—for example, both a SWAT team and a bomb squad. A significant portion of sworn officers were working Monday through Friday, 9:00 A.M.–5:00 P.M., in administrative tasks where they were indoors and behind desks as opposed to present in the community. The department had a solve rate of approximately 17% and making arrests was particularly difficult to do for homicides and shootings, which was attributed in part to mistrust and perceived illegitimacy from the community.

Thomson, under the cover and protection of AG Milgram, shook things up. Specialty units that were not contributing to crime reduction efforts, especially the aforementioned Traffic Unit, were disbanded. Officers sitting behind desks were transferred to the streets. Police presence in certain neighborhoods, previously nonexistent, was reestablished. Both Milgram and Interim Chief Thomson have reflected on how these simple changes were met with tremendous resistance. The changes disrupted the status quo and were not well received, particularly by both the police union leadership and the Camden City Council. Over a two-year period from 2008 to 2010, Thomson described how one hundred formal grievances and eight different lawsuits were filed against him (see also Arco, 2015). He has explained, "And all I was asking cops to do was get out of their squad cars and talk to people" (Arco, 2015). If not for the state oversight and the backing of the AG's Office, then it is likely that the reform efforts would have been dissolved. Thomson stated:

> When you're starting to hold people accountable, that's not welcomed with open arms. Not only did I have my own workforce that was upset about it, but I had virtually all of their relatives and friends who were in other departments throughout the city also not happy about it either. So it wasn't like I was getting support from the infrastructure within city hall in and of itself to boot, right? It was being appointed by you and having that cover, because they couldn't just. . . . If they could have just, with one council meeting, got rid of me, they would have. There's not a shadow of a doubt in my mind that would have occurred. But they couldn't because the state, the governor was providing 85% of the budget and you [Anne Milgram] were the attorney general and you had the say. (Kurlander, 2020)

The year 2008 was even worse for homicides with fifty-four compared to forty-two in 2007. But 2009 saw thirty-four homicides—a 40% year-over-year reduction. Some believed that despite still being the most violent city in the state, the tide was beginning to turn in a positive direction. AG Milgram formally appointed Thomson chief in an official capacity in 2010.

Corruption

The CPD from May 2007 to October 2009 suffered from a pocket of misconduct and corruption. Five officers in the Special Operations Unit, Fourth Platoon—an elite group tasked with addressing crime at hot spot locations—were charged with a slew of federal offenses involving depriving citizens of their civil rights. Three of the officers pled guilty in federal court, one was convicted by a jury at trial, and another was ultimately acquitted. According to a press release from the FBI and U.S. Attorney's Office of the District of New Jersey in October 2010 after one of the officers pled guilty:

> The officers conspired to deprive individuals of their due process rights by charging them with planted evidence and threatening certain individuals with arrest using planted evidence if they did not cooperate with law enforcement. The defendants are also charged with paying for cooperation and information with illegal drugs; conducting illegal searches without a search warrant or consent; and stealing money and drugs during illegal searches and arrests. The defendants also failed to report found drugs and stashed them to use as planted evidence—adding drugs to the amounts seized during arrests in order to make the arrests appear more significant and expose the targets to greater potential penalties. Additionally, the defendants used unreasonable force, unlawfully detained individuals, and prepared false police reports or testified falsely under oath to conceal their actions. (FBI, 2010)

The officers who pled guilty, including one who testified in the trial of his peer who was convicted, admitted to bogus arrests for drug possession and running from officers as well as conducting searches without warrants or consent; on between thirty and fifty occasions, they confessed, officers added drugs to the amount seized in order to make arrests seem more significant and twenty occasions when informants—particularly prostitutes—were paid with drugs in exchange for information.

The fallout from this scandal was noteworthy. Camden County Prosecutor Warren Faulk announced that 185 cases had been compromised by the officers in question and were consequently dropped (*New York Post*, 2010). Citizens claiming to be victims of the corrupt officers filed a number of lawsuits. Eventually, in January 2013, the Camden City Council approved a settlement to pay $3.5 million in damages to eighty-eight individuals whose convictions were overturned in the scandal involving the four officers who pled or were found guilty (ACLU, 2013). In addition to the $3.5 million awarded in the settlement, the city also spent millions of taxpayer dollars in legal fees. It is important to note that Chief Thomson alerted state and federal prosecutors when he was made aware of the allegations. While the egregious actions of the officers in the unit were likely not representative of the department, they indicated more systemic issues that had opened the door for the corruption to occur for approximately two and a half years. CPD's Internal Affairs unit clearly broke down due to understaffing and using antiquated systems, as a federal appellate court decision (*Forrest v. Parry*, 2019) uncovered. The ordeal certainly played a role in the dissolve and rebuild debates that would follow in 2011–2013.

The Great Recession and Governor Chris Christie

A change in state administration in 2010 reversed Camden's prospects. Governor John Corzine, a Democrat who had appointed Milgram as AG, lost his reelection bid to Republican Chris Christie, which meant she was out of the position. Christie, a former U.S. Attorney, ran on a fiscally responsible platform that included encouraging the state's five hundred-plus municipalities to consolidate or share services (Heininger, 2009), drastically cut the state budget—particularly, the Distressed City Act where financial aid closed the city's budget gaps (G. Gibson & Renshaw, 2011). It sent Camden into a downward financial spiral, which also set the stage for the 2011–2013 showdown.

Relatedly, the state of New Jersey was still reeling from the Great Recession that rocked the full United States in 2007–2009. On February 7, 2010, after being sworn in less than a month prior, Governor Christie issued an executive order declaring an unprecedented "state of fiscal emergency" in response to a projected $2.2 billion budget deficit for the remaining current fiscal year (Christie, 2010); the fiscal year in the state runs from July 1 through the following June 30. Facing yet another projected $10.7 billion shortfall for fiscal year 2011 (i.e., July 1, 2010, through June 30, 2011), Christie's administration proposed and ultimately passed a budget with massive cuts that reduced the amount of state aid to municipalities by $445 million (Arco, 2015). Camden, which had been struggling to balance its own budget and relying on state subsidies for decades, would be hit particularly hard in the next fiscal year.

In January 2011, Camden Mayor Dana Redd was forced to lay off 168 police officers—nearly half (approximately 46%) of the city's entire force (CNN, 2011; Luhby, 2011). The decision left Camden with just 204 officers—the department's smallest size since 1949 (Goldstein, 2011). Camden slashed the staffing of other city departments as well: 67 of Camden's 215 firefighters (approximately 31%) were also laid off. The layoffs were a last resort to make up for a $26.5 million budget deficit and failed negotiations between city officials and public safety unions. Mayor Redd asked for $8 million in concessions: specifically for police officers and firefighters to pay more for their health care, to freeze or reduce their salaries, and to take furlough days. To be fair and provide more context, by 2011, Camden police officers and firefighters had worked without contracts or raises since 2009 and 2008, respectively (Luhby, 2011). Homicides in the city rose to forty-seven in 2011 up from thirty-seven in 2010. Figures 3.1 and 3.2 showcase rates of both violent crime and murder, respectively, among major urban New Jersey cities from 2007 to 2012.

The state's 2012 fiscal year was not shaping up much better. During negotiations in the spring and summer of 2011, Governor Christie continued to battle New Jersey Democrats in the legislature over the budget. Christie

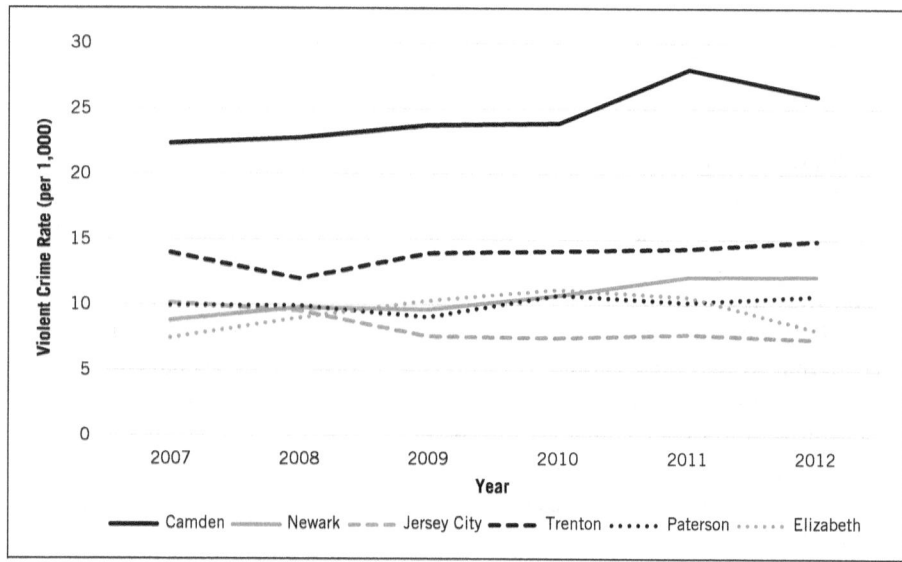

Figure 3.1 Violent crime rates (per 1,000) in New Jersey's "major urban" cities (2007–2012).

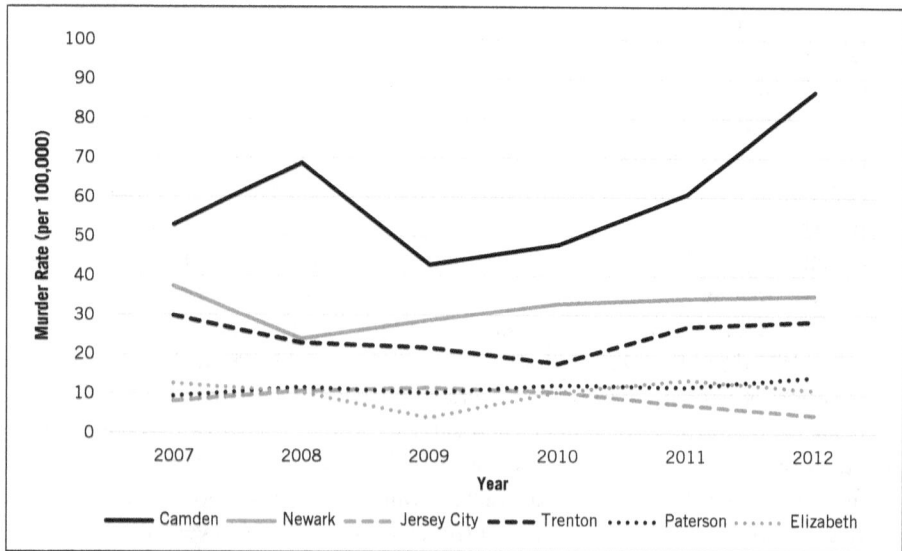

Figure 3.2 Murder rates (per 100,000) in New Jersey's "major urban" cities (2007–2012).

slashed approximately $900 million from the Democrats' spending plan—taking it from $30.6 billion to $29.7 billion—using the governor's authority of a line-item veto before signing the budget (G. Gibson & Renshaw, 2011; Renshaw, 2011). The cuts were broad and affected a multitude of areas from Medicaid to childcare and college tuition programs. State aid to distressed urban cities was substantially reduced. The transitional aid fund for the state's most distressed cities was to be scaled back from $149 million in fiscal year 2011 to $10 million in fiscal year 2012 (July 1, 2011, through June 30, 2012). That was $10 million to split between cities like Camden, Trenton, Newark, and Paterson, among others. Christie also vetoed $50 million to rehire police officers and firefighters throughout the state.

This timeline of events presents an exhaustive account of the broader financial and political context in the winter of 2011, when city and state officials debated the dissolving and rebuilding of the CPD. It was evident that the status quo, particularly financially, of Camden and its city-level police department was unsustainable. The intervening time period between early 2011 and August 2, 2012—the date when Mayor Redd formally announced plans for a new regional, countywide department—is largely a black box that can only be pieced together using public statements and local media reports, such as those from the *Philadelphia Inquirer*, *Newark Star-Ledger*, and the *Courier-Post*.

2011–2013

The plan for a regional, countywide police force to replace the Camden City Police Department was first proposed by the Camden County Board of Freeholders Director Louis Cappelli in January 2011—the same month when approximately one-half of Camden's police officers were laid off. By the end of the month, enough rumblings of a regional force led the editorial board of *The Star-Ledger* to pen a column titled, "Camden Needs Rescue from Regional Police," which expressed approval on the prospect (*The Star-Ledger*, 2011). On February 1, Camden County officials met with more than one hundred mayors and administrators as well as police and fire chiefs throughout the area to discuss their proposal (Osborne, 2011a). The meeting ended with plans to form an exploratory committee of mayors as well as police and fire chiefs to examine the utility of a county police force; that committee met several times through May 2011, where data was collected and shared. On May 23, documents from the exploratory committee leaked, including tentative timelines for dissolving the old department and creating a new countywide agency. The leaked documents created a political and media frenzy (D. Simon, 2011a). Figure 3.3 provides a timeline of relevant happenings from 2010 through 2013.

Not much is known about how the committee's plans developed over the summer of 2011. In late June 2011, Governor Christie used his line-item veto once again to drastically cut funding for the fiscal year 2012 budget (July 1, 2011–June 30, 2012). It was announced on August 2, 2011, that city, county, and state officials reached a memorandum of understanding to officially form a new regional police department with an intent to submit plans to the state for review by September 30, which is the deadline for municipalities to apply for state municipal aid (Baxter & Megerian, 2011; Vargas, 2011). The memorandum of understanding marked one of the first definitive commitments—with action—to dissolving the existing city department in exchange for a county agency. On the next day, August 3, the Camden County Board of Freeholders announced that John Timoney would be hired as a consultant for the planning of the new county police department (NBC 10 Philadelphia, 2011).

Timoney had a long career rising through the ranks of the New York Police Department (NYPD) to first deputy commissioner (i.e., second in command) under former Commissioner William Bratton before leading both the Philadelphia Police Department (PPD) as commissioner from 1998–2001 and the Miami Police Department as chief from 2003 to 2010. By many accounts, Timoney developed a reputation and was heralded as a police reformer for not only increasing accountability but also effectively reducing crime. A *New Yorker* exposé (E. Walsh, 2007) discusses several of his accomplishments at length, which include implementing data-driven, Compstat-style operations to address crime and quality of life issues as well as drastically reducing police shootings of citizens in every organization in which he was a leader. Timoney began working on a per diem basis on August 15 in which capacity he reviewed data, met with city and police officials, and visited neighborhoods in Camden (D. Simon, 2011b). Shortly thereafter, Timoney made public comments that the county should not necessarily expect a regionalized force to result in cost savings (D. Simon, 2011b). Of course, this was a major departure from one of the most consistent selling points made by Camden County officials—that such a change would cut costs and save money. In response to Timoney's comments, Camden County officials said the effort would still be worthwhile because it would increase the number of officers patrolling the streets of Camden (D. Simon, 2011b).

A few months later, on October 5, Timoney released a ten-page proposal for the new regional police department (D. Simon, 2011b). In it, he laid out his vision for the organization's structure and types of units. Perhaps the biggest takeaways included the substantial increases in overall staffing of both sworn officers and nonsworn civilian personnel—the former of which would improve the daily deployment of uniformed officers who had previously worked desk jobs. The proposal called for a change from the current reactive model to a more proactive policing style that focused on improving the quality of life for the community, an emphasis on partnerships with residents as the foundation of success as well as the establishment of a community policing division, and a completely revamped unit of command structure for operations of the new department that allowed for more flexibility for redeployments and reassignments of units to meet situational demands (see also den Heyer, 2016). Timoney's proposal also laid out his vision for a Real-Time Tactical Operations and Information Center (RT-TOIC), which included timely monitoring of crime trends as well as the ability to monitor officer deployment in the field and the use of CCTV and other surveillance cameras to conduct "virtual patrols" in target neighborhoods.

As shootings and homicides piled up over the following few months, plans remained uncertain. For example, during the first week of December, Camden City Council President Frank Moran called on Mayor Redd to press the state to send the National Guard into Camden or increase the number of NJ State Troopers assigned to the city (Osborne, 2011b). AG Paula Dow made no commitments to such actions upon visiting Camden in early December.

Finally, after months of silence, Mayor Redd announced on December 9 that she was moving forward with a county takeover of the city's police department. The announcement did not provide much detail; instead, she only mentioned that the city and county had exchanged financial information and "made notable progress" (Osborne, 2011b). Once Redd made this formal announcement, Governor Christie began publicly acknowledging how talks were underway to plan the county department (Observer, 2011). Activists and community organizations immediately started preparing petitions to create a voter referendum in the form of a ballot question—which would allow city residents to decide whether they were in favor of the county takeover (Rudolf, 2012). The year ended with forty-seven murders in the city.

Efforts were underway in early 2012 to "sell" the idea of the new county department, although they met with resistance. The Camden City clerk rejected the initial petition in February that sought to force a vote on the matter, citing technical flaws (Osborne & Simon, 2012). As of early March, Mayor Redd hosted nine community meetings where she made promotional presentations to residents (*Philadelphia Inquirer*, 2012). A newly formed activist group—Citizens' Community Committee for Public Safety—alongside the Camden Fraternal Order of Police held countermeetings with presentations outlining their opposition. On March 20, Camden County officials put out an advertisement in two local newspapers, the *Camden Courier-Post* and *Philadelphia Inquirer*, urging prospective applicants for the new department to send in their qualifications, which would be used to create an applicant

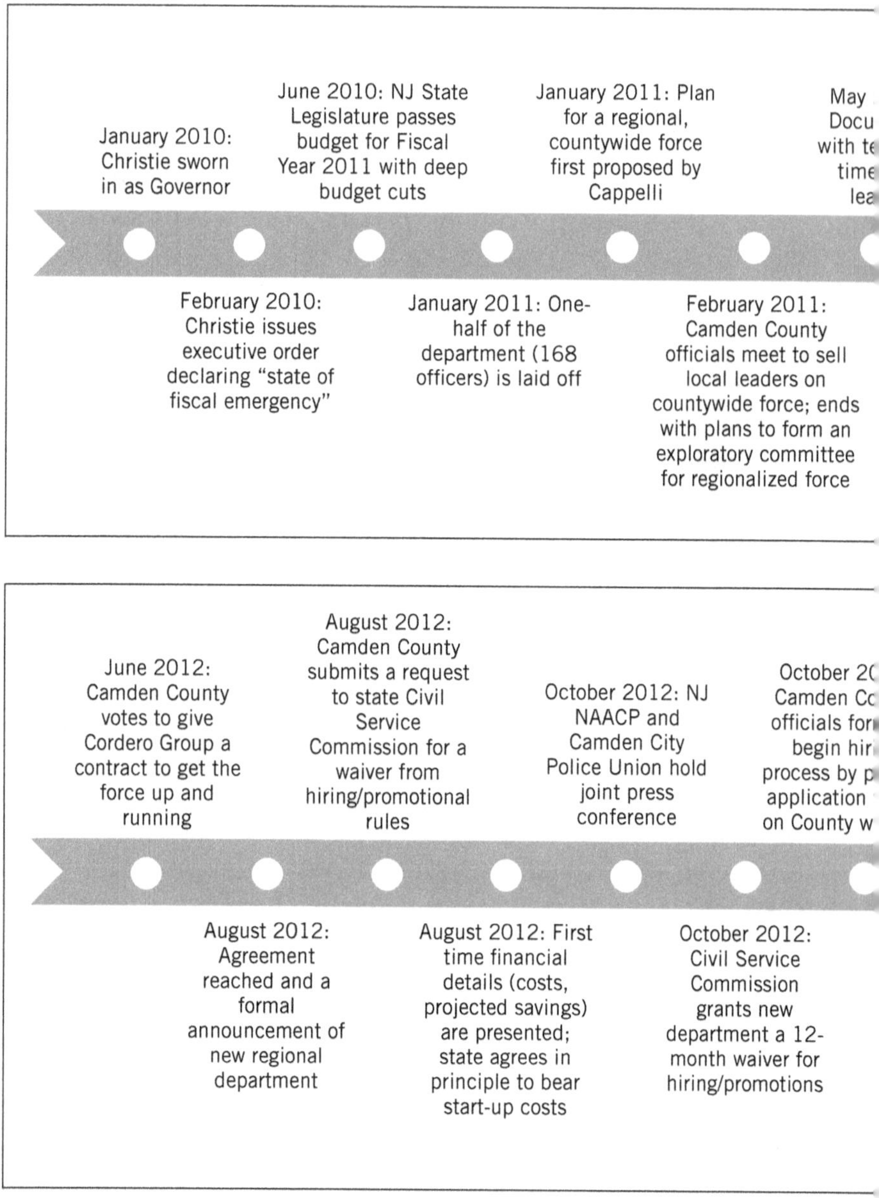

January 2010: Christie sworn in as Governor

June 2010: NJ State Legislature passes budget for Fiscal Year 2011 with deep budget cuts

January 2011: Plan for a regional, countywide force first proposed by Cappelli

May Docu with te time lea

February 2010: Christie issues executive order declaring "state of fiscal emergency"

January 2011: One-half of the department (168 officers) is laid off

February 2011: Camden County officials meet to sell local leaders on countywide force; ends with plans to form an exploratory committee for regionalized force

June 2012: Camden County votes to give Cordero Group a contract to get the force up and running

August 2012: Camden County submits a request to state Civil Service Commission for a waiver from hiring/promotional rules

October 2012: NJ NAACP and Camden City Police Union hold joint press conference

October 2012 Camden Co officials for begin hir process by p application on County w

August 2012: Agreement reached and a formal announcement of new regional department

August 2012: First time financial details (costs, projected savings) are presented; state agrees in principle to bear start-up costs

October 2012: Civil Service Commission grants new department a 12-month waiver for hiring/promotions

Figure 3.3 Timeline of relevant events from 2010 to 2013.

st 2011: ncement of andum of standing d to form regional artment

August 2011: Timoney hired as consultant for planning new department

October 2011: Timoney releases 10-page proposal for new department

December 2011: Mayor Redd announces plans to move forward with county takeover of city police force

February 2012: City clerk rejects petition to hold a ballot initiative to put question of county takeover to voters

March 2012: Camden County officials run newspaper advertisement urging potential applicants to "submit a letter of interest"

June 2012: NJ Superior Court judge rules against putting the matter before voters

---

ary 2013: den City l votes 6–1 off all city's fficers

January 2013: Camden City police officers receive layoff notices; vague promise to be hired onto new force

January 17, 2013; Camden County Police Department becomes official as County Board of Freeholders votes to establish it

January 2013: Camden's Fraternal Order of Police (FOP) members given ability to vote to approve terms to serve as the foundation of a new contract

April 30, 2013: Last day of the old Camden City Police Department (ending a 141-year run)

May 1, 2013: First official day of the Camden County Police Department

October 2013: Camden County Police Department is unionized

pool (Osborne & Simon, 2012). Opponents, meanwhile, pursued and prepared a second petition through the court system to hold a ballot question for voters in the next election that collected approximately twenty-seven hundred signatures from community members—the minimum number required by law (D. Simon, 2012a). Mayor Redd and Camden City Council President Frank Moran sued to block the petition, sending the matter to the NJ Superior Court to rule on (Maciag, 2014). Table 3.2 presents a list of those who supported, opposed, or were noncommittal to the county takeover of the police department based on public comments.

The summer of 2012 created a lot of momentum for the new department, when a legal decision dealt a huge blow to the opposition. A NJ Superior Court judge in mid-June ruled in favor of Mayor Redd and against putting the matter before city voters (Maciag, 2014; D. Simon, 2012a); however, the community and activist groups vowed to appeal that decision before the NJ Supreme Court (Blumgart, 2020). On June 21, the Camden County Board of Freeholders voted to offer a contract to a law enforcement, security, and technology consulting company: the Cordero Group (D. Simon, 2012a). The group's founder and chairman, Jose Cordero, a twenty-one-year veteran of the NYPD and with experience turning around other cities (e.g., East Orange, NJ), had assisted the CPD in 2008 during the supercession under AG Milgram. The contract paid the group approximately $20,000 per month for

TABLE 3.2 INDIVIDUALS AND GROUPS WHO SUPPORTED VERSUS OPPOSED THE COUNTY POLICE TAKEOVER		
Supported	Opposed	Noncommittal
Mayor Dana Redd	Camden Fraternal Order of Police, including President John Williamson	Camden County Prosecutor Warren Faulk
6 out of 7 city council members, including President Frank Moran		
Governor Chris Christie[a]	Brian Coleman, the sole dissenting city council member	State Police Benevolent Association spokesman Jim Ryan
Camden County Board of Freeholders Inc. Director Louis Cappelli Jr.	NJ NAACP President James Harris	
George Norcross III, businessman and Democratic Party organizer	Camden County NAACP President Colandus "Kelly" Francis	
U.S. Representative Rob Andrews of the 1st Legislative District serving Camden City and County	Select members of the Camden City Police Department[b]	
	Community groups/activists, including Citizens' Community Committee for Public Safety	

[a] Christie was the sole Republican; every other politician was a registered Democrat.
[b] Anonymous critical statements.

approximately one year—partly using money seized by the CCPO during arrests—with the goal of getting the new force up and running. Cordero assisted in creating policies, work rules, and hiring guidelines (D. Simon, 2012a; Vargas & Simon, 2013).

August was particularly notable. On August 2, an agreement was reached, and the official announcement of the new regional police department was made. Part of the announcement was that the current chief—Scott Thomson—would lead the new agency, and officials would be submitting plans to the state for review by September 30. Camden County officials submitted a request to the NJ Civil Service Commission (CSC) for a waiver from rules governing hiring and promotions (D. Simon & Vargas, 2012). August 30 marked the first time any type of financial details and projected annual savings were presented when they were sent to the *Philadelphia Inquirer*'s editorial board. County officials also announced that the state of New Jersey agreed in principle to bear the start-up costs for the new department.

Those who read it felt the financial details and projected savings announcement left a lot to be desired—putting it mildly. Media outlets and even a sitting Camden City Council member, Brian Coleman, criticized the lack of detailed explanation, documentation, and information on how Camden County officials arrived at the cost-saving figures. The announcement stated that the cost to launch the new department would be between $5 million and $6.5 million with much of these expenses going toward new police vehicles and uniforms, professional services to screen applicants, and recruitment materials (D. Simon & Vargas, 2012). It also claimed that the new department would save $14–$16 million per year by cutting out wasteful "fringe" pay to officers from the annual $60 million police budget (see also Rudolf, 2012). Camden County officials provided only brief details publicly and, it appears, to Camden's own city council. For example, the *Huffington Post* reported how a Camden County spokesman provided the outlet with a one-page email that outlined how "fringe" pay, which includes pension and health care benefits, cost $25 million in the current 2012 budget; yet, nearly 65% of these expenses would be eliminated under the new county plan (Rudolf, 2012).

There was no breakdown comparing specific categories of expenses in both the old and new departments in order to draw conclusions about whether the projected $14–$16 million in savings annually was possible. Coleman, the abovementioned city councilman, who was opposed to the new department, gave several statements to media outlets on the lack of financial transparency (D. Simon & Vargas, 2012). Speaking to the *Huffington Post*, Coleman mentioned that he tried and failed to get a full accounting of the police department's current spending, and how those planning the new police agency never provided its anticipated finances to the public or discussed them in detail with the city council. He stated, "I've asked for an explanation and requested documents, but they haven't turned them over.... The numbers don't add up. That's why they don't release them" (Rudolf, 2012). Coleman was not the only one to weigh in on the lack of financial transparency. Dr. Brendan O'Flaherty, a professor of economics at Columbia University with a research focus on urban finance, reviewed the one-page financial summary provided by the county to the *Huffington Post*—calling it "incomprehensible." According to Dr. O'Flaherty, "I don't see how anybody could have made an intelligent decision on this based on the information they've shared. It's a serious breach of normal standards of transparency" (quoted in Rudolf, 2012).

Despite this opacity, the controversial transition toward a county police department continued. On October 3, the CSC granted the new department a temporary twelve-month waiver from the traditional requirements for all hiring and promotional processes (Osborne, 2012). Such a waiver would free the new organization from the strict bounds of the CSC, a strategy previewed earlier with the hiring of interim and then full-time Chief Thomson in 2008. On October 15, Camden County officials formally began the hiring process for prospective recruits when they posted application forms on the Camden County website (D. Simon, 2012b). Resistance and opposition continued as well. The New Jersey chapter of the NAACP and CPD's Fraternal Order of Police held a joint press conference blasting the plans of a county takeover (Rudolf, 2012). The year 2012 ended with sixty-seven murders, a record high, up twenty from the forty-seven murders in 2011—a 43% increase.

New developments started quickly in 2013. On January 4, the Camden City Council voted to lay off the entire city police department in preparation for the new county department beginning in a few months. The meeting lasted two minutes with no debate before the 6–1 vote was cast (Tawa, 2013). Coleman was the lone "no" vote. All police officers, including Chief Thomson and the entire command staff, received layoff notices about a week later. County officials also released contract terms for laid off officers with a vague promise that they would all be hired onto the new force (D. Simon, 2013). The CCPD became official on January 17 when the Camden County Board of Freeholders voted to establish it; the vote also accepted the terms of a $5.5 million state grant to cover some expenses of the start-up costs, which was the first financial public commitment from Governor Christie (D. Simon, 2013; Vargas & Simon, 2013). Additionally, it was announced at this time that three senior officers in the city department would begin working on launching the new force, specifically assisting with background checks, overseeing training, and acting in supervisory roles.

In late January, the county made an offer to the Camden Fraternal Order of Police: if members approved the terms of what would serve as the foundation for a new contract under the forthcoming department, then it would "consider for hiring" all officers rather than up to the 49% that was set out by state law (D. Simon, 2013). Officers voted in favor. The next few months were hectic with hiring and the transition, which are covered in more detail in the next chapter. April 30, 2013, was the last day of the old CPD—ending its 141-year run of being controlled at the city level. May 1, 2013, marked the first official day of the CCPD—controlled by the county but only serving the jurisdiction of the city of Camden up until September 2024 when CCPD began coverage of neighboring Woodlynne (Hartman, 2024).

2015 NJ Supreme Court Ruling

In August 2015, more than two years later, the NJ Supreme Court ruled unanimously in favor of the community members and activists who proposed an ordinance to put the dissolution of the city's police force to a vote (Blumgart, 2020; Hernandez, 2015). Of course, the goal of the ordinance was to halt the county takeover and creation of the new police department. In their decision, the court ruled that the voter referendum in the form of a ballot question should have been allowed to take place during the general election in November 2012, and how the actions taken by both the city and Camden County in blocking the petition and stymieing the ordinance were illegal. However, the decision came a few years too late.

4

The Newly Formed CCPD

May 1, 2013, was the official start date of the CCPD. However, the wheels on the new operation began spinning much earlier—in late 2012 and the first few months of 2013. The purpose of this chapter is to provide an in-depth examination into how the CCPD got off the ground from a planning, financial, and logistical standpoint. New practices and technologies became a staple of the organization, so this chapter pays particular attention to the changes implemented, as both a storyline and a secondary analysis about the transition rather than an independent evaluation of each change conducted in real time. In this early period, CCPD would prove more efficient, responsive, and noticeably present throughout the city in the neighborhoods that needed it most.

Start-Up Costs and Budget

The successful creation and transition of the new CCPD hinged on clearing substantial start-up costs. The state of New Jersey provided generous funds that totaled $10 million (Queally, 2013). More specifically, the new police department would split a $5.5 million grant from the state Department of Community Affairs in the following manner: $4.3 million for salary and wages, $727,000 for twenty-eight new patrol vehicles, and $336,000 for professional services for hiring, such as background investigations and psychological tests (D. Simon, 2013). The state office of the AG also granted Camden an additional $2 million from monies seized in asset forfeiture

(D. Simon, 2013). The city of Camden would pay Camden County, which would oversee the new department, for the services with a combination of city tax dollars and state aid (Queally, 2013)—the same way the previous CPD was paid for.

The annual budget remained largely unchanged from previous years under the old department: the city of Camden would now pay Camden County approximately $62 million per year for operational costs (Maciag, 2014), although more recent estimates over the past few years put that figure around $70 million (see DiUlio, 2020). In a way, the cost-savings claims from Camden County officials that were repeated for two years (2011–2013) leading up to the new organization in support of the change never bore out; early estimates made by the likes of the late John Timoney appeared, with the benefit of hindsight, to be accurate. However, and to be fair, it seems as though the new annual budget did provide the new department with the ability to do more—both from a quantity (e.g., more officers) and quality (e.g., better technology) standpoint—with the same or a similar amount of funding. One of the most costly expenses for any organization is personnel. The old budget, for example, allowed for approximately 250 sworn officers whereas the same amount of money in the new budget allowed for over 400 sworn (Queally, 2013). Relying strictly on figures provided by a Camden County spokesperson for comparison, the average annual cost of a police officer in the old department was between $180,000 and $182,000 (Maciag, 2014; Queally, 2013). That figure was reduced by about one-half in the new department to approximately $93,000–$96,000 per officer per year. By many accounts provided, base compensation and salary remained comparable; however, some critics have claimed that CCPD officers, particularly the newly hired inexperienced ones, made significantly less money (see Colligan, 2015)—which was later confirmed (Borowski, 2024b). Personnel costs were reduced by addressing and cutting fringe benefits, overtime, shift differential pay, and the uniform allowance (Maciag, 2014; Queally, 2013; Thomson, 2020)—although more specific details on the exact financials were never provided to the public.

Hiring Process

On January 18, 2013, three senior officers, including Deputy Chief Michael Lynch, began launching the new department (D. Simon, 2013). They were tasked with overseeing training, assisting with background checks, and acting in supervisory roles. The hiring process for current city officers looking for employment in the new agency was rigorous. According to an op-ed penned in the summer of 2020 by former Chief Thompson, "Any officer who wanted to be considered for the new force, including me, had to fill out a fifty-page application, take psychological and physical tests and pass an interview process that was specifically created from community focus-group surveys about what community residents wanted in their police officers" (Thomson, 2020; see also Doubek, 2020; Oftelie, 2019).

Regarding this latter point, some community activists have taken issue with the assertion that community members have been involved in the CCPD from its inception through other critical decisions, including its new use of force policy. For example, Ojii BaBa Madi, a community activist, has argued that most community groups, such as the Concerned Black Clergy, have never been and continue to not be consulted on matters of the police department. He accuses Camden County representatives of handpicking select community members and groups that acquiesce to the department's wishes (Bauman & Chakrabarti, 2020). Police departments across the country do strategically select certain community members and groups to cultivate political capital and increase public legitimacy without sacrificing organizational independence (see Cheng, 2024).

Critically, the actual transition from the CPD to the CCPD occurred during the period from January to April 2013. The city department continued to function at this time even as the new county department was being built. The temporary headquarters during the early months of 2013 for the CCPD was a building roughly ten miles south of Camden in Blackwood, NJ. It once housed the county's youth services department. In early March, the CCPD was composed of fifteen police officers—Deputy Chief Lynch, three lieutenants, two sergeants, and nine detectives—and four administrative workers tasked with staffing and growing the new department in order for it to be ready for the turnover on May 1 (Laday, 2013a). These first fifteen officers handled the hiring process by screening applications—of which there were over 1,200 during the first few weeks of March 2013; 162 applicants were current CPD officers. More specifically, the fifteen officers conducted background checks and interviews with prospective members, while panels of retired judges as well as officers from the Camden County Sheriff and Prosecutor's Offices assisted with evaluating candidates (Laday, 2013a). Additionally, the officers prepared curriculum for a streamlined training program that included two weeks for learning the new CCPD's policies and procedures followed by hands-on field training in the beats across the city (Laday, 2013a).

Chief Thomson discussed the process of the former city department officers applying for positions in the new county agency on a few occasions (see, e.g., Manhattan Institute, 2020; Oftelie, 2019). He details how roughly three-quarters of the old department did, in fact, apply to the CCPD. Thomson categorized the other quarter, consisting of approximately forty to fifty officers who did not, as being problematic and actively trying to stymie the reorganization by dissuading their fellow officers from applying. Thomson described these officers as self-selecting out of the new department, which he viewed as beneficial, allowing for a truer reset.

By late March, 155 current Camden City police officers received and accepted offers to transfer to the new CCPD along with another more than 120 new officer hires from outside the old city department (Laday, 2013b); those officers who were currently under investigation were denied employment (Manhattan Institute, 2020). The latter group of new hires were already either police officers in other jurisdictions or police academy graduates. The aforementioned two-week training period for CCPD's policies and procedures began on March 25 with field training, which was led by the former city officers who transferred into the CCPD, starting on April 8 (Laday, 2013b). Throughout April, different batches of officers were sworn in to CCPD's ranks and began their deployments in field training in various neighborhoods (e.g., Parkside) (Laday, 2013c,d). There were essentially two departments operating in the city of Camden between April 8 and April 30, as the old force was phasing out and the new CCPD was expanding their responsibilities (Laday, 2013b).

Changes to the Union Contract and Collective Bargaining

The dissolving of the old city department on April 30, 2013, also eliminated the existing police union as well as its contracts and collective bargaining agreements. This ended Chief Thomson's tenuous and adversarial relationship with the old union leadership, which he has described as serving as "defense attorneys for bad cops" (Manhattan Institute, 2020). If you recall from Chapter 3, union leadership opposed Thomson's—as well as Anne Milgram's—every move dating back to 2008 (see also Kurlander, 2020). The old Fraternal Order of Police union filed one hundred grievances and eight lawsuits against him during his first six months as interim chief (Kurlander, 2020; Manhattan Institute, 2020; Oftelie, 2019). Resistance greeted Thomson's attempts to assign officers who handled administrative, desk duty tasks during the week's normal business hours into street/patrol assignments on nights and weekends. Thomson (2020) also discussed the difficulty of being bound by the old union contract and binding arbitrator decisions that prohibited him from holding officers accountable for misconduct and poor performance.

The officers under the new CCPD did not have union representation for a six-month period until October 1, 2013. When a new union was formed with a completely fresh collective bargaining agreement, the revamped department was able to change the problematic status quo that plagued the old organization. The relationship became more of a partnership between the new department and the new union leadership, who took an active role in helping facilitate organizational change rather than fight it. Thomson publicly discussed his relationship with the new union leadership, whom he believed shared a common vision for safer, better, and community-oriented policing (COP) (Oftelie, 2019, p. 14n.; see also Thomson, 2020). One example of a less adversarial and more collaborative relationship is evidenced by new union leadership accepting a seat at the table for discussions of a use of force and de-escalation policy rework with the ACLU-NJ and the Policing Project of NYU, which are discussed in Chapter 6.

Operational Changes

Staffing

Perhaps one of the biggest, most significant changes the new CCPD brought was to the department staffing. Remember that the "normal" levels of full-time sworn officers in the mid- to late 2000s ranged from the low 400s to the high to mid-300s; they had 366 officers in 2010 (Swan et al., 2020). Those numbers were reduced even lower to 265 and 268 in 2011 and 2012, respectively, amid budget shortfalls—not to mention an additional average daily absentee rate of 30% in late 2012 with officers calling in sick and using leave time (Chang, 2012; Zernike, 2012). Low staffing levels contributed to the old department's poor quality of response and the city's violence in the years immediately predating the CCPD:

- 67 homicides in 2012 (a 43% increase from the year prior), 53 of whom were fatally shot, with another 172 shooting victims who survived (CCPD, 2022; Thomson, 2020).
- Police response times for 911 calls for service averaging more than sixty minutes (Zernike, 2014).
- 175 open-air drug markets (Maciag, 2014).
- Occasionally, the entire city was policed by twelve officers at a time with the old department (Goldstein, 2011; Vice, 2014)—down from eighty officers in the late 1990s/early 2000s, which was described as problematic even back then (Peterson, 2000b).

Increasing police officer presence on the streets, particularly in the most violent sections of the city, was one of the foremost priorities for Thomson and the new organization. In a 2020 discussion with former NJ AG Anne Milgram, Thomson recollects his experiences with a largely absent police footprint during his time rising through the ranks of the old CPD:

> Now, when I was a lieutenant in the narcotic unit that we talked about, we did a high-level investigation into what is arguably . . . at

the time, it was one of the most violent streets in North America, and we had a pole cam put up, and it was a secret pole cam. Nobody knew, not even the Camden cops knew it was there. Myself and a few other agents and investigators knew about it. But I remember reviewing hours and hours and hours of tape of this criminal drug gang that operated there, and being embarrassed and amazed at the same time that the only time a Camden cop car drove down that street was when somebody got shot, and there was a lot of people getting shot. But absent somebody being shot, the police didn't patrol it. (Kurlander, 2020)

The lack of police presence from his personal experience is supported and confirmed by the slew of outside reviews from the AG's Office from the 1980s through the mid-2000s (see NJ Attorney General, 2006). Thomson continued:

I remember that thought and how it bothered me, and that was something that I knew we had to address at some point in time. I think that underscores and provides the example of one of the first dynamics that we changed when we did the immediate reorganization of the department and pushed everybody out on the street. It was to create a presence wherein there was none, and prior to that, the most violent people in the city would operate with an absolute sense of impunity on the public streets, which has caused the overwhelming majority of the population, which are good people, to abandon public space and never leave their homes. The disruption of shaking up the entire organization, pulling everybody out from behind the desk and putting them out on the street was in large part, even before we put systems of accountability in place, what gave us the ability to start to have reductions in violent crime immediately. (Kurlander, 2020)

Milgram, too, spoke and wrote about her observations of the lack of police presence during the old city regime in 2007–2008. She described her first ride along in 2007: "The one thing that I did not see that day was a single police officer on the streets of Camden" (Milgram, 2020).

The new CCPD started with approximately 200 sworn officers with another 50 hired quickly in May 2013 (Swan et al., 2020). Chief Thomson (2020) credited the additional 50 officers early on as enabling the new department to instantly boost its presence in the community. It took another year to return to pre-2011 staffing levels when 100 more officers were hired in 2014 (Swan et al., 2020; Thomson, 2020). An article in *Governing* focused on the change in staffing. According to Maciag (2014): "An analysis of police employment data indicates that in the course of a year, Camden has gone from a bare-bones force to having at or near the highest police presence of any larger U.S. city on a per capita basis. By the time the force is fully staffed, which the county expects will be later this summer (2014), Camden will have 411 full-time sworn officers, or about 53 for every 10,000 residents. Cities of populations exceeding 50,000 employed an average of 17 officers per 10,000 residents in the most recent 2012 data reported to the FBI. Only Washington, DC, recorded a higher tally that year—about 61 officers per 10,000 residents—than Camden will once its new force is fully up and running."

Some studies find that increases in the number of police officers in departments, such as from federal grant sources like the U.S. Department of Justice's Community Oriented Policing Services program (Evans & Owens, 2007; Mello, 2019), are associated with subsequent reductions in crime. Chalfin and colleagues (2022), for example, used police employment data from a sample of 242 large U.S. cities over a thirty-eight-year period (1981–2018) to study how changes in police force size affect homicide victimization. More officers saved lives, with every ten officers hired abating one homicide annually, and reductions were twice as large for Black murder victims (see also Chalfin, 2022). On the other hand, reductions in police force size from large layoffs of officers (Piza & Chillar, 2021) and strikes (Aziani, 2022) have been associated with rising levels of crime. Camden's most violent years in recent memory came between 2011 and 2013 when the size of the force was diminished, absenteeism among the remaining officers skyrocketed, and the city struggled to put enough police officers on the street.

Another major change among the new CCPD was the outsourcing and civilianization of a number of departmental tasks that were previously handled by sworn officers under the old city agency. These included hiring civilian staff for central booking and records management (Swan et al., 2020) as well as outsourcing crime-scene technicians, intelligence analysts, and an information technology specialist (Oftelie, 2019). In many cases, these personnel were hired as consultants on a part-time basis, which reduced costs compared to full-time staff. The outsourcing and civilianization allowed sworn officers to dedicate more time to traditional law enforcement duties in the neighborhoods that needed it most.

Deployment into Neighborhoods

Coupling the increase in staffing to now fulfill basic law enforcement functions increased the proportion of officers' time spent in communities rather than only entering when answering calls for service. Traditionally, in American policing, practical constraints, such as continuously driving around responding to dispatched 911 calls, prohibit officers from being able to engage in true community policing and problem-solving activities. For example, in most departments around the country, a small number or percentage of officers are assigned to a "community policing" unit, or an equivalent name, where they perform the relevant functions—hosting community meetings and forming partnerships, conducting citizen police academies, door-to-door canvassing—while all other officers handle the "business as usual" crime control–related functions (Mastrofski, 2006). Research has found that this approach, known as the specialist model, leads to one of the biggest drawbacks of creating such units: officers assume that community policing activities are already being covered by said unit that they remain isolated in the organization without changing how the agency as a whole conducts business (Maguire & Gantley, 2009). The old CPD followed this specialist model. CCPD drastically altered this ratio: 70%–80% of officers would be assigned to community policing functions through the creation of "Neighborhood Response Teams" (NRTs) with only 20%–30% of officers assigned to a traditional patrol division (CNA Analysis & Solutions, 2019; Oftelie, 2019), which, on paper and from an organizational chart framework, brings the CCPD into a generalist model, where the practice of community policing is more institutionalized (Maguire & Gantley, 2009).

The NRTs provided, arguably, one of the biggest changes to the street-level interactions between officers and citizens. Officers in NRTs were deployed into high crime "hot spots," or small concentrated geographic areas of significant criminal activity. A small portion of places—usually 5% of neighborhoods, street segments or intersections, or addresses—account for a disproportionate share of crime and violence, oftentimes in excess of 50% (Braga et al., 2019). Organizationally, the CCPD was better able to perform directed patrol—that is, in specific areas with a purpose—in lieu of a general police response that deploys officers randomly and equally throughout the patrol area. A sizable body of empirical research from across the country finds that hot spots and directed patrol strategies lead to modest crime reduction benefits with little evidence of displacement; instead; there is a "diffusion of crime control benefits" (lower crime) in the areas immediately adjacent to where these place-based tactics are employed (Braga et al., 2019; National Academies of Sciences, Engineering, and Medicine, 2018). The CCPD would later rename the small geographic areas where NRT officers were instructed to spend a majority of their time as "Guardian Zones" (CNA Analysis & Solutions, 2019).

Once there, the officers were expected to walk around and engage with the community by knocking on doors and visiting businesses as well as patrolling those areas on bike. A significant portion of their time was alleviated from responding to dispatched 911 calls for service, which freed them up to be more proactive in the community as opposed to moving from one call to another. They were not exempt from responding to dispatched calls; however, even if NRT officers did arrive on scene first, the call and subsequent paperwork was turned over to Patrol Division officers (CNA Analysis & Solutions, 2019). With the newfound unallocated time, the department hoped NRT officers would be better equipped to diagnose some of the underlying causes of crime, violence, and disorder. By these accounts, NRT officers now had both the time and the logistical cover to address the recurring problems in their areas of assignment—the bare minimum and absolutely necessary components needed to follow the SARA (scanning, analysis, response, and assessment) model and conduct true problem-oriented policing (POP).

Foot patrols were a staple of the new organization—only made possible by the increase in officers, the restructuring of the Patrol Division and NRTs, and more civilianization that alleviated tasks from the sworn personnel. One of the original policing tactics dating back to the 1800s before motor vehicles, foot patrol allows for more face time and interaction between officers and the community. It increases police visibility and presence, and research has largely found the tactic to bring both crime reduction and public perception benefits (National Academies of Sciences, Engineering, and Medicine, 2018). The geographic nature of Camden offers an advantage for reinvesting in foot patrols compared to more suburban and rural areas: the city is densely populated and only nine square miles. Reinvestment in the tactic was likely influenced by what was happening across the Delaware River. Chief Thomson often credits Charles Ramsey—the police commissioner in Philadelphia from 2008 to 2016—as being one of his closest mentors as a young chief (Oftelie, 2019). The PPD, under Ramsey's leadership, facilitated two separate foot patrol experiments and subsequent evaluations (Ratcliffe & Sorg, 2017; Ratcliffe et al., 2011).

Increased foot patrols began in Camden in mid-April 2013, a few weeks before the official launch of the CCPD on May 1, and focused on micro areas of hot spots in the Parkside neighborhood; in June 2013, they expanded to the Fairview neighborhood, specifically Yorkship Square (Swan et al., 2020; see also Queally, 2013). Starting in early 2014, foot patrols expanded to several other neighborhoods including North Camden, Whitman Park, Broadway, and the Center City area (Swan et al., 2020). Estimates describe the drastic improvements of officer visibility in the community, including a "75% increase in 'boots on the ground'" and an increased "street-presence" of five times compared to the old city agency at the end of its tenure (Oftelie, 2019). Figure 4.1 presents a map of the different neighborhoods in the city.

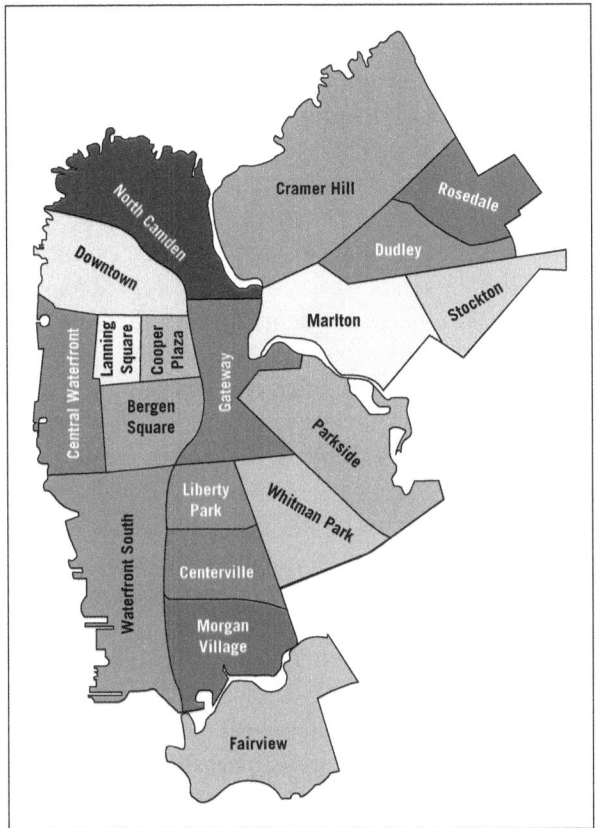

Figure 4.1 Neighborhoods in Camden, New Jersey. (*Schema-root.org*.)

A Specific Focus on Community Policing

Similarly, the increases in the number of sworn officers as well as the aforementioned operational restructuring that took place presented the CCPD with an ability to engage in more COP. While multifaceted and more of an abstract philosophy than a tangible tactic, COP generally should include five different components: (1) closer, more accessible deployment to citizens, (2) community revitalization and collaborative relationships between officers and the public, (3) an emphasis on problem-solving and addressing root causes, (4) valuing and incorporating community input, and (5) increasing legitimacy in order to boost credibility and public trust in police (PERF, 1996). Shortly after its start in May 2013, the CCPD dedicated more time, effort, and resources toward a host of activities and events that were not possible before, with such a limited police force that was stretched too thin—

particularly in the years right before the change (2011 on). These activities and events have been well publicized and include neighborhood cookouts, block parties, and other community events with Mr. Softee Ice-Cream Trucks along with other food vendors as well as having uniformed officers in classrooms reading to school children.

Such events have been criticized as simply being a public relations campaign for photo opportunities for the CCPD. However, CCPD officials including the former chief Thomson have responded by stating that the cookouts and barbeques serve multiple functions: (1) increasing residents' presence in public places, which puts more "eyes on the street" (Jacobs, 1961) and, historically, has been a problem in Camden with people abandoning space, staying indoors, and ceding that space to criminals and drug dealers; and (2) providing meals for a city that is largely poor and has been designated as a food desert by the state's Departments of Community Affairs and Agriculture as well as the Economic Development Authority (Skoufalos, 2022, see also Kurlander, 2020). Regarding this latter point, surveys of hunger in Camden find that upward of 65% of city residents experience some degree of food insecurity (Camden Food Access Work Group, 2020).

In terms of partnerships, CCPD's deputy chief at the time—Joseph Wysocki—helped create Project Guardian a few years later in 2015: a collaboration between CCPD and educational, religious, and social service groups that aims to bring counseling, support services, and life skills training to at-risk youths in the city (Caffrey, 2015; Hernandez, 2016; Hickey, 2017; Madden, 2017). Taking the form of a mix between a "call in" meeting from a focused deterrence intervention, sometimes called "pulling levers" (Braga & Weisburd, 2012) and the "Scared Straight" program, Project Guardian identifies juveniles who may be involved in gangs and offending more broadly from previous encounters with police and seeks parental consent for the youths to attend meetings where they hear from, among social workers and clergy, formerly incarcerated individuals who have turned their lives around. The program holds such meetings a few times each year. A focus on juveniles was an important impetus for Project Guardian as CCPD crime statistics indicated one-third of all violent crimes were being committed by those under eighteen (Caffrey, 2015).

Technology

Starting in 2010 and through the first month of the new agency in May 2013, Camden spent around $4.5 million dollars on technology to assist in crime control and public safety functions (Laday, 2013e, 2015c). These technological investments included a state-of-the-art Real-Time Crime Center (RTCC) called RT-TOIC, an AGDS, a network of 120 mounted surveillance cameras throughout the city, and automated license plate readers (ALPRs) for all patrol vehicles. As of 2021, that number rose to 221 mounted surveillance cameras (YouTube, 2021). It is clear that technology made up a huge component of CCPD's crime reduction plan.

RT-TOIC

The brains and central nervous system of CCPD's technology-based crime-fighting approach, the RT-TOIC represents one of the most recent innovations in public safety. RTCCs are central rooms that house and integrate a variety of technologies and information systems in order to assist police with field operations and decision-making. According to the Electronic Frontier Foundation's (2024) "Atlas of Surveillance" project, there are a total 146 RTCCs in the United States with three to eight new centers becoming operational since 2015 (Przeszlowski et al., 2023). CCPD's RT-TOIC was one of the first in the country. Only three studies have formally evaluated RTCCs' impact on crime reduction and investigative capabilities, and a survey of forty-four agencies with RTCCs found that less than half assessed any type of effect on crime or clearance rates (Przeszlowski et al., 2023). Despite the growth and the limited evidence base, RTCCs were associated with reductions in crime in Chicago (Hollywood et al., 2019), and improvements in clearance rates in Chicago (Arietti, 2024) and Miami (Guerette & Przeszlowski, 2023).

The RT-TOIC has been covered at length in media publications and videos, including during the visit by President Obama in May 2015 (see C-SPAN, 2015). It has also received some critical attention in the academic literature surrounding topics like big data policing and mass surveillance (McQuade, 2019; Wiig, 2018; see also Ferguson, 2017). RT-TOIC is a state-of-the-art room at CCPD's headquarters with several large forty-two-inch screens mounted for reviewing all types of information and staffed 24/7 by contracted non-sworn officers. Projected onto the big screens is video footage from a network of over two hundred mounted surveillance cameras in neighborhoods and business corridors throughout a color-coded map of the city. The cameras allow for staff within RT-TOIC to conduct "virtual patrols" and monitor the surveillance footage, verifying whether a sworn officer in the field is required in order to free them from responding to nonurgent and nonemergency calls. For example, a virtual patrol once detected a juvenile with a gun near a school, which led to an officer being dispatched and arriving on scene within a few minutes; such virtual patrols also allow for the tracking and surveillance of possible suspects until an officer can respond (CNA Analysis & Solutions, 2019). In addition to monitoring live surveillance camera footage, the RT-TOIC tracks AGDS and ALPR alerts—two new detection systems discussed in the coming pages—as well as displays the location of every police vehicle in real time using its GPS and color-coded maps of how long officers have spent within designated areas (CNA Analysis & Solutions, 2019). The GPS located on officers' department-issued cell phones and body-worn cameras would later track officer movement in the RT-TOIC when CCPD officers began wearing the latter in late 2015 to early 2016 (Adomaitis, 2015b; Borowski, 2023b; Oftelie, 2019).

Used in these ways, the RT-TOIC serves not only to assist with crime control but also to manage, monitor, and hold police officers accountable. Internal control mechanisms for officers, particularly uniformed frontline staff, became a staple of the new department and a deviation from the relative lack of accountability in the old city agency. The aforementioned color-coded maps projected on screens in RT-TOIC show green, yellow, or red areas based on the amount of time officers out in the field are inside the designated geographic areas—called "Guardian Zones" but also representing hot spots or areas of concentrated criminal activity—compared to the expected amount of time officers should be there. The maps turn from green to yellow and then to red as the actual time within the designated zones falls behind the expected time (CNA Analysis & Solutions, 2019). District commanders and field supervisors are able to access the color-coded maps with the real-time locations of all police vehicles and officers on foot or on bike. Such precise geographic locations of officers in the field also may facilitate safety in cases of emergencies when those officers are in trouble and require backup. These tools within RT-TOIC in totality, from the virtual patrols to the officer monitoring capabilities, help ensure more departmental efficiency as well as police presence and time spent within the neighborhoods that may need it most.

AGDS

From 2010 through the end of 2015, the entire city of Camden became covered by an AGDS network. An AGDS uses microphones to triangulate the location of gunfire. More specifically, the system places acoustic microphones or sensors at strategic geographic intervals to create a grid-like system throughout physical space, which is used to determine the point of origin of either the sound waves produced from a muzzle blast or the sonic boom generated from a bullet as it travels (see Mares, 2022, for a more detailed description of how AGDS work). Algorithms process and identify the sounds as either gunfire or other loud noises—fireworks, car exhaust backfires—and AGDS may have an additional human review of the sound. Once confirmed as gunfire, departments are notified—usually through a central communications system—and officers are dispatched to the precise location. This process can take between a few seconds and about one minute. Although there are a number of vendors that provide such AGDS services, SoundThinking (formerly known as ShotSpotter) is arguably the largest and most popular.

Camden installed its first SoundThinking microphones in the Whitman Park neighborhood in 2010 (Laday, 2013e, 2015a) with additional geographic coverage starting in 2013 (YouTube, 2019). As of June 2015, there were more than thirty AGDS microphones deployed throughout the city with plans to expand SoundThinking into a citywide program in all the remaining neighborhoods without AGDS—Waterfront South, Morgan Village, Fairview, Cramer Hill, and East Camden (Adomaitis, 2015b). The contract to expand SoundThinking citywide, which was approved by the Camden County Board of Freeholders in the summer of 2015, cost more than $600,000.

Camden is one of the more than 150 cities in the United States—usually those with concentrated gun violence problems—utilizing SoundThinking (2023). Estimated costs are between $70,000 and $85,000 per square mile per year for a leased system that includes human vendor review (Mares, 2022). Synthesizing the available research and based on his own evaluative work on the technology, Mares (2022) discusses how, although AGDS has been touted to provide a number of potential benefits—namely, faster response times and, subsequently, better victim assistance, such as quicker medical attention and hospital transport, more accurate locations of shootings and reporting of gunfire, and enhanced evidence recovery—these claims have not been subjected to much peer-reviewed testing and evaluation. A recent evaluation of SoundThinking in Kansas City, Missouri, found that the technology did not significantly influence the likelihood of evidence collection or case clearance in shooting incidents (Piza et al., 2023). Most striking, Mares notes, is how the research testing whether AGDS provides a deterrent effect and reduces gun crimes or violence is mixed at best.

In Camden's experience with SoundThinking, some figures as well as a medical study speak to how the technology has influenced gun violence response. According to information from SoundThinking, during a period when the technology was first installed, approximately 30% of gunshots were going unreported by residents (Laday, 2015a) when the detected gunfire incidents in the areas equipped with AGDS were compared to citizen calls to 911 regarding "shots fired" or a person being shot in those areas. Based on these comparisons, it appears that SoundThinking was beneficial, at least initially, in allowing CCPD officers to be aware of and respond to shootings that they would not otherwise have known about. Additionally, there is evidence that SoundThinking has allowed both the CCPD and local EMS to improve their ability to assist gunshot victims. Goldenberg and colleagues

(2019) explored shootings in Camden from 2010 to 2018 and compared those incidents in which SoundThinking detected and alerted first responders versus those where it did not. The AGDS technology was found to significantly reduce both emergency personnel response time as well as victim transport time to the hospital, although it did not significantly increase the likelihood of survivability (see also YouTube, 2019).

ALPRs

The CCPD also invested in ALPRs. ALPRs are cameras that scan the alphanumeric license plates of passing cars against existing databases, such as the National Crime Information Center or a state's Department of Motor Vehicles records, which lists stolen cars or registered owners who have open warrants (see Lum et al., 2010). When a match is made, which happens almost instantaneously upon the scan, the technology alerts users who can subsequently perform a traffic stop on the vehicle in question. ALPRs automate and speed up a process that was done manually by officers in the past. The technology has rapidly diffused since its inception in the early 2000s. By 2016, 68% of municipal law enforcement agencies with one hundred or more sworn officers had acquired ALPRs (Law Enforcement Management and Administrative Statistics, 2016). ALPRs can be deployed in two general ways: mobile units attached to police vehicles or fixed/stationary units that are mounted on light posts, traffic lights, and bridges. A majority of deployed ALPRs tend to be mobile units mounted on vehicles (Lum et al., 2019), although some agencies report employing both types of mobile and fixed units if they have the means to do so (Roberts & Casanova, 2012). Every CCPD patrol vehicle was equipped with a mobile ALPR as of May 2013—the initial launch of the new department (Laday, 2013e).

Despite the rapid diffusion of ALPRs, few studies have explored departmental outputs—arrests and stolen vehicles recovered—and the technology's impact on crime. ALPRs generally provide increased efficiency and lead to more arrests compared to conventional law enforcement practices (Jordan, 1997; Lum et al., 2019; Ozer, 2010; Roberts & Casanova, 2012). That is, they generate more "hits" for stolen vehicles or plates compared to officers manually investigating such crimes (Koper, Taylor, & Park, 2019; Potts, 2018), while arrests and automobile recoveries have been found to be two to three times more likely to occur during patrols where officers are using ALPRs (Koper, Taylor, & Park, 2019). Yet, ALPRs have not produced clear evidence of providing a deterrent effect in the form of reducing crime. Most rigorous evaluations find that treatment areas with ALPRs did not experience significant reductions in crime compared to control areas (or postintervention periods) (Kernahan & Valasik, 2019; Lum et al., 2011; Taylor, Koper, & Woods, 2012; but see Shjarback & Sarkos, 2025; Wheeler & Phillips, 2018, for exceptions), although these evaluations have been limited to only a few research sites (e.g., Mesa, AZ; Alexandria and Fairfax County, VA; Baton Rouge, LA; Buffalo, NY; Atlantic City, NJ).

The potential benefits of ALPRs may also extend to investigative efforts, such as identifying suspect movements and corroborating alibis (see Willis, Koper, & Lum, 2018) and, subsequently, improving solve or clearance rates (Koper & Lum, 2019). However, agencies thus far have indicated that they usually do not use the technology for these purposes. Only 10%–12% of large agencies with one hundred–plus sworn officers with ALPRs reported using the technology "always or almost always" for investigating crimes against persons and property (Lum et al., 2019). ALPRs, when employed in this manner, can add to existing information technologies since the data that they collect can be stored, shared, analyzed, searched, and retrieved (Byrne & Marx, 2011), although most departments do not have the large networks of fixed cameras throughout their jurisdictions to effectively facilitate such novel investigative efforts. Given that every patrol vehicle was outfitted with an ALPR starting in May 2013, it appears as though the CCPD possesses a big enough network to facilitate the technology for investigative purposes. It is simply another tool available to CCPD and its officers.

Summary

The actual transition from the CPD to the CCPD was incredibly complex with planning and logistical changes occurring well before May 1, 2013. Those changes covered staffing, operational strategy, and technology. This chapter synthesized and detailed the handoff from one organization to the other, and it points out how there were essentially two police departments operating at the same time—particularly in April 2013. The CCPD made many drastic changes from its very first days and months, including improvements not only in the raw numbers of sworn personnel but in the ways in which those officers were deployed geographically and from an organizational standpoint, such as the split between the NRTs and the Patrol Division. Other shifts, such as the outsourcing and civilianization of certain functions, freed up officers to do more police work: foot and bike patrol in crime hot spots and overall increases in proactivity, which had been lacking and deficient for quite some time. Investments in technology assisted the CCPD not only in addressing crime but in serving as internal control mechanisms to foster the accountability of officers being where they were supposed to be. Taken as a whole, the CCPD was able to do way more with similar levels of funding.

5

CCPD's Impact

Whereas the previous chapter explored the specific changes that the CCPD implemented, the purpose of this chapter is to examine the new organization's impact through a host of different measures. Did they work to curb crime—and how? Therefore, it is best viewed as a synthesis and secondary analysis of data, previous reports, and articles. It covers the CCPD's influence on officer response times, crime, and victimization as well as levels of enforcement and citizen complaints of excessive use of force. The CCPD made much progress on a number of fronts in comparison to the old city police department, which undoubtedly improved the lives of Camden residents through effects like fewer open-air drug markets and lower rates of both violent and property crime victimization. However, the CCPD and its officers also engaged in conduct that angered residents—leading to scrutiny from activists and media alike. The CCPD's story is complicated and nuanced, and it appears as though the organization progressed in a nonlinear fashion.

Daily Functions and Operations

Recall that the old CPD in 2011 through early 2013 was reduced to a skeleton crew that was unable to perform basic functions and operations. Low staffing of sworn officers—plus excessive absenteeism averaging 30% daily in 2012 (Chang, 2012; Zernike, 2012)—led to backlogs and mounting caseloads for detectives as well as extreme delays in responding to 911 calls for service. Chief Thomson explained in 2012, "We don't have property crime detectives anymore. You know, I have shooting investigations that are backlogging, like, burglary cases" (NPR, 2014). Additionally, he stated, "Our ability to police the city had been reduced to a triage unit going from emergency to emergency" (Maciag, 2014). Citizens waited an average of sixty minutes for officers to respond on scene at the very end of the old CPD's reign (Zernike, 2014). With all of CCPD's changes, particularly better staffing levels, the average response time was drastically reduced to 4.4 minutes in the summer of 2014—a little over a year into the newly created agency (Zernike, 2014).

Researchers at the Walter Rand Institute (WRI) at Rutgers University–Camden partnered with the CCPD to more thoroughly evaluate the new agency's impact on different aspects such as response times and crime reduction (see Swan et al., 2020). To date, this represents the lone independent evaluation conducted by outside researchers examining the department's efforts and its subsequent impact on crime reduction. Information on changes in calls for service and response times as well as whether foot patrols and multijurisdictional task force efforts were effective stem from the WRI evaluation, while all other data presented here is a secondary analysis of publicly available data. WRI reviewed all calls for service (CFS) from May through August—usually the busiest time of the year for departments in the late spring and summer months—for years 2013 through 2016. WRI researchers identified the top categories of CFS as: (1) disturbance of the peace, (2) vice complaint (drugs), (3) suspicious person (adult), (4) domestic disturbance, and (5) burglar alarm. CCPD's average response time, which is measured from the time a call is received by 911 to when an available officer is dispatched by the 911 operator, for all five types of calls was approximately 5.5 minutes; the average time between a call's reception and an officer arriving on scene was 13 minutes (Swan et al., 2020).

WRI also provided a more specific breakdown of three of the top CFS categories. The average response time for vice complaints for drugs was just over four minutes; twenty-two minutes from call reception to officer arrival. The average response time for a domestic incident involving two adults with either an injury or an offender was just over six minutes from call dispatch to officer arrival. And, perhaps, the category for which there is the highest level of urgency needed, the average response for possession of a firearm (i.e., "person with a gun") was just over three minutes from call dispatch to officer arrival. These statistics and figures suggest that much progress was made in a basic departmental function as simple as responding to citizens' calls for service in a timely manner.

Crime and Victimization

One of the most, if not the most, commonly touted changes regarding the transition from the old city agency to the CCPD is the drastic reduction in crime and victimization, particularly violent crime and gun violence. There is no doubt that the rates of violent crime victimization, and murder more specifically, have precipitously declined over the past thirteen years in the city. Figures 5.1 and 5.2 plot standardized rates of violent crime—murder, rape, robbery, and aggravated assault—and murder per capita, respectively, for each of the six cities categorized as "major urban" by the NJ State Police for years 2011 through 2020.

Camden not only saw overall declines in violent crime victimization since 2011 but also, as Figure 5.1 shows, managed to narrow the gap between itself and the others. Camden's violent crime rate dropped most steeply between 2013 and 2014. Despite the violent crime reduction and narrowing, Camden as of 2020 still had the highest rate of violent crime per 1,000 residents out of the six major urban cities in the state.

Moving on to murder rates per 100,000 residents, Camden's trend largely mirrors its broader violent crime rate. Aside from an increase in 2016, Camden's murder rate has declined every year since 2012. During 2011–2013, Camden stood in stark contrast to the other five cities in the state and well exceeded their rates; however, this trend began to change in 2014 when

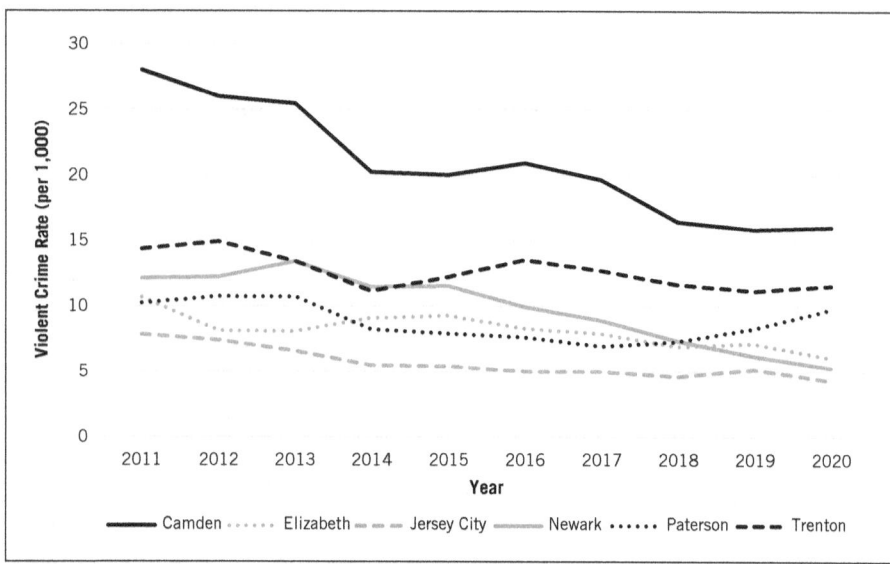

Figure 5.1 Violent crime per 1,000 residents in New Jersey's "major urban" cities (2011–2020).

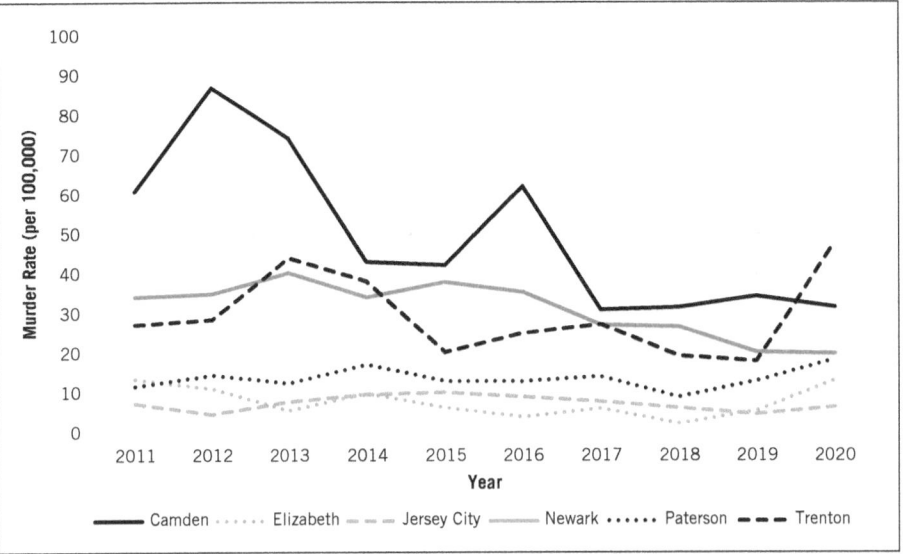

Figure 5.2 Murder rates per 100,000 residents in New Jersey's "major urban" cities (2011–2020).

Camden's murder rate was at least comparable and in a similar ballpark as the others—albeit still remaining the highest through 2019. The year 2020 was the first time during this period that Camden did not record New Jersey's highest murder rate and was surpassed by Trenton, which experienced a 167% increase from 2019 to 2020. The total number of murders decreased slightly from 2019 ($N = 25$) to 2020 ($N = 23$) in Camden, while 2020 represented the largest one-year increase—nearly 30%—in the nation's homicide rate following the COVID-19 pandemic and the social unrest from the murder of George Floyd (Asher, 2021).

Camden also reined in gun violence since the highs in 2012 and 2013. In addition to the CCPD's official statistics, another data source has been able to independently confirm the steep reductions in shootings from 2013 to 2014. SoundThinking, Camden's AGDS, released gunfire figures from all twenty-eight cities that used its technology in 2013–2014. Of the twenty-eight, Camden saw the third-largest reduction in gunshots detected by the SoundThinking system from 2013 (704 within the areas covered by the technology) to 2014 (366)—a 48% decline and well ahead of places like Chicago, Charlotte, NC, Milwaukee, WI, and Oakland, CA (Laday, 2015b). According to SoundThinking, the average reduction in gunfire for all the cities over the two-year period was 28.8% (see Laday, 2015b). Homicides by shooting, aggravated assaults with firearms, and number of incidents where someone was struck by gunfire but survives have all dropped, particularly from 2014 on; the steepest declines came in all categories from 2013 to 2014. Table 5.1 shows the totals for each category of gun crime from 2012 through 2020.

Figure 5.3 shows felony property crime rates—specifically, burglary, larceny, and motor vehicle theft—per 1,000 residents for each of the six "major urban" cities in New Jersey. Much like the patterns of violent crime and murder, property crime rates in Camden have gradually declined from 2011, with the gap between Camden and the other five cities narrowing over time. From 2017 through 2020, Camden no longer had the highest standardized property crime rate of the six cities tracked, with Elizabeth overtaking it each year and with Trenton coming close to exceeding Camden's rate in 2018 and 2020. Camden's property crime rate has been somewhat comparable—despite still being higher in most cases—to the other major urban cities in the state since 2016–2017.

TABLE 5.1 GUN VIOLENCE IN CAMDEN (2012–2020)									
Crime type	2012	2013	2014	2015	2016	2017	2018	2019	2020
Homicide-Shooting	53	52	28	31	42	20	22	18	17
Aggravated Assault with Firearm	381	379	257	296	288	298	235	250	304
Nonfatal Shooting Hit	172	143	90	109	92	95	81	81	86

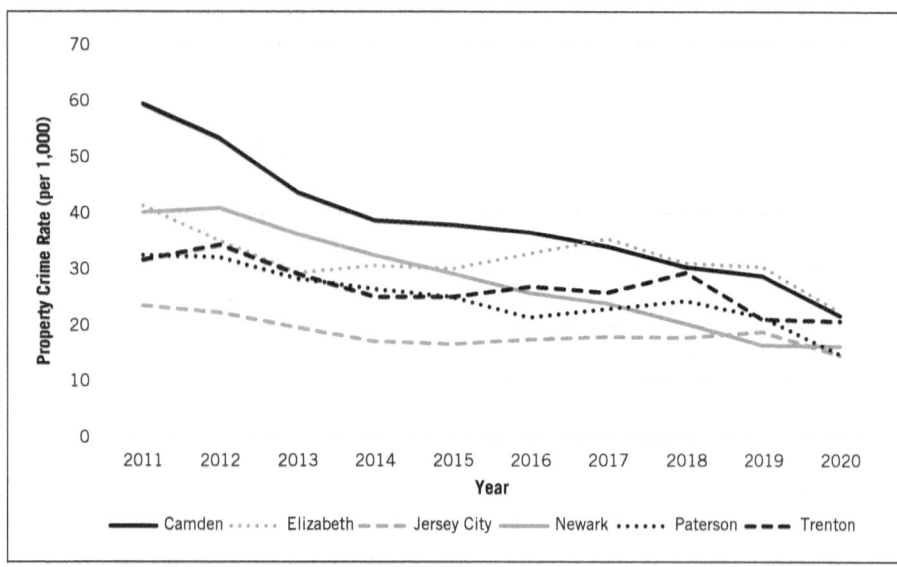

Figure 5.3 Property crime per 1,000 residents in New Jersey's "major urban" cities (2011–2020).

The CCPD made progress but continued to have a difficult time addressing drug crime. A common statistic cited is that Camden was once home to 175 open-air drug markets at its most recent peak in 2012 (Maciag, 2014; Thomson, 2020), which were down to below 40 by 2015 (Oftelie, 2019). The aforementioned WRI evaluation appears to substantiate this transition using citizens' 911 calls to the police regarding drugs. The total number of CFS categorized as vice complaints for drugs were compared from May through August in years 2013 to 2016. There were 3,232 CFS in the late spring through summer in 2013 and 3,287 in 2014, followed by 1,669 in 2015, and 1,650 in 2016—marking a 49% reduction from May–August 2013 to May–August 2016 (Swan et al., 2020).

Aside from simple descriptive changes over time, researchers at the WRI at Rutgers University–Camden performed a more rigorous evaluation of CCPD's efforts. WRI focused primarily on two factors: foot patrols and multijurisdictional task forces and their impact on crime (see Swan et al., 2020). Foot patrol strategies began in mid-April of 2013—about a half-month before CCPD was officially launched. WRI analyzed their effectiveness, including comparisons of treatment areas that received the foot patrols versus comparable control areas that did not as well as an interrupted time series analysis of pre- and post–foot patrols in the assigned areas. Each analysis found that foot patrols had statistically significant crime reduction benefits, especially on violent crime, specifically aggravated assaults and robberies with a firearm. Property crime was also significantly reduced following foot patrols and in the areas where police stepped up patrols, although the reductions were weaker compared to those of violent crime. WRI researchers also found a decline in reported crime in the buffer areas around the foot patrols' targeted zones, which provide continued and consistent evidence of a "diffusion of crime control benefits" in the areas surrounding and adjacent to the treatment zones (Braga et al., 2019; National Academies of Sciences, Engineering, and Medicine, 2018).

WRI additionally measured the impact of five multijurisdictional task force operations that targeted major drug networks. Using an interrupted time series analysis of crime in the geographic areas targeted before and after each operation, researchers determined these efforts led to short-term reductions (e.g., three to six months) in crime and violence. For context, these operations were long-form investigations—several months to over a year—in which four to over forty individuals were charged with drug trafficking and racketeering (see Swan et al., 2020, p. 21). Such operations are similar to the "gang takedown" approach used by the NYPD in recent years that is more precise in its focus on a small targeted number of individuals or groups disproportionately involved in crime and violence (Chalfin, 2022; Chalfin, LaForest, & Kaplan, 2021). Such investigations look to build major cases through wiretaps, monitoring social media activity, cameras and other technology, and undercover officers as opposed to a more broad-brushed and sometimes indiscriminate use of police interventions that may ensnare a larger group of individuals.

Holding Offenders Accountable

The CCPD also experienced higher levels of success over the years in holding offenders accountable for the most serious crimes: homicides. Like with many other CCPD metrics, such as excessive force complaints and the use of tickets—to be discussed in the coming pages—progress is not always linear. One of the best measures of holding offenders accountable can be calculated using the clearance or solve rates—that is, the percentage of arrests made for a particular crime type that is reported to the police or that an agency is aware of. Clearance rates for homicides committed in the city of Camden have gradually improved; however, it is important to keep in mind that credit for such successes must also be paid to other organizations and the collaborative efforts between them.

In 2015, Chief Thomson sought assistance for CCPD's homicide detectives. He reached out and set up a visit from a homicide prosecutor—John Colello—in the Los Angeles County District Attorney's Office (Boren & Steele, 2016). After a site visit, Colello reported that CCPD's homicide detectives were "stretched a little thin" by their caseloads. He subsequently recommended assigning one group of detectives to investigate homicides and a separate group, nonfatal shootings, which a few studies have shown promise in increasing the clearance rates of, particularly, for the latter (Braga, 2021). Thomson, at the time, responded that such a recommendation and reducing caseloads for detectives was difficult to implement given CCPD's challenges with staffing: the department had 354 sworn officers, well below its goal, and had lost nearly 150 officers in its first two years to resignations and retirements. Staffing levels and issues of retaining officers is a topic discussed in more detail in Chapter 8.

Another collaboration, the Camden County Crime Coalition, began operation in 2010 during a time of dwindling resources and staffing under the old city department and survived the transfer to the CCPD in 2013. It started as a partnership between the city agency, the CCPO, and the U.S. Attorney's Office, a number of federal agencies (including the FBI, DEA, ATF, and U.S. Marshals Service), nearby municipal police departments (including Cherry Hill and Lindenwold), and probation and parole departments (Joyce & Pearson, 2019). It is partially funded by the Philadelphia/Camden High Intensity Drug Trafficking Area (HIDTA) program. Serving primarily as a forum to share intelligence and foster collaboration, the Camden County

Crime Coalition takes the form of periodic meetings to discuss, review, and build cases for investigations and prosecutions regarding violent crime, guns, and drug-trafficking organizations (Joyce & Pearson, 2019).

In addition to the Camden County Crime Coalition partnership, detectives from the CCPO deserve credit for holding offenders accountable and improving the solve and clearance rates in Camden. Detectives from both the CCPD and the CCPO work together to jointly investigate homicides and other crimes—the vast majority of the cases they tackle occur in the city of Camden. Camden city, for instance, accounted for twenty-three out of the county's thirty-one total homicides in 2020 (74%) (CCPO, 2021). CCPO detectives in the Homicide Unit work on homicides, while detectives in CCPO's Major Crimes Unit investigate nonfatal shootings and attempted murders (CCPO, 2023). Table 5.2 presents the homicide clearance/solve rates by year for the city of Camden, which were derived from both CCPO press releases and media reports.

The new initiatives eventually seemed to yield results in the form of cleared cases. The year 2020 seemed to be a turning point when arrests were made in twenty-two out of the twenty-three homicides in the city that year—yielding a clearance rate of 95.7%. The CCPO credited the agency's unprecedented success to a change in their homicide division's rotation for on-call detectives, which allowed them more time to work cases before being

TABLE 5.2 CLEARANCE RATES FOR HOMICIDE	
Year	Clearance rate
2005–2011[a]	High 40%–Mid 50%; 60% in 2006
2012[a]	53%
2013[b]	15%
2014[a]	38%
2015[a]	37%
2016[b]	76%
2017[c]	—
2018[c]	—
2019[d]	65%
2020[e]	95.7%
2021[c]	—
2022[f]	65%
2023[f]	63.5%

[a] Boren & Steele (2016).
[b] Joyce & Pearson (2019).
[c] Unavailable.
[d] Napoliello (2021); number represents Camden County's homicide clearance rate.
[e] CCPO (2021).
[f] Borowski (2024a).

assigned additional ones (Napoliello, 2021). The CCPO (2021) elaborated on those administrative changes in a press release, which stated:

> "In Feb. of 2020, we began a new on-call rotation for our seven homicide detectives that would essentially move a detective to the bottom of the list so they could dedicate as much time as possible toward solving that case before they were assigned another," said Capt. John Hunsinger, who served as Lieutenant of the Homicide Unit until 2021.
>
> "Previously this rotation was done using a formula that sometimes meant a detective could be back on call within 2–3 weeks, and thus increase the likelihood of that detective getting another homicide in that short period of time. We think this change has played an important role in allowing detectives the ability to identify and track leads more quickly. Not being on the rotation allows them the time to focus on their most recent case during those crucial first days."

In addition to solving (defined as making arrests of suspects) the highest percentage of homicides in the department's history in 2020, the CCPO also made note of the speed with which arrests were made in cases countywide. "Of the 29 homicides solved, 21 arrests were made within one month and another six arrests happened within two months of a homicide" (CCPO, 2021). The success of 2020, however, may be an anomaly since homicide clearance rates in the city declined to 65% and 63.5% in 2022 and 2023, respectively (Borowski, 2024a).

Taking nothing away from the hard work and dedication of detectives in both the CCPD and the CCPO as well as prosecutors in the CCPO, the coverage of this topic would be remiss without a discussion of technology and surveillance. Investigators and those tasked with prosecuting offenders benefit from the near—if not absolute—ubiquity of cameras and other tools that track movement throughout the entire city of Camden. There is no shortage of media, activist, and academic reporting on the topics of "big data policing" and "mass surveillance," particularly in Camden (McQuade, 2019; Rutgers Center for Security, Race and Rights, 2023; Wiig, 2018). Camden has even been dubbed the "Surveillance City" (Friedersdorf, 2013; Vice, 2014). At last count, the city had 221 surveillance cameras (Napoliello, 2021), plus the ability to tap into video and CCTV footage from businesses and residents as well as the ALPRs on all CCPD vehicles, which scan and record every license plate they pass. According to CCPD Detective Edward Gonzalez, "Video footage helps lay the groundwork for the detectives' first moves in a homicide investigation" (Napoliello, 2021). Detective Gonzalez added, "When the police develop a suspect, it's usually easy to spot that person." It also likely reduces the chances of identifying the wrong person as a suspect.

Community Engagement

For all of the positive attention and favorable coverage that the CCPD has received for their efforts toward community policing, there are few—if any—systematic and empirical methods to explore whether public perception and perceived legitimacy has improved over time. This is not unique to the CCPD, as the vast majority of police departments across the country do not formally track how the community views the organization and whether progress is being made in this crucial area. Very few police departments survey their citizenry in a meaningful way in order to gauge the successes (or lack thereof) of various community policing initiatives and strategies. In the rare instances in which citizen interviews or surveys are done, there is usually collaboration with independent researchers, where generous grant funding is involved (e.g., Peyton, Sierra-Arévalo, & Rand, 2019; Weisburd et al., 2022).

Perhaps citizen behaviors can serve as proxy measures for their perceptions of their respective police departments. Indicators such as calling the police to report crime and victimization as well as other less serious disputes may tap into those attitudes of trust and legitimacy, and studies have attempted to explore changes in this type of citizen behavior in the wake of high-profile, critical incidents involving local police (Desmond, Papachristos, & Kirk, 2016; Moyer, 2022). But how do researchers separate an increase in citizens' willingness to call the police from a possible increase in crimes that spur a call? A recent working paper suggests an innovative measure for comparing citizens' calls alongside the incidents motivating them in the same system: the ratio of police-related 911 calls to gunshots detected by SoundThinking or another AGDS technology (Ang et al., 2021). This measure provides an opportunity to track how citizens' calls to 911 for police services converges or diverges over time in places that have other technologies detecting an incident, like SoundThinking, which can serve as a point of reference. A growing gap in the 911 call to SoundThinking alert ratio could potentially be picking up a reduction in citizen behavior to invoke the police, and, thus, declining citizen engagement.

Relatedly, some are concerned that as law enforcement personnel rely more and more on technology, they may engage less with the community. Although evaluation work on the topic is limited, a study from St. Louis, Missouri, uncovered that AGDS implementation was related to reductions in citizens' calls for reporting gunfire (Blackburn & Mares, 2019; Mares & Blackburn, 2021). The findings suggest that, over time, residents may come to rely on the technology for a police response as opposed to calling 911. Data from SoundThinking, or another AGDS, can be compared to explore whether, and the degree to which, citizens are underreporting gunfire (see Mares, 2022).

Press releases by the CCPO detail how CCPD officers were alerted to fatal shootings, allowing for a cursory examination of trends in citizen engagement for reporting these shootings compared to such AGDS technology. Camden installed its first AGDS microphones in the Whitman Park neighborhood in 2010, and there were more than thirty microphones deployed throughout the city by the summer of 2015; by the end of 2015, the AGDS network covered the entire city. In late November 2014, the CCPD's press releases describing firearm homicides began providing better, more detailed descriptions for how police were notified of each fatal shooting as opposed to the broad and generic information it would have released without the AGDS data: "Police responded to the 1500 block of Federal Street." This level of detail continues to the present day. As such, all CCPO press releases from November 2014 on describing fatal shootings in the city of Camden were qualitatively coded to extract the exact method(s) with which CCPD officers were alerted to fatal shooting incidents:

1. Citizen initiated (e.g., "police responded to a 911 call for reports of gunfire")
2. AGDS initiated (e.g., "police were notified of a ShotSpotter activation")
3. Police officers hearing gunfire
4. Shooting victims arriving at a hospital
5. A combination of sources (e.g., citizen 911 call and a ShotSpotter alert)

A fatal shooting of an eighteen-year-old male in April 2015 was the first explicit mention of the AGDS alerting police in a CCPO press release. Table 5.3 presents the results of the qualitative analysis broken down by year, and, subsequently, Figure 5.4 plots the total proportion of citizen-initiated and AGDS-initiated alerts for fatal shootings over time. In a small number of incidents depending on the year, CCPO press releases did not provide enough information for how police were alerted to the fatal shooting event.

Despite year-to-year fluctuations and the small base numbers of fatal shootings being examined, there is a general downward trend in the proportion of total citizen-initiated alerts. Total AGDS-initiated alerts experienced a steep increase from 2015 to 2016—the latter being the first full year the entire city had coverage—before falling again during a period of relative stability. Both citizen- and AGDS-initiated alerts seem to have converged around 40%–50% in recent years. It is also relatively rare now for CCPD officers to either hear gunfire (3%–11% depending on the year) or have shooting victims who later die show up at the hospital (0%–6%) without any other alerting mechanism(s).

TABLE 5.3 MANNER(S) IN WHICH CCPD WAS ALERTED TO FATAL SHOOTINGS OVER TIME

	2014	2015	2016	2017	2018	2019	2020	2021	2022	2023
Single modality										
Citizen initiated	75%	61%	39%	50%	55%	44%	53%	35%	39%	38%
AGDS	—	23%	37%	15%	18%	39%	29%	53%	39%	35%
Police hear gunfire	—	6%	—	—	9%	11%	6%	6%	4%	4%
Arrived at hospital	—	—	—	—	—	6%	6%	—	—	—
Other (e.g., car crash with gunshot victim inside)	—	—	—	—	—	—	—	—	—	8%
Not enough information	25%	3%	—	—	—	—	—	6%	9%	8%
Combination										
Citizen & AGDS	—	6%	21%	30%	18%	—	6%	—	9%	4%
AGDS & police hear gunfire	—	—	3%	5%	—	—	—	—	—	4%
Totals										
Total citizen-initiated	75%	67%	60%	80%	73%	44%	59%	35%	48%	42%
Total AGDS-initiated	—	29%	61%	50%	36%	39%	35%	53%	48%	42%

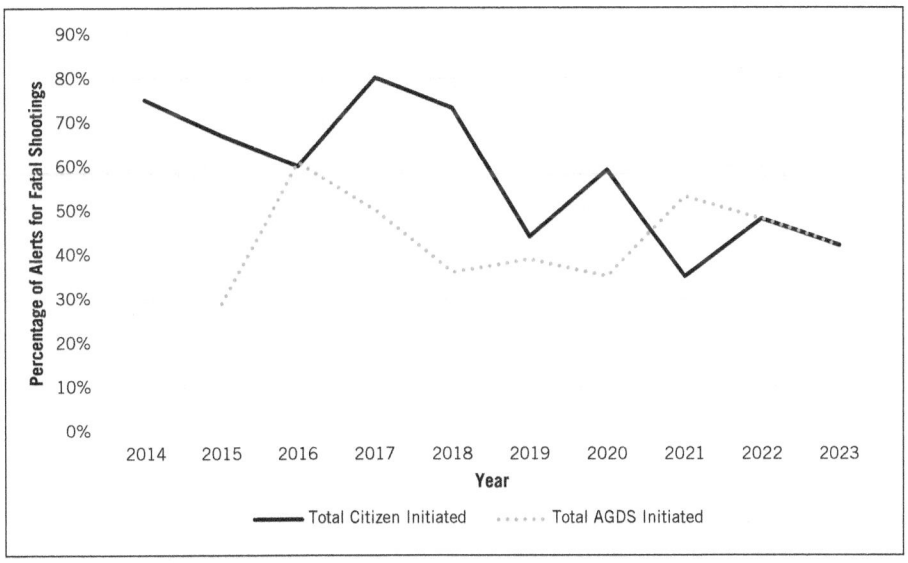

Figure 5.4 Proportion of total citizen-initiated and AGDS-initiated alerts to CCPD for fatal shootings over time (2014–2023).

However, whether increases in technology—specifically AGDS—reduced community engagement remains inconclusive. Ideally, a broader universe of gun violence and 911 shooting calls that includes nonfatal injurious shootings could be compared to AGDS alerts. Yet, those indicators of how CCPD officers are alerted in nonfatal shootings or, more broadly, all "shots fired" calls are not publicly available.

Vehicle and Pedestrian Stops

With more officers as well as improvements in operational and internal accountability, there is evidence that the CCPD engaged in much more proactive policing than the old city agency managed in its final years. Increased staffing as well as the civilianization and outsourcing of certain tasks—central booking, records management, crime-scene evidence collection—allowed for more uniformed officers to be deployed into neighborhoods: utilizing foot patrol and place-based hot spots policing approaches while making more pedestrian and vehicle stops. Any increase in officer productivity metrics would be apparent compared to the minimal output from when the department was stretched too thin, particularly from 2011 through early 2013, but even in the years before then (Kurlander, 2020; Milgram, 2020; NJ Attorney General, 2006). However, those stops and interactions between officers and community members were not always amicable at first. Data from a number of sources shows a tremendous growth in police-citizen encounters with signs pointing to aggressive enforcement tactics during the first year or two of the CCPD.

The Stanford Open Policing Project provides measures of total CCPD stops as well as a breakdown into pedestrian (person on foot) and vehicle stops for years 2013 through mid-2018. Researchers from Stanford University accessed these figures from public records requests (see Pierson et al., 2020)—specifically, the OPRA under New Jersey state law. Figure 5.5 presents the annual totals from May 2013 through mid-June 2018. For example, the raw data indicate the CCPD made 15,113 total stops from May 1, 2013, through the end of the year: 11,159 vehicle stops and 3,954 pedestrian stops. These annual numbers exploded in 2014 with 60,352 total stops broken down into 43,610 vehicle stops and 16,742 pedestrian stops. Still, this is not a fair apples-to-apples comparison. When examining May 1, 2013, through the end of the year, to May 1, 2014, through the end of 2014, there was a 143% year-over-year increase in total stops in 2014, a 135% increase in vehicle stops, and a 164% increase in pedestrian stops. An increase in CCPD officers in 2014 certainly played a role in the dramatic rise in total stops and police-citizen interactions.

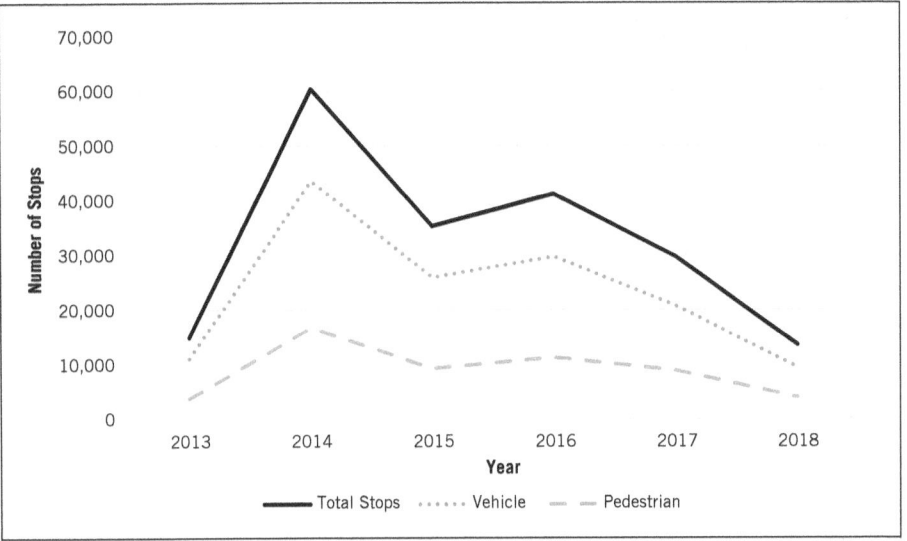

Figure 5.5 Total, vehicle, and pedestrian stops (2013–2018). (*Note: Data for 2013 start on May 1; 2018's numbers only run through June 13.*)

The number and unprecedented increase in pedestrian stops in 2014 warrants additional coverage. When using Camden's population estimate of 77,317 from the U.S. Census Bureau's "American Community Survey" in that year, the rate of stopped pedestrians is 216.6 per 1,000 residents. To put this into context, standardized rates of pedestrian stops were calculated in other major cities that came under scrutiny and, ultimately, federal or court-related intervention during each of their respective peak years using the following formula: (# of stops × 1,000) / population. Table 5.4 presents these comparisons between Camden, New York City, Philadelphia, and Chicago. New York City's peak year for pedestrian stops was 2011 when the NYPD made a total of 685,724 documented stops (ACLU-NY, 2012). Using their population estimate that year of 8,244,910, the NYPD's rate of pedestrian stops equates to 83.2 per 1,000 residents. Similarly, in 2009 the PPD made 253,333 documented stops (ACLU-PA, 2010), which—when using the population estimate of 1,528,306—comes out to a rate of 165.8 per 1,000. Only the Chicago Police Department stopped those walking on foot at higher rates than that of the CCPD in 2014. Chicago PD made more than 718,000 documented pedestrian stops in 2014 (Skogan, 2022), which equals 263.7 residents per 1,000 when using the population estimate of 2,722,407 in that year.

An important caveat to keep in mind is that these calculations use U.S. census population estimates at the city level in order to arrive at benchmarks, which are less than ideal (see Ridgeway & MacDonald, 2010). However,

TABLE 5.4 TOTAL NUMBER AND RATES OF PEDESTRIAN STOPS PER 1,000 RESIDENTS

City	Pedestrian stops	Population estimate	Rates per 1,000
Camden			
2014	**16,742**	77,317	**216.6**
2015	9,241	76,131	121.4
2016	11,328	74,417	152.2
2017	8,822	74,534	118.4
New York City (2011)	685,724	8,244,910	83.2
Philadelphia (2009)	253,333	1,528,306	165.8
Chicago (2014)	718,000	2,722,407	263.7

Sources: All population estimates come from Table DP05, American Community Survey (one-year estimates). Philadelphia's population estimate was 2010 instead of 2009 (did not exist online).

these population estimates are one of the few consistent measures that exist to make such cross-city comparisons. These benchmarks fail to take visitors and nonresidents into account. There is ample evidence that those categories have a significant impact on Camden's numbers. Camden, historically, has drawn outsiders from the nearby suburbs to buy drugs from the city's many open-air markets—a trend that has continued in more recent years. For example, during the years 2011–2012 when the old CPD recorded 175 open-air drug markets, officials reported that approximately 80% of the city's drug arrests were of nonresidents (Maciag, 2014). High numbers of nonresidents entering into Camden to buy drugs and subsequently being stopped by police—either in vehicles or on foot—would undoubtedly inflate those per capita rates.

To account for this missing context, the total number of drug arrests made countywide in 2014 should be added to the aforementioned Camden population in order to adjust the benchmark. The NJ State Police compiles annual reports on drug arrests; however, those figures are aggregated to the county level. In 2014, there were 5,062 drug arrests made in Camden County: 1,394 for the sale and manufacture and 3,668 for the possession and use of drugs (NJ State Police, 2014). When the 5,062 total drug arrests are added to the 2014 population estimate for the city of Camden of 77,317, the new benchmark estimate is 82,379—resulting in a per capita pedestrian stop rate of 203.2 per 1,000, which is an incredibly conservative estimate that takes into account every single drug arrest in the entire county in 2014. Even if this number is somewhat below the 216.6 per capita stop rate that does not account for the role city visitors play in drug arrests, it is still well above the per capita rates of pedestrian stops in both New York City (83.2 per 1,000) and Philadelphia (165.8 per 1,000) in their peak years, when they each drew investigation and intervention that led to reforms.

This high rate of pedestrian stops does not necessarily mean that Camden residents themselves were overpoliced relative to citizens of other cities, although it gives credence to residents who felt that way during this period. Outsiders may account for a large portion of those stops, although there is no simple way to differentiate between Camden residents and nonresidents across the totality of stops. However, the jump still speaks to a sudden rise in police confrontations on the streets of Camden, demanding more attention to what emerged from those confrontations and how they would change over time. This 2014 peak in CCPD stops appears to be short lived as annual totals precipitously declined in 2015. The rates of pedestrian stops per 1,000 residents were reduced from 216.6 in 2014 to 121.4 the next year—a 44% decline. After an uptick in 2016 (152.2 per 1,000), the rate declined once again in 2017 (118.4 per 1,000) to slightly lower levels than in 2015. Despite the reductions from 2014, the rates through 2017 continued to be high—worse than New York City's peak in 2011.

Low-Level Enforcement Using Tickets and Citations

The aforementioned increase in department and officer activity was accompanied by a steep rise in enforcement for low-level offenses. This has been well documented by community and activist groups who worried about the fairness of such a high level of police scrutiny as well as the local media using data from Camden's Municipal Court system. For example, during fiscal year 2013, which ran from July 2012 through June 2013, mostly still under the old city department, there were 97,000 cases filed in the municipal court (Boren, 2014). The next fiscal year—July 2013, two months after the CCPD began, through June 2014—saw an increase to almost 125,000 cases filed. Such an increase in volume led the city to add more municipal court personnel to the payroll, including another judge, a prosecutor, two public defenders, and approximately fifteen administrative staff. Table 5.5 breaks down the specific types of violations among those cases and their fiscal year-over-year changes. The numbers suggest a significant leap in highly discretionary citations given out in the first year or so of the new organization. CCPD officers handed out 99 tickets for riding bicycles without bells from July 2013 through June 2014, while there was only a single citation for riding a bicycle without a bell during the previous fiscal year. Similarly, the number of tickets for riding a bicycle without a light was 240, up from 2 the previous year. Tickets for tinted car windows (948 vs. 197) and failure to maintain lights or reflectors in vehicles (2,579 vs. 495) increased by 381% and 421%, respectively.

On May 18, 2015—the same day then-President Obama visited Camden—the ACLU-NJ put out a press release that highlighted many of these year-over-year changes. It concluded by comparing the new caseload with

TABLE 5.5 TICKETS IN CAMDEN MUNICIPAL COURT (FYS 2013 AND 2014)			
Category	7/12–6/13	7/13–6/14	Percent change
Total cases	97,000	125,000	+29%
Riding bicycle without a bell	1	99	—
Riding bicycle without a light	2	240	—
Disorderly conduct	1,766	2,521	+43%
Failure to maintain lights/reflectors—vehicle	495	2,579	+421%
Tinted car windows	197	948	+381%
Sources: ACLU-NJ (2015); Boren (2014) from Camden Municipal Court. Notes: Base rates too low for first two categories.			

the number of total residents of Camden, unfavorably: "In other words, even if every single Camden resident—adult and child—were hauled into Municipal Court, there would still be an additional 50,000 cases approximately [before caseloads reached the number achieved in 2014]" (ACLU-NJ, 2015). The sheer volume of tickets in fiscal year 2014 is exacerbated by the fact that such fines likely placed harmful and undue financial burdens on Camden residents—many of whom live below the poverty line.

Use of Force and Citizen Complaints of Excessive Force

While frequent stops from officers and high numbers of discretionary citations factor into perceptions of excessive policing, community wariness about the police presence also concerns whether police use force unjustly. The next chapter covers how the department addressed this rising concern, but it is important first to measure how the transition affected the use of force.

Data from NJ Advance Media's *The Force Report* was used to examine trends in use of force among the CPD during the organization's last year or so (January 1, 2012, through April 30, 2013) versus the first few years of the CCPD (from May 1, 2013, on). *The Force Report* was the culmination of a sixteen-month investigation that obtained all use of force reports from every municipal police department and the NJ State Police for the years 2012–2016 through OPRA requests (McCarthy & Stirling, 2018; Nelson, 2018). The number of individuals who experienced some documented level of police force—from compliance holds and grabs and takedowns to more serious categories such as strikes with hands, feet, and batons—increased each year from 2012 through 2014. In 2012, 295 people experienced use of force from officers in the old city department followed by 365 individuals, in the year of transition between the CPD and CCPD, in 2013, and 495 individuals did in 2014—a 36% increase from the previous year.

Local media and activist groups have additionally covered citizen complaints of excessive force, which were derived from information obtained through OPRA requests. As is discussed further in Chapter 6, in 2012, the last full year of the CPD when the agency had fewer than 270 officers, there were forty-one citizen complaints alleging excessive force (Boren, 2015). During 2013, the year of transition from the city to the county department on May 1, there were thirty-five such complaints. However, excessive force complaints made by citizens increased by 86% in 2014 to a total of sixty-five (Boren, 2015). It appears that the rise in enforcement in and around 2014—total, vehicle, and pedestrian police stops as well as the use of tickets for relatively low-level infractions—was accompanied by an increase in the frequency both in which force was used and in the excessive force complaints made.

Summary

The CCPD had a tremendous impact in its first few years on a number of different measures when compared to the old city department. For one, it became a functioning agency that was better able to respond to urgent community needs as it improved on the previously exorbitant dispatch and arrival times. Violent crime—specifically, gun violence and murder—property crime, and open-air drug dealing were all dramatically reduced from the record highs during 2011–2012, despite the fact that Camden has remained one of the most—if not the most—violent cities in the state and country. Much of this progress in the realm of crime and victimization has been independently verified from the evaluation work of researchers at the WRI as well as from SoundThinking's AGDS technology.

Still, other indicators of change are either inconclusive or show problematic levels of policing. There are very few data mechanisms for evaluating CCPD's community policing efforts and any potential impact on public perception and perceived legitimacy—an area for which the organization has received much positive attention. Officer proactivity in the form of vehicle and pedestrian stops, ticketing for low-level violations, use of force and citizen complaints of excessive levels of force all garnered community, activist, and media attention in 2013 and 2014 in particular. Taken as a whole, the CCPD's transition during its first few years was complicated, nuanced, and progressed in a nonlinear fashion. What was clear by the end of 2014 and beginning of 2015 was that the organization and its leaders needed to address the city's perception that the new regime was overpolicing Camden's citizens and change course.

6

CCPD's Course Correction

While there were things that the CCPD did well and deserve credit for—particularly, eliminating response and arrival time delays, increasing officer presence and foot patrols within neighborhoods, and making dents in the high levels of crime and victimization—many community members and organizations, activist groups, and media outlets raised concerns about the *level* of policing that people within the city experienced in the new department's first year and a half to two years. To be fair to CCPD and its leadership and officers, the old city department was consistently criticized for not doing enough policing: too few officers visible throughout the city and no way for supervisors to hold those officers accountable if they were not doing their jobs. Additionally, there was a tremendous amount of political pressure for the new organization to reduce crime and violence, which will be discussed in more detail in chapter nine. Such criticism and pressure were likely front and center when the CCPD had a chance to reset with a new organizational structure, enhanced technology, and internal accountability mechanisms—like GPS devices tracking and mapping officers' time and movement—allowing for officers to dedicate more time in communities and engage in proactive policing activities.

The scale of police stops, the extreme use of ticketing for low-level offenses, and the use of force as well as complaints of excessive levels of force angered the community and alerted the ACLU-NJ and local media alike. They wanted the CCPD to address the aforementioned concerns—a call that the agency largely obliged. The purpose of this chapter is to describe CCPD's course correction in light of community feedback with a focus on training and policy, among other changes. In many ways, it is how the CCPD responded to these initial concerns that has shaped the way the organization has been covered, overwhelmingly favorably, in the wake of the murder of George Floyd in 2020 and beyond.

Training

Beginning in the spring of 2015, the CCPD employed a combination of two different types of de-escalation training for officers: the "Ethical Protector" course from Resolution Group International followed by "Integrating Communications, Assessment, and Tactics" (ICAT) from the Police Executive Research Forum (PERF). Chief Thomson met Jack Hoban—a retired U.S. Marine Corps officer and the president of Resolution Group International—in 2014 and later approached him to provide training to the then two-year-old department with the goal of making officers "ethically-driven, effective communicators, and tactically proficient in a very challenging environment" (Hoban & Gourlie, 2019). Hoban asked Thomson to select his twenty most respected and charismatic officers—those who were looked up to by their peers in the department (Hoban & Gourlie, 2019; see also PERF, 2016, p. 19). Thomson's first choice was the new lead training instructor and former U.S. Marine Kevin Lutz. Together, Lutz and Hoban selected the next nineteen officers—a few lieutenants and sergeants with the rest being patrol officers. Resolution Group International trained those selected officers in the Ethical Protector course in May 2015.

Designed by Hoban, the Ethical Protector training focused on community policing methodologies, tactics, and communication and de-escalation skills—some of which Hogan adapted from the Marine Corps' "Winning Hearts and Minds" efforts abroad (Hoban & Gourlie, 2019). Respect for the sanctity of life was a core tenet woven throughout. Following an introductory lecture, the training was composed of three days with physical, hands-on experience. Resolution Group International continued to train CCPD officers on a few additional occasions during the summer and through the end of 2015 (Adomaitis, 2015c; Moselle, 2015). Approximately twenty to twenty-five CCPD officers at a time received the training with a total of seventy-one completing it (Goh, 2021; Hoban & Gourlie, 2019).

In September 2016, PERF began offering their new ICAT de-escalation training to the CCPD. In fact, Camden was one of the first pilot departments in the country to receive ICAT. Chief Thomson had close ties to PERF as he was elected as the organization's president in 2015. The CCPD, specifically, then-Lieutenant Lutz, also assisted in the development of the ICAT program in April 2016 as a participant and working group member tasked with creating the training curriculum (see PERF, 2016a). Batches of officers underwent ICAT training in fourteen different sessions through the end of 2017 by which time all CCPD officers had received it (Goh, 2021). During this time period, CCPD provided ICAT both as an initial curriculum for all officers and as reinforcement retraining for those officers who had engaged in above-average levels of use of force. Later, all new CCPD recruits would receive ICAT training in the police academy (Bender, 2020).

The planning origins of what would become PERF's ICAT training began in 2014 following a series of high-profile police shootings of citizens. PERF identified a critical training gap at the time for a particular set of police-citizen circumstances: those interactions in which a person is perceived to be behaving erratically—due to either mental illness or an emotional episode, substance abuse, or an intellectual or developmental disability—and is potentially dangerous although unarmed or with a nonfirearm weapon such as a knife or a blunt object (PERF, 2015, 2016a). Officers nationwide described receiving relatively less training on topics such as de-escalation, crisis intervention, tactical communications, and less-lethal alternatives to deadly force. Additionally, police training is rife with outdated and, arguably, questionable concepts that may contribute to police shootings and the escalation of force, such as the "21-foot rule" and "drawing a line in the sand" (Sierra-Arévalo, 2024; S. Simon, 2023). PERF, as a result, consulted leading training experts from around the country as well as abroad from Police Scotland and the Greater Manchester Police in England. Officers in the United Kingdom rarely carry firearms, yet they resolve the vast majority of—if not nearly all—incidents with knives, edged weapons, and blunt objects without deadly force. Therefore, PERF relied heavily on the training regimen implemented in the United Kingdom in their creation of ICAT's model curriculum.

ICAT was designed to bridge the gap between the previous types of communications skills offered by Crisis Intervention Team training and the practical tactical skills needed to de-escalate and resolve certain encounters without deadly force. PERF's (2016a) training guide covers six modules: an introduction, the critical decision-making model (CDM), crisis recognition and response, tactical communications, operational safety tactics, and integration and practice. In addition to lectures and discussion, the training relies on hands on, physical instruction with role-playing scenarios. Perhaps the most integral component of ICAT is the CDM. Developed in the United Kingdom and historically used by SWAT teams in the United States, the CDM focuses on a different style of thinking than the traditionally taught use of force continuum. The CDM is based on a circular thought process designed to help officers develop and think through their options in a situation using five-steps centered around an agency's core values and ethics and the sanctity of human life (PERF, 2015, 2016a). Officers are taught tangible and tactical skills, such as "slowing interactions down" and buying more time until additional specialized resources can arrive on scene as well as creating distance, taking cover, and tactically retreating.

Although there is a limited research base, the few evaluations of ICAT have yielded promising findings—including one in Camden. A test of officers' perceptions among the University of Cincinnati Police Department found participants held positive views of the training, with 71.6% willing to recommend it to others and 63.5% interested in a follow-up course (Isaza et al., 2019). In terms of officer behavior, ICAT evaluations of both the Louisville Metro Police Department and the CCPD uncovered statistically significant reductions in police use of force. Both research designs were rigorous. Engel and colleagues (2022a) employed a stepped-wedge randomized controlled trial design in Louisville where officers received the ICAT training at different intervals—allowing a comparison not only across time but also among those who had received the training versus those who had not. ICAT in Louisville was associated with reductions in not only use of force incidents and citizen injuries but also officer injuries in the post-training period. Goh (2021) performed a similar individual-officer analysis in Camden as well as a department-level synthetic control comparison of use of force among the CCPD compared to thirty-five other large municipal departments in New Jersey who had not received the ICAT training. The results of the individual-officer analysis found no significant effects; however, the synthetic control analysis suggested that the de-escalation training led to a 40% reduction in serious use of force incidents.

These preliminary findings must be qualified. There have been very few tests of de-escalation training in law enforcement broadly (Engel, McManus, & Herold, 2020), let alone of PERF's ICAT, and evaluations are not uniform in their effectiveness at both changing officer attitudes and reducing use of force (see Council on Criminal Justice, 2021). An evaluation, for example, of Polis Solutions' T3 (Tact, Tactics, and Trust) de-escalation program in Tucson, Arizona, and Fayetteville, North Carolina, found that, although participating officers were more likely to have improved attitudes, there was no evidence that the training altered officer behavior regarding the use of force (see McLean et al., 2020; Wolfe et al., 2020). White and colleagues (2021a) found similar benefits to officer perceptions in their evaluation of a department-created de-escalation training in the Tempe (AZ) Police Department—of which they included bits and pieces from both ICAT and T3. Patrol officers who took part in the training differed in their behavior from those who did not: they were less likely to use a condescending or patronizing tone and charged or imposing body language, while they were more likely to attempt to build rapport with citizens and resolve encounters informally, without issuing a ticket or citation (see White et al., 2021b; White, Orosco, & Watts, 2023a). Additionally, citizens were less likely to be injured during use of force encounters with officers who received the de-escalation training (White, Orosco, & Watts, 2023b).

More specifically, regarding officers' perceptions following both the ICAT and the T3 programs, those officers who were receptive and intrinsically motivated to train were more satisfied and more likely to place higher priorities on de-escalation tactics and procedurally fair communication during citizen encounters (Engel et al., 2021; Wolfe et al., 2020). The officers most likely to embrace the training could be self-selecting into the programs being evaluated in these studies or could be reporting what they believe their supervisors to be looking for. A more nuanced analysis highlights the importance of the selection and quality of the specific trainers in affecting officer receptivity to the training regimen. During the ICAT and T3 evaluations, respectively, officers' perceptions of their immediate supervisors' receptivity to the training as well as their perceptions of organizational justice—defined as subordinates' evaluations of fairness in processes, outcomes, and treatment by supervisors and leaders, and the agency more broadly (Wolfe & Lawson, 2020)—were found to influence their own levels of satisfaction with and their degree of attitudinal changes after the training (Engel et al., 2022b; Wolfe et al., 2022). Those officers who felt that their supervisors and command staff were not receptive, did not communicate the value of the training, did not seek their opinions about the training, and failed to ensure the training was administered fairly were less satisfied with the training and did not experience as many attitudinal changes. Altogether, there is reason to be hopeful about the influence of new training but also reason to be skeptical.

There are a number of lessons to glean from CCPD's apparent success with their de-escalation training as well as the preliminary literature on the topic more broadly. First, training effectiveness is likely contingent on the individual department. Those that have top-down buy-in and support from leadership—as was the case in Camden with Chief Thomson—may increase their chances. Next, the right collection of officers from within each organization, continuing to buy-in themselves, must be the ones to deliver such training. They should, ideally, be well respected by their fellow officers—much like then-Lieutenant Lutz and the others who were carefully selected in 2015. In fact, a component of White and colleagues' (2021b) experience in Tempe was that officers peer-nominated the top de-escalators in the department, who were then incorporated into the planning phases of the de-escalation curriculum. Departments, leaders, and immediate supervisors that foster perceptions of organizational justice on the part of frontline staff as well as those who are themselves receptive to innovative training tenets are in a better position to reap the potential benefits. Training, however, is only one side of the coin that must be complemented with policy and other related accountability mechanisms.

Administrative Policy, Data Documentation, and Review

People are influenced by the organizations that they work for. This applies not only to police officers but to members of any profession. If you have worked for multiple companies or even supervisors, then you are likely to have experienced varying levels of monitoring and accountability. In some organizations, there is a free-for-all with a lack of supervision and little-to-no tracking of employee performance. In others, it is the complete opposite end of the spectrum. Over time in such systems, people generally start to recognize what they can and cannot get away with. Policing is no different in that the role of each respective department is of the utmost importance, which taps into the concept of an "organizational culture" (Paoline & Terrill, 2014; J. Wilson, 1968).

Policing literature is ripe with examples highlighting how officer behavior, particularly as it relates to use of force and highly discretionary self-initiated activities like vehicle and pedestrian stops, differs across the organizations in which they work. Empirical studies have focused on administrative policy, internal sources of review investigating and adjudicating critical incidents such as police shootings, and more formal documentation and data collection standards. The NYPD is credited with beginning this movement toward stricter departmental policy that narrowed officer discretion along with better data collection mechanisms and after-incident review standards. In August 1972, NYPD Commissioner Patrick V. Murphy introduced a new policy restricting the use of deadly force (Temporary Operating Procedure 237; see Fyfe, 1979). Whereas officers were previously allowed to shoot to prevent the escape of a criminal to effect an arrest—the traditional "fleeing felon" rule—Murphy narrowed officer shooting discretion to be used only in situations involving the defense of life. That is, situations when there is a risk of death or serious bodily injury to themselves or others. He additionally created new directives for the documentation of firearms discharges as well as the Firearms Discharge Review Board to investigate such incidents.

James Fyfe (1978, 1979), a former lieutenant in the NYPD, examined the impact of the directive and found that the NYPD's intervention resulted in a considerable reduction in the frequency with which officers used their firearms. Other metropolitan departments uncovered similar patterns of reductions in police shootings following more restrictive policy changes as well as documentation and review protocols, including Los Angeles (Meyer, 1980) and Philadelphia (White, 2000), among other cities (Oakland, Atlanta, Kansas City, MO, and Omaha, NE; see Geller & Scott, 1992; Sherman,

1980, 2018; Walker, 1993). Alternatively, studies show that police shootings increase during administrative permissiveness when restrictions are relaxed (White, 2001). These studies generally find no negative impact on officer safety following more restrictive firearms policies (see, e.g., Sherman, 1980; Walker, 1993).

In addition to reducing the total number of police shootings in general, stricter administrative policies governing firearms usage were also found to affect the most controversial and highly discretionary incidents. Examining firearms discharges from both the NYPD and the Memphis Police Department, Fyfe (1982) classified incidents into two categories: "elective," in which the officer involved can choose to shoot or not at little or no risk to oneself or others, versus "non-elective," where the officer has little real choice but to shoot or to risk death or serious injury to oneself or others. He found that the Memphis Police Department, which had a less restrictive policy, engaged in more "elective" shootings, specifically of "fleeing felons," while the NYPD with their more restrictive policy engaged in more "nonelective" defense of life shootings (see also Fyfe, 1979). Differences also manifested in the disproportionate use of deadly force against Black Americans. Racial disparities were greatest for elective shootings in Memphis, where Blacks who were unarmed and nonassaultive were killed at a rate that was eighteen times greater than that of their white counterparts. Upon synthesizing the available research at the time, Walker (1993, 32) concluded:

> Administrative rules have successfully limited police shooting discretion, with positive results in terms of social policy. Fewer people are being shot and killed, racial disparities in shootings have been reduced, and police officers are in no greater danger because of these restrictions.

An initial study has also found departments that adopted restrictions in the form of more constraining policy language regarding shooting at moving vehicle threats engaged in fewer of such deadly force incidents among a sample of the 100 largest local/municipal police departments in the United States (Shjarback & Ward, 2025).

Extending beyond the documentation and review standards for firearms discharges, a recent standard over the past few years requires mandatory reporting when officers directly *point* their guns at citizens but do not fire. A number of large agencies currently mandate this type of documentation—including the Dallas, Baltimore, Cleveland, New Orleans, and Chicago Police Departments—and it has been recommended as a best practice by the National Policing Institute (2019) for agencies to better understand how often and under which circumstances their officers are engaged in such behavior. Two studies thus far have found that "point and report" policies and documentation requirements are associated with fewer police shootings of citizens (Jennings & Rubado, 2017; Shjarback, White, & Bishopp, 2021). Changes in the Dallas Police Department in 2013 resulted not only in fewer police shootings in general but also in reductions in "threat perception failure" shootings (i.e., those where an officer mistakes an item in a person's hand for a gun) (Shjarback, White, & Bishopp, 2021).

Stricter administrative policy has also been shown to have an impact on less-than-lethal weapons and nonlethal force in general. When conducted energy devices, such as TASERs, and Oleoresin Capsicum (pepper spray) are placed higher on a department's use of force continuum—and, therefore, limiting the circumstances that warrant deployment—officers rely on them less frequently (Bishopp, Klinger, & Morris, 2015; Ferdik et al., 2014; Morabito & Doerner, 1997; Terrill & Paoline, 2017; Thomas, Collins, & Lovrich, 2010). For example, the Dallas Police Department once permitted their officers to deploy TASERs when met with "defensive resistance" (i.e., noncompliance against a lawful order; e.g., refusing to stand up when ordered to do so if seated). The Dallas Police Department's use of force policy was then changed to limit the use of TASERs to only during "active aggression" scenarios, such as a physical action directed at an officer or an innocent citizen, including attacking, grabbing, punching, and/or kicking an officer (Bishopp, Klinger, & Morris, 2015), a change that resulted in fewer TASER deployments. Finally, Terrill and Paoline (2017) examined the impact of administrative policy on the full spectrum of nonlethal force, where they uncovered that officers working in departments with more restrictive policies employ force less readily compared to officers working in agencies with more permissive and lenient policies. These findings mirror the studies that have tested the influence of administrative policy on police use of deadly force. Taken together, this body of research underscores the importance of stricter administrative policy governing what officers can and cannot do coupled with rigorous data collection and review standards, highlighting the importance of administrative policy reform to results on the ground.

Police Use of Force in New Jersey

As discussed in previous chapters, New Jersey is in a unique position because the state's AG has tremendous power and influence over local policing matters. The state constitution as well as the Criminal Justice Act of 1970 (N.J.S.A. 52:17B-97 to -117) grants the authority for the general supervision of criminal justice affairs to the AG as the chief law enforcement officer of the state.

The purpose of the act is to provide for the uniform and efficient enforcement of the criminal law and the administration of justice throughout New Jersey. Therefore, the state of New Jersey has *one* model use of force policy that is set by the AG's Office, and all five hundred–plus law enforcement departments in the state must follow its guidelines. This model presents a number of benefits—namely, that the AG can institute swift changes for

_____ POLICE DEPARTMENT
USE OF FORCE REPORT

A. Incident Information

Date	Time	Day of Week	Location	INCIDENT NUMBER

Type of Incident
☐ Crime in progress   ☐ Domestic   ☐ Other dispute   ☐ Suspicious person   ☐ Traffic stop
☐ Other (specify)

B. Officer Information

Name (Last, First, Middle)		Badge #	Sex	Race	Age	Injured Y/N	Killed Y/N
Rank	Duty assignment	Years of service		On-Duty Y/N		Uniform Y/N	

C1. Subject 1 (List only the person who was the subject of the use of force by the officer listed in Section B.)

Name (Last, First, Middle)	Sex	Race	Age	Weapon Y/N	Injured Y/N	Killed Y/N
☐ Under the influence ☐ Other unusual condition (specify)	Arrested Y/N		Charges			

Subject's actions (check all that apply)	Officer's use of force toward this subject (check all that apply)	
☐ Resisted police officer control	☐ Compliance hold	Firearms Discharge
☐ Physical threat/attack on officer or another	☐ Hands/fists	☐ Intentional
☐ Threatened/attacked officer or another with blunt object	☐ Kicks/feet	☐ Accidental
☐ Threatened/attacked officer or another with knife/cutting object	☐ Chemical/natural agent	
☐ Threatened/attacked officer or another with motor vehicle	☐ Strike/use baton or other object	Number of Shots Fired ____
☐ Threatened officer or another with firearm	☐ Canine	Number of Hits ____
☐ Fired at officer or another		[Use 'UNK' if unknown]
☐ Other (specify)	☐ Other (specify)	

C2. Subject 2 (List only the person who was the subject of the use of force by the officer listed in Section B.)

Name (Last, First, Middle)	Sex	Race	Age	Weapon Y/N	Injured Y/N	Killed Y/N
☐ Under the influence ☐ Other unusual condition (specify)	Arrested Y/N		Charges			

Subject's actions (check all that apply)	Officer's use of force toward this subject (check all that apply)	
☐ Resisted police officer control	☐ Compliance hold	Firearms Discharge
☐ Physical threat/attack on officer or another	☐ Hands/fists	☐ Intentional
☐ Threatened/attacked officer or another with blunt object	☐ Kicks/feet	☐ Accidental
☐ Threatened/attacked officer or another with knife/cutting object	☐ Chemical/natural agent	
☐ Threatened/attacked officer or another with motor vehicle	☐ Strike/use baton or other object	Number of Shots Fired ____
☐ Threatened officer or another with firearm	☐ Canine	Number of Hits ____
☐ Fired at officer or another		[Use 'UNK' if unknown]
☐ Other (specify)	☐ Other (specify)	

▶ If this officer used force against more than two subjects in this incident, attach additional USE OF FORCE REPORTS.

Signature:	Date:
Print Supervisor Name:	Supervisor Signature:

7/2001

Figure 6.1 Stock use of force reporting form from the NJ Attorney General (2000).

policing matters in a timely fashion, often with the simple stroke of a pen. Additionally, police departments' use of force policy is consistent (at least on paper) in New Jersey as opposed to other states where much variation exists in terms of when officers can use different levels of force in response to disparate levels of resistance.

While this system presented an opportunity for New Jersey to drive reform in Camden, in this case, the state would follow the city's lead. At the time of the Camden transformation in 2013, through the first few years after, the NJ AG's model use of force policy was woefully outdated. The last time the policy was meaningfully revised was in June 2000. The policy echoed the same tone and language described in the U.S. Supreme Court's decisions in *Tennessee v. Garner* (1985) and *Graham v. Connor* (1989). For example, it stated the standard points, including how "use of force must be objectively reasonable from the perspective of the officer." Like many other use of force policies, it was vague and ambiguous to the untrained eye and provided little guidance to officers regarding what they could and could not do. Discretion is understandable: police-citizen encounters are dynamic and transactional with no two use of force scenarios being comparable; it would be impossible to factor in all the different variables at work. But the same mechanisms used to track the use of force functioned to justify that force. In the 2000 revision, agencies were now required to report all use of force incidents to the AG's Office using a stock form that collected basic descriptive information on the situational characteristics of each incident—location, day, time—and officer and citizen demographic characteristics, and applied categories that justified the use of force. Figure 6.1 presents the stock NJ AG form.

CCPD's Policy Change

In response to the aforementioned community and activist groups' pushback in 2014-2015, specifically from the ACLU-NJ, the CCPD began the process of trying to address its problematic uses of force—specifically, the 86% increase in excessive force complaints from thirty-five to sixty-five in 2014—through changes in its policy. The CCPD leadership began a collaborative effort with the Policing Project at NYU School of Law and its founder Barry Friedman to revise its current use of force policy. It shared the resulting policy with every other agency within the state. The changes made in the eighteen-page revised policy drastically went above and beyond both the NJ AG's use of force guidelines at the time and the U.S. Supreme Court's minimum standards set forth in case law, such as *Tennessee v. Garner* (1985) and *Graham v. Connor* (1989). Figure 6.2 presents a side-by-side view of the major differences between CCPD's old and revised use of force policy that was created by the Policing Project.

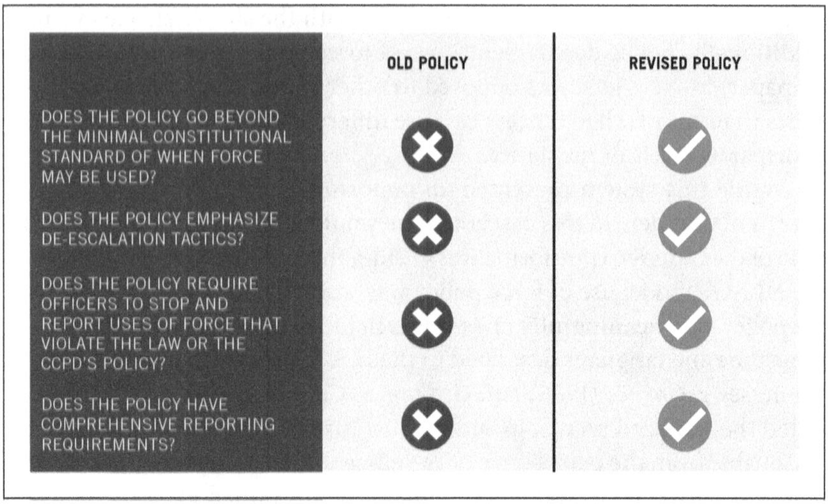

	OLD POLICY	REVISED POLICY
DOES THE POLICY GO BEYOND THE MINIMAL CONSTITUTIONAL STANDARD OF WHEN FORCE MAY BE USED?	✗	✓
DOES THE POLICY EMPHASIZE DE-ESCALATION TACTICS?	✗	✓
DOES THE POLICY REQUIRE OFFICERS TO STOP AND REPORT USES OF FORCE THAT VIOLATE THE LAW OR THE CCPD'S POLICY?	✗	✓
DOES THE POLICY HAVE COMPREHENSIVE REPORTING REQUIREMENTS?	✗	✓

Figure 6.2 Differences between CCPD's old and revised use of force policies. (*Source: Policing Project, 2020a.*)

For example, rather than simply echo the Supreme Court's constitutional principles—namely, that an officer may only use force that a reasonable officer would when facing similar circumstances—the new policy clearly spells out how officers "must do everything possible to respect and preserve the sanctity of all human life, avoid unnecessary uses of force, and minimize the force that is used, while still protecting themselves and the public" (Policing Project, n.d.). The policy encourages de-escalation throughout police-citizen encounters and provides officers with articulable standards in terms of what levels of force and tools—conducted energy devices, batons—are permitted in certain circumstances given the level of subject resistance (Policing Project, 2020b). It also explains what is not permitted, such as chokeholds and strangleholds, while restricting officers from shooting at moving vehicles except in unique situations.

During their assistance, the Policing Project compared the CCPD's new use of force policy with that of twenty-five other big-city departments across eight different metrics. The results of those comparisons can be found in Figure 6.3, which was also created by the Policing Project. The light gray boxes denote whether an agency's use of force policy had specific language addressing each metric, while the dark gray boxes denote that they did not. They found that while many of these agencies include language and address a few components, only the CCPD's revised policy as well as the San Francisco Police Department focuses attention on all eight areas (see Policing Project, 2020a). More specifically, CCPD's revised policy:

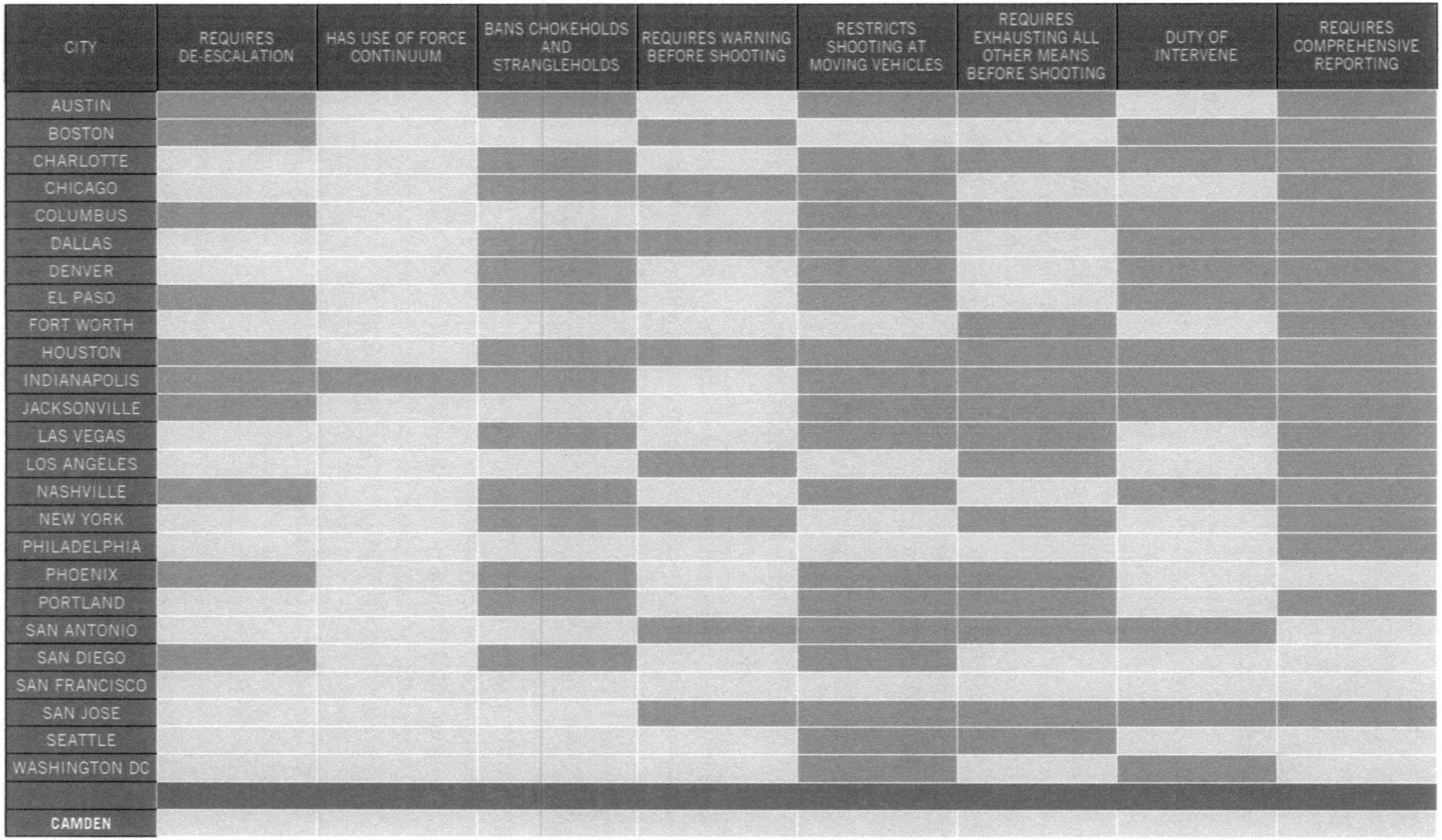

Figure 6.3 CCPD's revised use of force policy in relation to twenty-five other major cities. (*Note: Light gray shading indicates that it is included in the use of force policy, and dark gray shading indicates that it is not included in the use of force policy.*)

- Requires de-escalation
- Has a use of force continuum
- Bans chokeholds and strangleholds
- Requires officers to warn before shooting
- Restricts shooting at moving vehicles
- Requires deadly force be the last option
- Specifies that officers have a duty to intervene in any uses of force that violate applicable laws and/or CCPD directives
- Requires comprehensive reporting of uses of force

In addition to the Policing Project, the ACLU-NJ, select community groups and members, and the CCPD's new local chapter of the Fraternal Order of Police all provided input during the development with both the ACLU-NJ and the local Fraternal Order of Police vetting and accepting the final version of the new policy (Policing Project, 2020a, b, n.d.). The policy is consistent with and modeled after "PERF's 30 Guiding Principles on Use of Force" in their 2016b report. There are six principles in the CCPD's revised policy that hold the sanctity of all human life at the core of them. They are:

1. Officers may use force to accomplish only specific law enforcement objectives.
2. Whenever feasible, officers should attempt to de-escalate confrontations with the goal of resolving encounters without force. Officers may use force that is only objectively reasonable, necessary, and as a last resort.
3. Officers must use only the amount of force that is proportional to the circumstances.
4. Deadly force is authorized only as a last resort and only in strict accordance with this directive.
5. Officers must promptly provide or request medical aid.
6. Employees have a duty to stop and report the uses of force that violate any applicable law and/or this directive.

The CCPD's new use of force policy was even used as a model when the NJ AG's Office amended and revised its own statewide use of force policy, in 2020, for the first time in two decades. Much of the language in the AG's revised policy mirrors that of the CCPD, including an emphasis on de-escalation, exhausting all other options, and relying on use of force as a last resort, prohibitions against firing weapons at moving vehicles, a "duty to intervene" on other officers' behalf when witnessing illegal or excessive force, and a requirement to—when appropriate—render medical aid to citizens following an incident (NJ Attorney General, 2020). In a press conference to

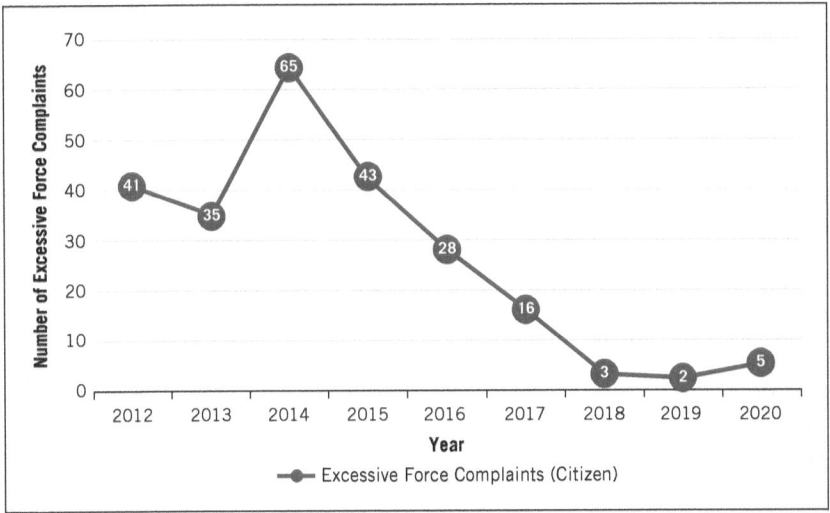

Figure 6.4 Excessive use of force complaints generated from citizens (2012–2020).

unveil the revised guidelines, then-AG Gurbir Grewal heralded the CCPD's use of force policy: "Their use of force has since declined while relationships between cops in the community and public safety have all improved" (Shaw, 2020).

There is evidence that the CCPD was able to rein in use of force in general and citizen complaints of excessive force following changes in both training and policy. If you recall from the previous chapter, excessive force complaints totaled sixty-five in 2014—an 86% increase from the thirty-five complaints a year prior in 2013. Figure 6.4 plots the annual number of citizen complaints for excessive force from 2012 through 2020, which shows how they have precipitously declined from their peak in 2014. In 2015, the CCPD ended the year with forty-three citizen complaints alleging excessive force—a 34% reduction from the previous year, followed by twenty-eight in 2016, sixteen in 2017, three in 2018, two in 2019, and five in 2020. "There's lots of things to praise," stated Alexander Shalom, senior supervising attorney at the ACLU-NJ, citing the reforms to the use of force, an emphasis on de-escalation, and the steep drop in excessive force complaints (Newton, 2020).

Technology to Assist Training and Policy

Supplementing the de-escalation training and use of force policy changes, the CCPD possesses a VirTra V-300® simulator. This state-of-the-art technology includes an elevated stage and five floor-to-ceiling screens covering three hundred degrees to portray true-to-life and reality-based situations to users (VirTra, n.d.). The system allows officers and other participants to practice how they would respond to lifelike scenarios, which are often based on actual police-citizen encounters, including "shoot-don't shoot" simulations where users must react to potentially deadly threats and decide to use their firearm or not. It is another valuable tool to reinforce classroom training and policy review, while honing one's skills in situational awareness and de-escalation tactics. According to CCPD training officer Sergeant Ralph Thorton, "Officers use the simulator to learn how to properly respond to situations that traditionally would warrant deadly force but do not necessarily require it" (Policing Project, 2020a). Additionally, former lead training officer Kevin Lutz described how CCPD officers wear heart rate monitors that show their body's reactions to stress situations while using the VirTra V-300®. According to Lutz, "We're teaching them how to bring their heart rate back down and talk through conflict. . . . So that when they get into a situation like this, more often than not, it's not their first time experiencing it" (J. Walsh, 2021).

Two use of force incidents in which deadly force was avoided, while anecdotal, highlight the potential impact of CCPD's training and policy changes.

"Broadway and Mickle"

On November 9, 2015, CCPD officers responded to a report of a man with a knife who threatened employees and customers at a Crown Fried Chicken restaurant on Broadway Avenue before leaving on foot. The forty-eight-year-old man was showing signs of mental illness when he was approached by police officers. He ignored officers' commands to "drop the knife" and continued to walk away from them—occasionally making slashing motions through the air. Officers held their gunfire while pursuing the man from a safe distance. For upward of seven minutes, fifteen officers and two police vehicles followed the man for several blocks as they created a buffer around him. Traffic was cleared in the areas directly ahead of where he was walking. One officer eventually closed enough distance to deploy his TASER, which dropped the man and incapacitated him to allow officers to place him in handcuffs. Much of the original incident inside the Crown Fried Chicken as well as the police-citizen interaction on the streets can be viewed on YouTube through a collection of surveillance, CCTV, and officer body-worn camera video footage (YouTube, 2015b).

The encounter was resolved without death or serious injury for both the man and responding officers. Leaders within the CCPD later commented on how the tactics employed and the outcome were unimaginable just a few years prior. Chief Scott Thomson told the *New York Times* that, had this incident taken place a year earlier, "We would more than likely have deployed deadly force and moved on" (Goldstein, 2017). Lieutenant Lutz echoed a similar sentiment stating, "Five, six, seven years ago, prior to this training, prior to the culture that we created, that most definitely ends in a police-involved shooting" (Cuellar, 2019). At the time of the nonshooting incident in November 2015, approximately seventy-one CCPD officers had completed the aforementioned "Ethical Protector" de-escalation training.

September 2020 Use of Force Incident

A similar, less publicized, police-citizen encounter occurred in September 2020. Body-worn camera footage from this incident can also be viewed on YouTube (2020b). It shows how a woman flagged down a CCPD officer to report that she had just been sexually assaulted by a man with a knife (see also Everett, 2020b; J. Walsh, 2021). Once the officer assists the woman into his vehicle, the suspect can be seen and heard tapping on the officer's driver's side front window with a knife. The officer slowly drives away, while the thirty-seven-year-old male suspect then gets into his vehicle and takes off. The suspect stopped his vehicle and exited several times—all while ignoring commands to drop the knife before getting back into the vehicle and driving off. Upon parking and exiting the vehicle a third time, he continued to ignore verbal commands to drop the knife. When he advanced on one of the pursuing officers, another deployed a TASER, which dropped the suspect—allowing officers to handcuff the suspect and place him in custody. The entire encounter lasted thirteen minutes.

CCPD officers followed their de-escalation training and use of force policies to a T. From the outset, the first officer repositioned himself by driving away and not exiting the vehicle; he did not immediately confront the suspect. Officers on their body-worn cameras can be seen using police vehicles as cover and not getting too close positionally. The watch commander monitoring the situation remotely can be heard over the radio reinforcing de-escalation tactics to the officers: "Maintain a safe distance, continue to de-escalate the male, and engage in conversation." Officers throughout the encounter appear to make active choices to avoid "officer-created jeopardy/danger," not placing themselves in situations that contribute to police shootings (Borodkin, 2022). Ultimately, the CCPD officers engaged with a noncompliant individual with a deadly weapon who was wanted for a violent crime. If they did shoot him, then there is no doubt that it would have been considered a "lawful but awful" deadly force encounter—that is, legally justified given the facts and circumstances based on what a reasonable officer on the scene would do rather than with the benefit of hindsight (*Graham v. Connor*). However, the key distinction here, according to then-Captain Lutz, who was in charge of training for many years, was that, although the suspect posed a "potential threat," it was not an "imminent" one (see J. Walsh, 2021); the PERF's ICAT de-escalation training applied here due to there being a nonfirearm weapon threat. Overall, this incident showcases how CCPD's reform efforts are sustainable: it occurred more than five years after the de-escalation training began and over a year after the policy changes were made while under the leadership of a new chief.

Other Changes (Internal Affairs and Use of Tickets/Citations)

In addition to addressing problematic levels of the use of force through training, policy, and enhanced technology, the CCPD took steps to dissuade officers from issuing excessive tickets and citations. It accomplished this reduction by directing the Internal Affairs Unit to focus attention on such officer behaviors and outputs. Former chief Thomson (2020) discussed this in an op-ed written in the *Washington Post* a few weeks after the fallout from the murder of George Floyd:

> Part of this was about eliminating counterproductive policing routines: I directed internal affairs to investigate the department's top five ticket-writing cops each month, because handing a hefty traffic fine to someone who's scraping by can be life-altering, and not in a way that protects the community. Our preference was to issue warnings. The state American Civil Liberties Union chapter and community residents explained that some of our low-level-offense enforcements were making things worse. We listened.

Shalom of the ACLU-NJ reiterated that then-Chief Thomson took steps to lower the number of tickets after being made aware of the issue (Breslauer et al., 2020; Newton, 2020).

Data and measures from the Stanford Open Policing Project, which were discussed earlier in Chapter 5, independently verify the dramatic scaling back of CCPD's use of citations from 2015 on. Excluding all those stops made for investigatory purposes in which the final disposition was usually categorized as "field contact" or "community intelligence" cards, all enforcement-eligible CCPD stops were examined from May 1, 2013, through June 13, 2018. An enforcement-eligible stop indicates, based on the data reported, that officers had the discretion to either make an arrest, issue a ticket or summons, or let the citizen off with a warning for some type of crime or other violation. The numbers and percentages of enforcement-eligible police stops

TABLE 6.1 ENFORCEMENT-ELIGIBLE POLICE STOPS						
	2013[a]	2014	2015	2016	2017	2018[b]
Arrests	396 (6%)	587 (3%)	218 (1%)	217 (0.9%)	80 (0.5%)	26 (0.4%)
Citations	6,252 (94%)	19,070 (97%)	8,646 (55%)	7,504 (30%)	4,617 (26%)	1,561 (22%)
Warnings	0 (0%)	0 (0%)	6,790 (43%)	17,672 (70%)	12,910 (73%)	5,511 (78%)
[a] Data collection begins May 1, 2013.						
[b] Data collection ends June 13, 2018.						
Source: Stanford Open Policing Project.						

for each year are presented in Table 6.1, including the breakdown into three broad categories: arrests, citations, and warnings.

In 2013 and 2014, CCPD officers either made arrests or issued citations for all enforcement-eligible vehicle and pedestrian stops. The Stanford Open Policing Project data indicates that zero warnings were issued for these enforcement-eligible stops during these years. This pattern appears to change in 2015 when warnings finally picked up in the data. Starting in 2015, the total number of citations begins decreasing with stark differences from 2014 ($N = 19,070$) to 2015 ($N = 8,646$). In addition to the raw numbers, the percentage of enforcement-eligible stops in which a citation is issued also begins to precipitously decline: from 97% in 2014 to 55% in 2015, followed by 30% in 2016, 26% in 2017, and 22% through June 13, 2018. The use of warnings follows the inverse pattern. Starting in 2015, the percentage of enforcement-eligible stops for which CCPD issued a warning in lieu of a citation increased to 43% followed by 70% in 2016, 73% in 2017, and 78% through June 2018. CCPD clearly and successfully reversed course on one of its most controversial practices.

Summary

Despite a rocky start to the level of policing administered in its first two years, the CCPD responded to calls for change and course corrected. Community, activist, and media attention must be recognized for bringing attention to those concerns (see Danley, 2020); however, it is also important to credit the CCPD's leadership, officers, and organization as a whole for taking a number of proactive steps to remedy problematic levels of policing. The CCPD sought out innovative de-escalation training and even served as a guinea pig for PERF's new and, at the time, untested ICAT program. The CCPD completely revamped their use of force policy—making it more restrictive by limiting officer discretion and providing more guidance to officers—despite the fact that they were under no legal obligation to do so. In that regard, they collaborated with academics and law professors at the Policing Project to construct a revised policy that later served as a model for the entire state of New Jersey and perhaps other departments around the country. And they took active steps to curtail the excessive use of citations by employing Internal Affairs to perform a novel and nontraditional function of investigating those officers writing the most tickets.

7

DID THE CHANGES TAKE?

The previous few chapters detailed how the CCPD began and what it did—organizationally and strategically—during its first few years. They covered the new department's impact and the initial challenges as well as how the CCPD changed course in response to community pushback. One question continually posed since 2013 is whether there was a culture change from the CPD to the CCPD. Former Chief Thomson, among other Camden County officials (e.g., Gagis, 2019), has written and spoken about his perceived culture changes among the CCPD. According to Thomson, "As of May 1, 2013, we had the luxury of building culture rather than the challenge of changing it" (Arco, 2015; see also Thomson, 2020). In fact, the difficulty of addressing problematic organizational culture and the failures of past reform efforts have opened the door for the defund and abolish movements—spurring places like Minneapolis (Phelps, 2024; Romo, 2020) and Ithaca, NY (Lowery, 2021) to mull following Camden's lead and start anew. While assessing department culture is beyond the scope of this project—especially short of qualitative interviews with those who were part of both organizations or an ethnography of the CCPD—the purpose of this chapter is to examine and weigh in on a related question: Did things change from one agency to the next? As the CCPD updated operations, technology, and policy, how did their approach to policing change?

By most metrics and accounts, the newly minted CCPD needed to address and reform two related aspects: (1) apathy, lethargy, and overall ineffectiveness in tackling crime, and (2) accountability. For example, much was said in the years immediately leading up to 2013 about the lack of police work and even police visibility in neighborhoods as well as the problems with pockets of corruption. These dueling dilemmas meant that the CCPD, from its origination, was tasked with a herculean effort, which should make the changes it eventually made even more impressive.

Apathy, Lethargy, and Overall Ineffectiveness in Tackling Crime

Camden dealt with underenforcement issues dating back to 2007–2008. At the time, the CPD had an appropriate number of sworn officers on their force; however, too few were deployed on the streets in the community, while many worked inside, behind a desk doing administrative tasks. Efforts from both the AG Anne Milgram and Chief Thomson to address this lack of visibility on the street during nonbusiness hours was met with swift resistance from police union leadership. Such resistance and the extreme difficulty of making basic operational changes may best signal the toxic organizational culture that came to embody the old department. After all, it is not a promising sign when the leader of an organization—let alone the chief law enforcement officer in the state in the form of the AG—cannot easily get things done. Additionally, Chief Thomson has reflected on the lack of standards and accountability mechanisms during this time, whereby there were few ways of making sure officers were where they were supposed to be or to compel them to do their jobs (Kurlander, 2020).

When the Great Recession finally took its toll in 2011 and nearly half of its sworn officers were laid off, Camden's police force was utterly decimated. Those officers who remained—as well as those who were eventually rehired—suffered from being stretched too thin and the numbers showed it: from rising response times, eventually averaging sixty minutes (Zernike, 2014), to steep increases in violent crime, most evident by a record-high sixty-seven homicides in 2012 (CCPD, 2022). Camden was *under*policed, in no uncertain terms, in the years leading up to the 2013 formation of the CCPD. Drastic action needed to boost the number of sworn officers and, perhaps more importantly, their visibility in neighborhoods—at the same time ensuring that those officers were doing police work while there. More specifically, there needed to be an increase in uniformed officer presence, particularly out on foot or on bikes, in the most violent and problematic areas through a directed patrol or "hot spots" policing strategic framework. Additionally, the department needed a rigorous set of internal controls to ensure that the officers were actually spending the necessary amount of time in those designated areas. There is evidence that this happened—particularly through the creation of the NRTs, restructuring of the patrol division, and civilianizing and outsourcing tasks (see Oftelie, 2019; Swan et al., 2020)—and it was an essential first step in addressing the apathy and lethargy that came to characterize the city department.

A growing body of research has found that increasing police personnel and subsequent improvements in presence and visibility within communities has crime reduction benefits, although such increases may exacerbate low-level enforcement of minor crimes and violations. This body of research is above and beyond that of the sizable directed patrol and hot spots policing literature and other place-based policing strategies (e.g., Braga et al., 2019; National Academies of Sciences, Engineering, and Medicine, 2018). Camden's experience in the first few years following the May 2013 start of the CCPD largely mirrored these broader crime reduction trends, particularly violent crime and homicide, and also that of ramping up low-level enforcement. Both the benefits in terms of crime declines for serious offenses as well as the increases in arrests and citations for less serious offenses disproportionately impact disadvantaged and minority communities. A study from Chalfin and colleagues (2022), using the longitudinal data of 243 large U.S. cities and their police departments from 1981 through 2018, found that increases in police force sizes intensified low-level "quality of life" arrests, particularly of Black people (see also Chalfin et al., 2021). Declines in police expenditures and personnel have been found to reduce low-level misdemeanor arrests rates nationwide (Beck et al., 2023). This general pattern of more cops and less crime—and vice versa, less cops and more crime—has been attributed to a number of different methods and research designs as well as unique natural and quasi experiments.

While it has long been assumed that the increased police presence from tactics like hot spots policing works through its impact on peoples' perceptions of arrest certainty or risk, this link has not been subjected to much evaluation research. The same goes for the inverse: that perceptions of arrest certainty are reduced by both personal and vicarious experience of "punishment avoidance" (Stafford & Warr, 1993) or not getting caught. A recent study provided one of the first direct tests of increased police presence during a hot spots initiative on active offenders' perceptions of arrest risk. Bucci (2023) examined a longitudinal sample of serious adolescent offenders in Philadelphia that coincided with the PPD's Operation Safe Streets, which placed uniformed officers at two hundred to three hundred geographic locations of concentrated criminal activity in an effort to increase visibility to reduce offending in open-air drug markets. Results uncovered that the Operation Safe Streets intervention did, indeed, increase individuals' perceptions of arrest risk—suggesting that a likely intervening mechanism at work for policing tactics that improve officer presence is through perceptions of certainty of arrest. One of the more consistent themes from community interviews during the 2013–2015 years of the new CCPD is the noticeable rise in police visibility (see, e.g., Bauman & Chakrabarti, 2020). The improvement in officer presence alone starting in April–May 2013 was probably a salient shock to residents' and would-be offenders' perceptions as well as a much-needed shift for CCPD's working culture.

Policing's Duel-Edged Sword of Benefits and Costs

The city of Camden and its residents had much to gain from the changes stemming from CCPD—namely, a new department that actively engaged in street police work—but not all of those changes were initially welcomed by segments of the community. The fact that tension over the increased police presence played out in Camden during the first couple years (2013–2014) is not surprising since all policing has both benefits and costs, and it is difficult—if not impossible—to have one without the other. Many criminologists share this viewpoint, including Wesley Skogan (2022), Aaron Chalfin (2022), and Andy Wheeler (2020), among others. However, most individuals and politicians fail to recognize the full picture and only acknowledge one while ignoring the other. Depending on a person's political perspective and life experiences, some see only policing's benefits whereas others only see the harm and costs. More officers in the community, which expanded their level of proactivity in the use of vehicle and pedestrian stops, impacted levels of crime and violence in Camden and reduced the number of open-air drug markets—or, at the very least, pushed them indoors. For the first time in a long time, residents were able to retake portions of public spaces that were ceded due to fear of violence and criminal activity. As Jane Jacobs (1961) described, additional residents frequenting these areas added more "eyes on the street," which could potentially increase the level of capable guardianship in those places (Cohen & Felson, 1979)—therefore, changing the way both residents and offenders perceive physical space (J. Wilson & Kelling, 1982). Despite these benefits, there is little doubt that there were also costs associated with Camden's experiment: near-ubiquitous surveillance through technology as well as very high levels of police stops and the excessive use of ticketing early on.

The key and goal for police agencies is to strike the right balance with their level of enforcement while maximizing the benefits of the job and minimizing the harm or costs. Sometimes police presence alone might be enough without having to resort to much enforcement activity. Moreover, police enforcement varies on a spectrum, which can be viewed in Figure 7.1. On the one end, using pedestrian stops as an example, officers might do very little or close to nothing—either from laziness and incompetence or depolicing (see Shjarback et al., 2017b) due to the sociopolitical climate and fear of consequences for simply doing one's job. There are repercussions for this lack of policing that may take the form of inviting more individuals to carry illegal firearms due to the perception of the low risk of being stopped and caught with them and overall punishment avoidance. At the other end of the enforcement spectrum, officers do way too much in the form of stopping too many innocent people who are simply going about their daily functions. If done without the reasonable suspicion necessary, then they risk violating individuals' constitutional rights, not to mention alienating citizens and eroding trust in law enforcement. Targeted enforcement, including stop, question, and frisk, done in a more precise manner—as opposed to broad, indiscriminate use—can be an effective tool for police. However, the data from many cities show that targeted enforcement sometimes devolves into *the* tool, which is incredibly harmful (see, e.g., Skogan, 2022).

Policy, training, supervision, and accountability should be used to maximize policing's benefits and mitigate its harm. Regarding the harm, there are ways to safeguard against low-level enforcement from running amok—such as having officers provide more description on the reasons for a pedestrian stop or increased data collection of officer outputs more broadly followed by more rigorous review procedures by supervisors (Mummolo, 2018). The numbers and figures presented in Chapters 5 and 6 paint a picture of CCPD's costs in terms of the high rates of pedestrian stops and the use of high-volume ticketing practices that appeared to peak in 2014. Community members and activist groups—including the ACLU-NJ—made it clear that they did not appreciate that particular degree of enforcement. To CCPD's credit, signs of a turnaround and a response to those concerns are evident by the reductions in the rates of pedestrian stops and the increased use of warnings in lieu of tickets starting in 2015. Central to the drastic cutting

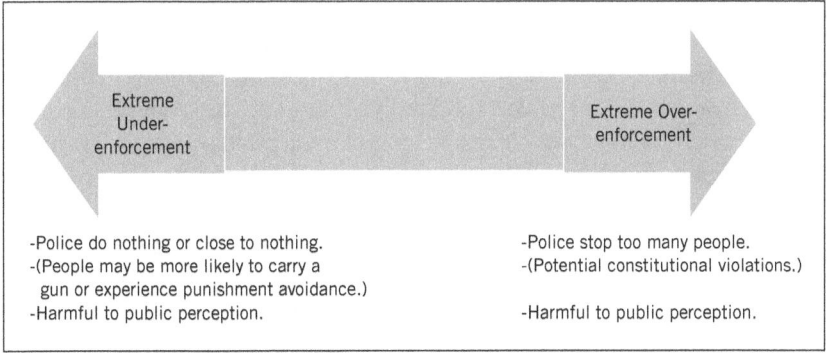

Figure 7.1 Spectrum of police behavior and enforcement.

back of citations was Chief Thomson's (2020) move to use CCPD's Internal Affairs division to investigate those officers who issued the most tickets.

A Word on Police Enforcement of Drugs and Their Markets

Throughout Camden's experiment, much has been made about the CCPD's level of enforcement activity, particularly in the early years. There was media coverage on the level of police stops, citations for seemingly innocuous violations like bicycles without bells or lights, and arrests for relatively minor crimes such as "loitering to commit a controlled dangerous substance (CDS)" offenses. While many may view these efforts as overly aggressive and not deserving of CCPD officers' time—think of a person condescendingly asking an officer, "Don't you have better things to do like fight serious crime?"—it is important to note that significant portions of the community *do* want police to address low levels of crime and the social disorder that comes along with it. This includes open-air drug dealing, illegal sex work, and individuals using drugs on the streets or in vacant buildings after purchase. Communities and their residents are not a monolith, and, therefore, there is variation in how they view an increased police presence and the particular tactics that officers use as well as the priorities placed on "low-level" drug enforcement.

An exchange on W. Kamau Bell's *United Shades of America* highlights this point. Bell dedicated an entire episode to policing in Camden, which aired in 2016. At one point, Bell asks a lifelong Camden resident if she has seen the city change in her lifetime to which she replies, "Well, it's getting a little better. I mean, we've got a lot of work to do, so." Upon probing her on the work to be done, she states, "Like get these people off the corners. Some people park on the side of my house using drugs all the time" (*United Shades of America*, 2016). Peoples' perceptions of law enforcement are complex and multifaceted. In the case of the aforementioned woman, along with most others, their perceptions of the local police are influenced, in part, by how they view their effectiveness or the lack thereof. Are they addressing the problems in the community—no matter how low-level they may appear to others? Are police responsive to said problems and do they provide adequate levels of safety and security? Negative citizen perceptions of law enforcement are as much a function of the underenforcement of the law—a failure to protect individuals from victimization—as they are a function of overenforcement or too much policing (see Kennedy, 1997). One of the key takeaways from Figure 7.1 is that both extremes on the spectrum of police enforcement—doing little to nothing as well as way too much—can be harmful to public perceptions and perceivied legitimacy.

New Internal Controls to Ensure Officer Accountability

Related to the issue of addressing previous bouts with apathy, lethargy, and overall ineffectiveness with the old city agency, CCPD relied on advances in technology to hold officers accountable to—at the very least—spend time inside their designated geographic assignments. A lack of officer presence and, more importantly, the inability to address it undoubtedly contributed to the high levels of crime and violence in the city. This is best illustrated by the secret pole camera set up on what Chief Thomson described as one of the most violent streets in North America in Chapter 4 (Kurlander, 2020). Absent 911 calls for a person being shot, there were virtually no signs of police activity on that street in the hours of footage that Chief Thomson observed. GPS devices in all police vehicles and officers' department-issued cell phones (Adomaitis, 2015b; Borowski, 2023b; Oftelie, 2019) as well as later in officers' body-worn cameras, in conjunction with a color-coded system that tracked officers time within designated boundaries in the RT-TOIC (CNA Analysis & Solutions, 2019), allowed supervisory officers to monitor and assess compliance within those locations. It is likely one of the biggest organizational and accountability-related changes—deviating from the old city agency—that facilitated CCPD's mission of placing more officers in the neighborhoods and specific areas within that needed it most.

Overall Agency Accountability

In addition to individual-officer accountability related to presence within desired geographic locations, the preponderance of the evidence suggests that the CCPD—as a whole—became more accountable to community and outside desires. Chief Thomson credits much of CCPD's ability to change and switch course to the fact that the organization was now building rather than changing culture: "It's swimming with the current as opposed to swimming against it" (Arco, 2015; see also Thomson, 2020). Moreover, he credits changes in union leadership that came along with the new organization in October 2013 with a renewed partnership and openness to address operational issues, policy, and training. Perhaps nowhere is this juxtaposition more evident than when comparing the difficulty Thomson had with amending the misappropriation of resources in the old city department's Traffic Unit as well as trying to reassign officers from administrative assignments to spending time on the streets (Oftelie, 2019; YouTube, 2020a).

Much, if not all, of what the CCPD has been able to accomplish over the years has been due to the collaborative relationship with the new union leadership rather than the previous adversarial tone that stymied and resisted efforts to change. In his op-ed in the *Washington Post*, Chief Thomson (2020) references the new leadership: "When the union reappeared, I enjoyed a partnership with leaders there who cared about the community as much as the welfare of their member officers." Additionally, "I could now accomplish in a few days policy and operational changes—things like codifying the requirement that officers de-escalate encounters before using force—that would have taken years in the old department." He is referring to the role that CCPD's union leadership played in working together with the Policing Project at NYU School of Law to completely revamp the department's use of force policy that was discussed in detail in the previous chapter.

Overall, the CCPD has been able to address a slew of factors and pivot relatively quickly in its first twelve years. Example after example highlights an ability to make changes in response to both internal and external demands. For one, they addressed police use of force and reduced citizens' complaints of excessive force through de-escalation training and revised administrative policy. The "Ethical Protector" training, beginning in 2015, followed by ICAT at the end of 2016, theoretically, served to make officers more ethically driven and effective communicators, who were tactically better able to resolve incidents with the least amount of force and without having to resort to deadly force. The revised use of force policy codified much, like respect for the sanctity of life, of what the de-escalation training and the department had been doing informally for years; plus, technology like the VirTra V-300® simulator allowed officers to practice and hone the skills and tactics they had been taught. All of these changes sought to shift the culture of the department as well as individual officers' mindsets from "warriors" to "guardians." And while it is difficult to empirically test and state definitively whether that occurred, the two nonshooting incidents—the Broadway and Mickle in November 2015 and the sexual assault suspect in September 2020—provide some anecdotal examples that CCPD is following a number of those tenets such as the Hippocratic Oath of Policing. Quotes from CCPD leaders following both of these incidents—namely, that "X years ago this would have more likely than not ended in a police shooting" (paraphrased; Cuellar, 2019; Goldstein, 2017)—might indicate a culture change.

Moreover, the CCPD was able to address their problematic levels of police stops and rein in the high degree of ticketing after community groups and the ACLU-NJ raised concerns. The number and rate of police stops, particularly of those on foot, and the steep rise in tickets peaked in 2014. That fact that these factors were amenable to change in a relatively quick manner—around 2015 being key—offers a data point for analysts looking for evidence of an organizational shift (or lack thereof). Can an organization change, and, if so, how quickly, in response to intentional internal and external attempts to do it? After all, this is the goal of all reform efforts, particularly at the federal level, when the Department of Justice's Civil Rights Division intervenes on behalf of local police agencies. The CCPD has shown they can do so for both use of force–related issues and their level of enforcement for low-level violations. Again, this stands in stark contrast to the unhealthy and stubborn organizational climate that came to define the old CPD where basic organizational factors were seemingly impervious to change. The use of warnings, in lieu of tickets, and handling interactions with citizens in more informal ways might also be indicative of policy changes shifting individual execution from "warrior" to "guardian."

Areas in Need of Improvement

While the preponderance of evidence suggests growth and a healthier organizational culture compared to that of the old CPD, there are some areas where the CCPD has fallen short from the statements and promises it initially made. Even basic comments made by President Obama during his May 2015 visit and speech were misleading or never came to fruition. Obama (2015) stated, "They [CCPD] doubled the size of the force—while keeping it unionized." Scott Thomson, the former chief from 2008 through 2019 who was at the helm of both organizations, clarified this point in an op-ed he wrote in June 2020. Thomson (2020) stated, "Although the police officer's union has since returned, initially the new officers came on without a union contract." Similarly, Obama announced how the CCPD had volunteered to be a part of the Police Data Initiative—an effort by the National Policing Institute to promote the use of "open" (i.e., publicly available) data, such as use of force and officer-involved shootings; citizen complaints; and stops, citations, and arrests, for enhanced accountability and transparency. Camden was listed as a PDI-participating agency as of 2020 among more than 130 other law enforcement organizations; however, the city and the department never posted or shared any data that has appeared on the NPI's PDI platform (Burke, 2017; Deblasio, 2019). If such transparency is one indicator of an agency's overall level of accountability to the public (see Walker, 2014), then CCPD surely misses the mark in this regard compared to many other departments around the country.

Summary

This chapter set out to perform a broad and cursory synthesis of whether there were notable and observable changes among the new CCPD and its officers. A proper and rigorous examination—such as qualitative interviews with those who were part of both organizations or an ethnography of the CCPD—was beyond the scope of this project. Instead, it examined proxy measures and indicators for data points about changes in behaviors: comparing the old city agency to the county department as well as those changes within the CCPD from the first few years and beyond. It appears as though the CCPD, through a multitude of different mechanisms, including growing and restructuring and using improved technology to aid internal accountability, was, indeed, able to reform from an agency characterized as apathetic and ineffective to one that began actually policing. Additionally, the CCPD became more responsive and made true changes to intentional internal and external demands. If being able to pivot relatively seamlessly—as was the case regarding excessive force complaints and the high-volume ticketing practices—is any indication of a healthier organization, then CCPD's ability to change showed development. Central to those shifts was the role that the new police union leadership played in assisting rather than resisting change.

8

Next Frontiers and Broader Police Reform Efforts

Despite its movement in a positive direction following some initial challenges in its first two years, there are still a few threats to the CCPD's overall progress. These extend beyond any one entity and require coordination with departments, regulatory bodies, and governments outside of Camden. In these challenges, Camden feels the broader possibilities of and obstacles to police reform acutely. The department, for example, has always struggled with officer turnover and general retention issues—a problem that is now shared by many police departments in the United States (PERF, 2023). How does Camden's struggle to retain officers reflect a national issue, and how is it unique to Camden and its reorganization efforts? The purpose of this chapter is to situate some of CCPD's challenges within the broader context and discussion of police reform across the country. Topics to be discussed include front-end versus back-end accountability and at what level—local, state, or federal—do police reform efforts have the best chance of success.

Turnover and Other Workforce-Related Issues

Officer turnover is one of the primary challenges for the CCPD—leading the organization to consistently fall short of full staffing. The CCPD is authorized to have 426 full-time sworn officers but has rarely if ever achieved that level of staffing for sustained periods of time. About two years in, around May 2015 when then-President Obama came to visit, the *Philadelphia Inquirer* ran a story about how the department had already been contending with 117 departures: 27 retirements with 90 resignations (Boren & Wood, 2015; see also Beym, 2015). By October 2015, there were more than 100 resignations with at least half of those officers taking jobs at other police departments across the state (S. Wood & Boren, 2015). As of August 2016, there were 151 resignations in addition to the 36 retirements since CCPD began a little over three years prior (Adomaitis, 2016). These resignation figures were massive and unparalleled throughout the state. The *Philadelphia Inquirer*'s investigation found that over the same two-year period from May 2013 to May 2015, only 15 officers resigned from the Paterson Police Department, 2 officers resigned from the Jersey City Police Department, and 0 officers resigned from the Atlantic City Police Department (Boren & Wood, 2015). Such a high volume of resignations has ripple effects, including filtering into every organizational facet of the agency: from detectives and investigators to the inability to keep all specialty units fully staffed.

Critics, particularly from the Camden County chapter of the NAACP, have been vocal about the turnover, while also, relatedly, lamenting about the fact that officers in the new CCPD were not as representative of the community compared to the old city department. For example, the late Colandus "Kelly" Francis, former president of the Camden County NAACP and one of the city's longest and most ardent champions, called the department a "revolving door" (Boren & Wood, 2015) and stated: "The word gets around. Go to Camden. Get the free training, it won't cost you anything, and you come back to your home base" (S. Wood & Boren, 2015). Darnell Hardwick, a former vice president of the Camden County NAACP also stated, "There's still a long list of people who want to transfer out" (Adomaitis, 2016). Both were referring to the ostensibly questionable practice of recruits using the CCPD as an opportunity to get trained as a police officer before seeking law enforcement jobs elsewhere in the state—one of the reasons provided for the high turnover by representatives of Camden and representatives of the CCPD themselves (see, e.g., Adomaitis, 2016; S. Wood & Boren, 2015). The reasons cited by those resigning from CCPD are, undoubtedly, diverse with some factors within the control of the organization, such as long shifts and a perception of unfair discipline, and others being external, such as better pay, a location closer to the departing officer's primary residence, or overall issues with the state's civil service test and commission. It is worth reiterating the multitude of internal accountability controls like GPS tracking from earlier chapters to which the CCPD subjects its officers: officers might not appreciate that degree of scrutiny from supervisors. They are less likely to contend with such issues in departments in safer and wealthier suburbs. Additionally, Hardwick and the late-Francis were also critical of how the new department in its early years lacked the racial diversity that the CPD boasted prior to 2013. Whereas more than 71% of officers in the old department represented racial minority groups just before being disbanded, more than 60% of the new CCPD's officers were white in 2015 (Adomaitis, 2015d; Zaremba, 2015).

There are obvious financial implications to so many resignations, particularly when Camden sponsors its recruits to train at the police academy. It costs a significant amount of money to initially train a police officer in the state of New Jersey and, more broadly, across the United States, which is why departments sometimes prefer hiring lateral transfers from other departments who already have academy training and law enforcement experience. In 2015, this training academy figure was estimated at approximately $14,000 per officer in the state. Therefore, it is incredibly expensive to hire and put officers through academy training only for them to leave the organization within a few months to a few years later. As a result, Camden County has tried to recoup some or, in select cases, all of the money spent on academy training, including filing lawsuits against a few towns that refused reimbursement. New Jersey state law "mandates that if an officer is trained in a municipality, and quits in less than two years and then joins another police force within 120 days, the new municipality owes all or some of the cost of training the officer" (S. Wood & Boren, 2015). For example, if an officer works for a municipality between 30 days and less than two years before moving elsewhere, then the new municipality is responsible for reimbursing approximately one-half of the training costs; municipalities must reimburse the full amount if an officer only works for less than 30 days.

In October 2015, the *Philadelphia Inquirer* reported on how Camden County sought to recover nearly $166,000 from other municipalities that hired officers who had resigned from the CCPD following short stints within the agency (S. Wood & Boren, 2015). One case was particularly troublesome. An officer graduated from the police academy in December and was a CCPD officer for less than thirty days before resigning on January 3—two days before swearing in as a lateral transfer in a bordering municipality. Given that the officer worked for the CCPD for less than thirty days, Camden County sought the full amount—$13,972—of the cost for academy training from the bordering municipality (S. Wood & Boren, 2015). The recruitment of Camden's officers by other departments is made possible, in part, by certain oversights or, perhaps, even a loophole within the state's CSC. For example, once a prospective officer who has taken the civil service exam joins a police force, the officer's name remains on the civil service list for a year—allowing other civil service–participating departments to engage in "poaching."

Turnover and retention are still an issue for the CCPD well into the 2020s. Looking back through media reports, which relied on OPRA requests, there have been many occasions since 2015 when the total number of full-time sworn officers falls short of the total number of authorized officers: 426. In late August 2016, for one, the CCPD had only 358 full-time sworn officers (Adomaitis, 2016). And officers continue to resign in high numbers only to join other police departments. According to Borowski (2023a), an "estimated 64 police officers in Camden resigned in 2022, with many going to other law enforcement jobs." It is imperative for the CCPD as well as officials from throughout the state, such as the CSC, to address what has essentially become a revolving door. The cycle puts Camden in a difficult situation: the CCPD is usually below its authorized number of sworn officers; therefore, it is consistently hiring. Would-be recruits looking to get their foot in the door to be sponsored by an agency for training costs can always rely on Camden before resigning and transferring to other departments.

A Word on Size and the Total Number of Officers

Most research that relies on secondary data and measures of the total number of sworn officers should also be viewed cautiously. The rates of police forces per capita are tapping into the absolute best-case scenario that all able-bodied officers are working. It does not take into account those officers who are pulled off the street and assigned to administrative work following critical incidents such as citizen complaints regarding use of force, officers who must report to court, those undergoing in-service training or other functions, those taking vacation or personal time, or those who are injured or out on disability and unable to work. Regarding this latter point, policing is dangerous, and officers are often injured performing their duties. American police, for example, experience the second-highest number of workplace homicides (behind cashiers) (Bureau of Labor Statistics, 2018) and the highest occupational rate of nonfatal victimization (Duhart, 2001; Fridell et al., 2009); approximately 10% of officers are assaulted in a given year, albeit most sustaining minor injuries (Bierie, 2017). Recent investigations into staffing levels within the PPD have blown the lid off of the idea that the number of sworn officers in an agency reflects the number of officers who are "active" and working—let alone present in the community.

In February 2022, the *Philadelphia Inquirer* published the first of several articles from their investigation into PPD's problematic use of a state disability benefit known as the Pennsylvania Heart and Lung Act (Gambacorta, Laker, & Bender, 2022a). Statewide since 2003, it allows all police officers and firefighters injured in the line of duty to collect 100% of their salaries while not paying state or federal taxes—a 20% raise at a minimum—and continuing to accrue vacation, unlimited sick time, and years served toward their pensions. Additionally, in a rare move that was negotiated by

PPD's Fraternal Order of Police Lodge 5, the doctors who see and treat the injured officers are selected exclusively by the police union—making determinations of how long they will be out and what level of work those officers can perform. The number of PPD officers claiming the disability and even being out on "no duty" (i.e., unable to handle tasks such as answering phones and filing paperwork) steadily grew over time. Starting from just 19 in 2003, when Charles Ramsey arrived in Philadelphia in 2008 to become PPD's Commissioner, there were 300 officers listed as injured on duty. Ramsey complained about the system and later described it as "the biggest scam going," although the total number of officers listed as injured and unavailable did decrease toward the end of his tenure in 2016 (Bender, Gambacorta, & Laker, 2022).

The *Inquirer*'s investigation found that the number of officers injured on duty and not working more than doubled after Ramsey's departure with 652 total from 2017 to 2021 (Gambacorta, Laker, & Bender, 2022b). The union's doctors designated 90% (587) of those as "no duty." All told, in 2021, approximately 14% of patrol officers—one in seven—were unavailable and out of work on the list compared to other cities where far smaller percentages of officers are out of work due to injuries (Bender, Gambacorta, & Laker, 2022; Gambacorta, Laker, & Bender, 2022a). A subsequent audit by the Philadelphia Office of the Controller (2022) mirrored the *Philadelphia Inquirer*'s findings. To make matters worse, the city controller's audit also found that PPD did not designate enough officers to uniformed patrol and many officers assigned to specialty units are conducting administrative work such as delivering mail between precincts—similar to the issues Chief Thomson had to contend with in 2007–2008 with the old city department.

While coming from a different department across the river, this example illustrates Camden and many other police departments' dilemmas. Sometimes the number of full-time sworn officers is deceiving. Viewing only the total number of officers in a department rather than a more accurate figure can obscure the severity of staffing shortages. One thing is clear: police organizations need an adequate number of officers—well-trained and experienced ones at that—to function appropriately. Understaffing might be one of the biggest—if not the biggest—threats to police accountability and reform efforts facing the profession in the twenty-first century. The problem only compounds when departments relax their hiring standards and bring in inexperienced officers with questionable character issues (see Adams, Nix, & Mourtgos, 2023). Understaffing and difficulties in recruiting and retaining quality officers filtered into the Memphis Police Department's "Street Crimes Operations to Restore Peace in Our Neighborhoods" (SCORPION) unit, highlighted recently with the brutal beating and killing of Tyre Nichols in January 2023. The five officers initially criminally charged in his death were incredibly inexperienced with only three to five years of tenure with the department; at least two had criminal records (Sainz, Mustian, & Condon, 2023). Ten to fifteen years ago, those five officers in question would be nowhere near this type of assignment—as indicated by retired Memphis Police Department officers who said the department once required at least seven years on the job before joining a specialty unit like SCORPION (Schuppe, Schapiro, & Ali, 2023). Given the persistent scale of turnover, officer retention and adequate staffing levels remain a significant challenge for the CCPD.

Front-End versus Back-End Accountability

Camden and the CCPD have become staples within debates surrounding police reform. Contemporary reform discussions and efforts toward increasing accountability have been ongoing for the past eleven years following Ferguson in 2014 and certainly the murder of George Floyd in 2020. Reformers within and outside of policing have suggested a slew of proposals for reform with varying degrees of attention and policy movement. However, not all accountability mechanisms are created equally. They range from untested "run of the mill" options that seem to be echoed following each wave of police scrutiny, such as increasing minority diversity among law enforcement ranks (see Shjarback, 2023; Shjarback et al., 2017a), to evidence-based strategies with a proven track record of success. We should focus our political and policy efforts toward the latter. Additionally, reform and accountability mechanisms fall on a spectrum of what the Policing Project at NYU School of Law calls "front-end versus back-end accountability" (Policing Project, 2020b), reflecting the benefit when a department extends a culture of responsibility throughout officer careers. It remains one of the most effective frameworks for critically assessing the potential impact of police reform. Table 8.1 presents examples of accountability mechanisms falling under the front end versus back end.

Front-end accountability includes innovative and effective training, strong departmental policies and practices, and internal controls to create a culture of organizational accountability before things go wrong. The

TABLE 8.1 FRONT-END VERSUS BACK-END ACCOUNTABILITY	
Front end	Back end
Innovative training	Civilian oversight/review
Strict administrative policy	Special or independent prosecutors
Early intervention systems	Consent decrees/federal intervention
Internal controls for documentation and monitoring	National Decertification Index (NDI)

CCPD has made the majority of its investments in front-end accountability mechanisms. While most police training has not been subjected to much evaluation, some formal de-escalation programs such as PERF's ICAT program, discussed in Chapter 6 and procedural justice offerings are promising (Weisburd et al., 2022; G. Wood Tyler, & Papachristos, 2020). Moreover, there are a few innovative training programs that have not been rigorously tested but do offer to address culture by having officers intervene on each other's behalf to prevent unnecessary and excessive force, such as the New Orleans Police Department's "Ethical Policing Is Courageous" and Georgetown University's "Active Bystandership for Law Enforcement" (ABLE). CCPD officers, like in all departments in the state of New Jersey, are required to receive both ICAT and ABLE training.

Strict administrative policy narrows officer discretion and limits the circumstances and situations under which they can do certain things. Policies can restrict, while not entirely prohibiting, behavior, particularly when it comes to officers using their firearms and other less-than-lethal devices such as TASERs or pepper spray as well as high-speed vehicle and foot pursuits. For example, a department policy that provides explicit language and guidance for when officers can and cannot shoot at moving motor vehicles—like limited exceptions when a driver is using the vehicle as a weapon of mass destruction, as in the terrorist attack with a box truck in Nice, France, in 2016, and the Christmas parade incident in Waukesha, Wisconsin, in 2021, or when an officer is being carried or dragged by the vehicle and cannot disengage. In all other scenarios when an officer can safety get out of the way, there is a policy expectation not to shoot. The CCPD as well as both the Dallas and the Denver Police Departments, among others, possess this type of firearm restriction, which follows the model policy from the PERF (2016) and a national consensus of eleven leadership organizations including the International Association of Chiefs of Police, and the National Organization of Black Law Enforcement Executives (see National Consensus Policy on Use of Force, 2020). Preliminary research suggests departments with more restrictive policies through constraining language regarding shooting at moving vehicles engaged in fewer of these types of deadly force incidents (Shjarback & Ward, 2025). In addition to strict standards governing the use of force and firearms, the CCPD (2023) provides incredibly detailed standard operating procedures surrounding topics such as arrest and transportation, vehicle pursuits, body-worn cameras, conducted energy devices, drug testing, and both its early warning system and internal affairs unit.

Other examples of front-end accountability measures include a functioning early intervention system that is well designed and maintained with adequate organizational resources (see Shjarback, 2015, 2020) and internal controls that stress monitoring and supervision for basic tasks and documentation up and down the chain of command. Regarding the former, an early intervention system is a nonpunitive tool that allows departments to monitor, identify, and correct problematic officer behavior before it escalates, while also improving the role of supervisors and providing enhanced monitoring capabilities for the organization as a whole. Standard operating procedures and guidelines that call for supervising officers to review reports written by line-level officers—including reports explaining the use of force and pedestrian or vehicle stops—and watching a portion of their available dash or body-worn camera footage creates and maintains a culture of heightened accountability. In one study out of New York City, a new NYPD directive mandated officers to write a few sentences to a paragraph explaining the justification for making a pedestrian stop, which also called for supervisors to review those descriptions at the end of shifts. An interrupted time series analysis found that the directive led to an immediate increase in the rate of stops producing evidence of suspected crimes: stops became more efficient (Mummolo, 2018). Interviewed officers indicated that the change signaled more managerial scrutiny, which led them to adopt more conservative tactics in selecting suspected pedestrians for inquiry.

Back-end measures, on the other hand, reflect after-the-fact, reactionary methods largely for holding *individual* officers responsible for their misdeeds. Civilian oversight and review bodies, special or independent prosecutors for matters of deadly force and in-custody deaths, consent decrees and broader federal intervention, and the National Decertification Index (NDI) or state-based equivalencies, like police licensing and revocation processes, all can be best categorized as back-end accountability mechanisms. There are currently no civilian oversight and review bodies for law enforcement in the state of New Jersey. Some of these mechanisms are necessary steps forward, but their mere existence is likely insufficient to produce real change, because they might not directly address *systemic* organizational issues or affect culture. It is possible, however, for back-end accountability mechanisms to produce feedback loops to front-end accountability as the back-end measures influence or prevent future problematic behavior.

For example, if a police officer is fired for cause from one agency that subsequently reports the information to the NDI—an electronic database that contains searchable records of officers who have been decertified from across the country (Atherley & Hickman, 2013)—and another agency consults the NDI for any information on said officer before making the lateral hire, then perhaps such due diligence will preclude the secondary agency from offering a job to a problematic officer with a history of issues. This hypothetical scenario would only work if there was comprehensive reporting to and consulting of the NDI, which is not mandatory at the moment. Ultimately, though, meaningful police reform will require more of the often-neglected front-end accountability mechanisms that target institutional and organizational issues.

There are other reform mechanisms that are more difficult to place on this front- versus back-end spectrum. Officer body-worn cameras, for instance, may reduce the likelihood that an officer steps out of bounds and thus serves as a front-end accountability mechanism. Yet, the audio and visual footage from body-worn cameras might also be used to hold officers accountable following a critical incident or a citizen or fellow officer's complaint.

Such accountability mechanisms are not foolproof. Policing, at the end of the day, is performed by individuals who may make the wrong decisions when under a high-degree of pressure and forced to act quickly under less-than-ideal conditions. Even those accountability mechanisms with more of a proven track record and evidence base—such as strict administrative policies governing firearms and the use of force more broadly—have their own limitations. These policies—after all—are simply words on a page unless they are reinforced through training and other mechanisms and there is an organizational commitment to them. However, those agencies that incorporate more accountability mechanisms—particularly on the front-end—are at least actively working to reduce the likelihood that they will experience problems and events that threaten police legitimacy. There are a few "low hanging fruit" issues from a back-end standpoint that can be easily addressed, such as reducing "wandering officers."

Wandering Officers

Wandering officers move from department to department—often due to firings and dismissals or being forced to resign (Grunwald & Rappaport, 2020). There have been a number of high-profile wandering officers over the past few years, which has led to more scrutiny on the gaps in the system that allow for problematic officers to fall through the cracks. For example, Timothy Loehmann is the former Cleveland police officer who shot and killed twelve-year-old Tamir Rice in November 2014. Prior to arriving at the Cleveland Police Department, Loehmann was dismissed from the police department in Independence, Ohio, after being deemed "unfit to serve." Cleveland PD ultimately fired him in May 2017 for failing to disclose the previous dismissal on his job application. Following his firing in Cleveland, Loehmann was offered employment by both the Bellaire, Ohio, and Tioga, Pennsylvania, police departments; however, those offers were either rescinded or he resigned shortly after being hired due to public backlash (Burke &

Cohen, 2022). Sean Grayson, the former Sangamon County, Illinois sheriff's deputy who shot and killed Sonya Massey in her own home while she was unarmed and experiencing a mental health crisis in 2024, was on his sixth department in four years (Griffith, 2024). Grayson, additionally, had two prior convictions for driving under the influence and received a general discharge from the military that cited "misconduct (serious offense)."

Like many other departments around the county, the CCPD has employed wandering officers at some point in their careers. One was former CCPD officer Douglas Dickinson, who was hired in 2014 and began patrolling the city in January 2015. Dickinson was criminally charged in June 2016 with several counts of simple assault and filing false reports stemming from two incidents that occurred in July and November 2015, respectively. In both incidents, Dickinson arrested individuals and used force on them. One, Carlos Pacheco, spent eleven months in jail, while the other, Quinzelle Bethea, spent three weeks in jail. Fellow members of the CCPD and Chief Thomson ultimately reported Dickinson's misconduct to prosecutors (Steele, 2016), which may signal a healthier organizational climate of officers reporting misconduct or excessive force as opposed to the traditional blue wall of silence (see also Saul, 2020). The Camden County Prosecutor dismissed the charges against both Pacheco and Bethea as well as a total of thirty-nine people for whom Dickinson was the sole sworn witness (J. Walsh, 2018).

While awaiting the adjudication of his charges, Dickinson moved to Florida where he applied to and was hired in September 2016 by the Wilton Manors Police Department—a suburb in the Miami metropolitan area (Trischitta, 2017). The next month—October 2016—he pled guilty to simple assault in New Jersey and was officially fired by the CCPD (J. Walsh, 2018). Dickinson was fired from the Wilton Manors PD in April 2017 and subsequently criminally charged in September 2017 for "uttering a forged instrument." The charges stem from when he produced three forged letters of recommendation from the CCPD during the hiring process, at which point he also failed to disclose that he was under investigation and had pending charges in Camden. Dickinson pled guilty and received an eighteen-month probation term in Florida in January 2018. Under the terms of the plea agreement, he surrendered his Florida law enforcement certificate. In June 2018, Camden County settled two lawsuits for approximately $200,000 in which Carlos Pacheco and Quinzelle Bethea were plaintiffs.

Another wandering officer's timeline is particularly egregious. In June 2020, in the weeks immediately following the murder of George Floyd and national fallout, Woodlynne, NJ, police officer Ryan Dubiel was caught on video pepper spraying a group of teens sitting on a porch stoop in an unprovoked and unjustified manner. Woodlynne is a small municipality of less than three thousand residents that shares a border with Camden; as of September 2024, the Woodlynne Police Department was disbanded and it is now policed by the CCPD. The cell phone footage went viral, which led to a deep dive into Dubiel's previous tenures as a police officer in the state. It was his ninth police department, including a stint in Camden from March 2013—during CCPD's large hiring wave a few months before the agency officially began—through 2015 (Callimachi, 2020; Vogt, 2020). Dubiel's employment history was riddled with problematic and questionable behavior. He resigned from one agency in 2012 before completing all of his training. A *New York Times* investigation in 2020 quoted the current chief of that agency as saying, "He just wasn't meeting our standards—we didn't feel comfortable with him being out there by himself" (Callimachi, 2020). In Camden, one source requesting anonymity cited that he had a history of disciplinary infractions; Lou Cappelli Jr., the Camden County elected executive who oversees the CCPD, also stated in 2020, "Dubiel washed out of the system in Camden because of our police reforms, which imposed a more stringent code of conduct and a higher level of oversight" (Callimachi, 2020). He was fired from a subsequent department within three months.

The fact that Dubiel bounced from department to department is indicative of broader systematic gaps, including the lack of sharing disciplinary records among police agencies through the end of 2019 and New Jersey's failure to have a state licensing process up until 2022. The same *New York Times* investigation uncovered that one police chief found no disciplinary problems in Dubiel's previous employments when his application was reviewed; Woodlynne officials were unaware of the previous firing (Callimachi, 2020). Prior to December 2019, stringent confidentiality rules surrounding Internal Affairs investigations precluded departments from sharing most officers' personnel records in the state. These policies were amended by New Jersey's then-AG Gurbir Grewal to allow for such personnel records to be more easily shared among departments. In the summer of 2022, New Jersey finally joined forty-six other states by beginning a process of creating a licensing program to issue and, therefore, revoke a police officer's certification throughout the state (Biryukov, 2022; State of New Jersey, 2022). If such a licensing program existed earlier and there was better sharing of personnel records pre-December 2019, then Camden and other police departments throughout New Jersey might have had an easier time building a culture of accountability in policing. Again, back-end accountability mechanisms provide a welcomed complement to the front-end measures, and they shore up a few of the gaps necessary for reform and accountability.

Areas of Reform: Federal, State, and Local Levels

Police reform and accountability efforts can and should take place at all three levels of government: federal, state, and local. In fact, many have made this case in academic and policy circles but also in writing for general public audiences (e.g., Stoughton, Noble, & Alpert, 2020). However, while better policing in the United States requires movement and changes at all three levels, these three levels of governance each vary in their appetite for reform, the likelihood of success, and the potential impact they will have. Americans are unlikely to see their federal government take a leadership role in police reform—largely due to its continued failure to pass meaningful legislation as well as an inability to encourage basic national data collection efforts for policing outcomes. Additionally, federal investigation and intervention into police departments through the U.S. Department of Justice's Civil Rights Division—while important and warranted in some cases—has only impacted a few dozen agencies since the 1990s and is dependent on the presidential administration in office at the time. Studies regarding federal intervention, such as the use of consent decrees, show mixed findings with evidence that it is difficult to sustain reform efforts (Alpert, McLean, & Wolfe, 2017; Chanin, 2015; Devi & Fryer, 2020; Goh, 2020; Powell, Meitl, & Worrall, 2017). On the other end of the spectrum, police reform and accountability efforts can be implemented more easily at the local level, such as through chiefs or city councils changing policy, but there are far too many agencies—approximately eighteen thousand across the country—that need to do so in order to make meaningful and tangible progress. The sweet spot in terms of the best bang for your buck action on police reform and accountability will likely come from the states.

States hold the most promise for a number of reasons. For one, each state's Peace Officer Standards and Training commission or their equivalent entities set minimum standards for the hiring and training of law enforcement officers throughout their respective states. This means they each can amend both the total number of police academy hours and the specific training content. It would be possible to add to the police academy curricula mandatory crisis intervention training or de-escalation training offerings, among other promising ones, such as procedural justice, for all new recruits as well as all current officers throughout the state. In 2021, for example, New Jersey mandated that all police officers would receive PERF's ICAT as well as Georgetown University's ABLE training (State of New Jersey, 2021). States are also in a better position—relative to the federal government—to launch comprehensive data collection systems tracking policing outcomes, such as firearm use and force more broadly as well as misconduct and traffic stops. These data collection mechanisms might add an additional level of scrutiny and oversight. Moreover, states have the opportunity to address arbitration processes and make changes to their law enforcement officers' bill of rights if they have one.

Summary

Many of the CCPD's primary challenges extend throughout the broader context of police reform. The agency struggles from an unprecedented and unparalleled level of turnover in the form of recruits hired and trained by CCPD moving on to other law enforcement departments a few months to a few years later. High turnover threatens the overall progress of any organization, while affecting all departmental functions and operations. In fact, Chief Thomson cited the high turnover as a reason why he was unable to staff more detectives in 2015–2016 (Boren & Steele, 2016). Recruitment and hiring as well as retention issues are complex and likely influenced by factors both within and outside of an agency's control. In the case of police departments throughout New Jersey, closer attention should be paid to the CSC and its role in potentially exacerbating turnover among the CCPD.

Departments such as the CCPD can work to achieve more responsible and disciplined policing throughout officers' tenure through both front- and back-end accountability mechanisms and through police reform efforts at varying levels of government. Many of these reforms require coordination among multiple departments throughout the state and country, or additional government coordination. The CCPD employs a number of front-end accountability mechanisms, including innovative training such as PERF's ICAT, and it possesses incredibly strict administrative policies that provide officers with clear guidance on a host of operating procedures. Yet, the CCPD and law enforcement throughout New Jersey do not have many back-end accountability mechanisms: until recently, there was no state licensing and revocation program and there are currently no civilian oversight bodies (see Shearn, 2020). While front-end accountability mechanisms create the greatest chance of reform success since they target more systemic organizational factors and culture, back-end measures are also important to shore up and provide additional layers of accountability—think the Swiss cheese model of accident causation (Reason, 1990)—and perhaps feedback loops. State-based efforts, compared to those at the local or federal levels, offer the most realistic and tangible steps toward reform and accountability that will impact the largest amount of police agencies. Although federal legislation would be ideal—like national use of force standards and comprehensive reporting requirements—state-level efforts are where reformers should focus our attention.

9

Expanding the Narrow Focus on Public Safety and Economic Revitalization Efforts

The primary aim of this book is to explore the police reform efforts in Camden, NJ, including both the positive changes the city achieved as well as the early and continued struggles. It largely concentrates on the transition and differences from one department—once controlled by the city of Camden—to a completely new agency that has been operated by Camden County since May 1, 2013. The CCPD received the lion's share of attention and credit for the crime-reduction benefits post-2012, and the agency's coverage was front and center in both national and international spotlights on police reform in the summer of 2020 and beyond.

Analysts of crime trends, however, tend to present a narrow view of crime-fighting efforts by focusing almost exclusively on law enforcement and relatively neglecting other nonpolicing justice system entities that can and do have an impact on crime, violence, and quality of life issues. Additionally, policing and departments are influenced by their broader social contexts, particularly different levels of politics. The success or failure of the CCPD or any policing agency may ultimately depend not only on the work done by its law enforcement officers and their managers but on the health of the broader social fabric of the city. The purpose of this chapter is twofold: (1) to direct more attention toward community-based solutions to public safety in an effort to spur a more comprehensive approach to tackling crime and violence. And (2) to properly couch the policing in Camden within the larger discussion of the tremendous political pressure to successfully reduce crime and overall economic revitalization efforts.

Expanding the Credit beyond Law Enforcement

This book has detailed the progress that the CCPD made in reducing crime and violence in Camden. In the media coverage from the summer of 2020, most articles only focused on what the new police force did to address crime—failing to recognize the other entities that may have contributed to the crime control benefits. The CCPD could not possibly have done the job by itself and has relied on its partnerships with the CCPO as well as a slew of federal law enforcement agencies, including the FBI, DEA, and U.S. Marshals Service. Regarding the latter, a review of CCPO press releases for homicides in the city provides example after example of the U.S. Marshals Fugitive Task Forces successfully locating and taking suspects accused of murder into custody from around the state and as far as Baltimore, Norfolk, VA, and Florida. Law enforcement is but one of many pieces involved in addressing the crime control and public safety puzzle, yet the policing profession remains a central piece.

It is important to also acknowledge all of the other non–law enforcement organizations and efforts that undoubtedly played a role in the crime reduction in Camden over the past twelve years. There are countless community and nonprofit groups dedicated to serving the city's families and youths with focuses including but not limited to fighting hunger and assisting with housing and employment. Research conducted by Sharkey, Torrats-Espinosa, and Takyar (2017) found a causal effect of local nonprofit organizations on crime. Using longitudinal data from a sample of 264 large U.S. cities, they estimate that every ten additional organizations focused on crime and community life in a city led to 9%, 6%, and 4% reductions in the murder rate, violent crime rate, and property crime rate, respectively.

One particular community-based program is deserving of attention. Cure4Camden was officially launched in 2014 under the umbrella of the city's Center for Family Services. Modeled after Chicago's "Cure Violence" program, Cure4Camden is a community-based violence intervention program aimed to stop shootings and violence using a public health approach: detecting and interrupting conflicts, identifying and treating high-risk individuals, and changing community norms (Center for Family Services, n.d.). The team consists of trained violence interrupters and outreach workers who are from the city—some of whom may have even been involved in crime, gangs, and drugs in the past—who act as "credible messengers" and try to mediate conflicts and prevent retaliatory violence (see also YouTube, 2016). In addition to this detection and interruption function, they also try to identify, work with, and redirect those individuals in the community who are—due to their past behavior and their social networks—most likely to either be shot or commit a shooting.

While Cure4Camden has not yet been formally evaluated, research on the Cure Violence and Advance Peace models—those that rely on community outreach and direct interruption or mediation of neighborhood conflicts by trained individuals known to the neighborhood and trusted by residents—is beginning to produce promising evidence of success in reducing gun violence and addressing social norms around the acceptance of violence (John Jay College Research Advisory Group on Preventing and Reducing Community Violence, 2020). Cure Violence and their inspired programs were associated with significant declines in shootings and violence in Chicago (Skogan et al., 2008); New York City (Delgado, Alsabahi, & Butts, 2017); Philadelphia (Roman, Klein, & Wolff, 2018), and Port of Spain, Trinidad and Tobago (Maguire, Oakley, & Corsaro, 2018). However, a few studies were found not to be as successful, including a Cure Violence–modeled program in Baltimore (Webster et al., 2013) and an Advance Peace–modeled program in Richmond, CA (Matthay et al., 2019). Researchers in New York City also conducted three waves of surveys with samples of young males (eighteen to thirty) in both the treatment areas that received Cure Violence and the control areas. The respondents' inclination to use violence for serious disputes and support for violence in petty disputes significantly decreased in the neighborhoods with Cure Violence (Butts & Delgado, 2017). Similar findings were uncovered among another sample of young men (eighteen to twenty-four) in two violent communities in Baltimore—suggesting Cure Violence and related programs may help participants embrace nonviolent responses to interpersonal conflict (Milam et al., 2018). So there is hope for Cure4Camden based on the mixed but largely positive results of the model.

In 2020, the NJ AG announced that Camden's Center for Family Services was awarded funding as one of nine sites in the state for a hospital-based violence intervention program (HVIP) pilot program (NJ Attorney General, 2021). Center for Family Services would partner with Cooper University Hospital in Camden—the city's only Level 1 Trauma Center—to offer intensive case management to patients sustaining a gunshot injury. The goal of such programs is to intervene on behalf of victims and their friends and family by offering supportive services and encouraging them to refrain from retaliatory violence. The partnership would be an extension of Cure4Camden's ongoing community violence intervention strategies; however, the effort was significantly delayed due to the COVID-19 pandemic. Research on HVIPs is even more limited than that of community-based programs like Cure Violence. Still, the preliminary findings offer support. Victims seen by crisis intervention specialists in hospitals were less likely to be arrested in follow-up periods (Becker et al., 2004; Cooper, Eslinger, & Stolley, 2006) as well as less likely to be reinjured and rehospitalized post-HVIP (Juillard et al., 2016; Zun, Downey, & Rosen, 2006). This collaboration has the opportunity to extend Cure4Camden's efforts by alerting their outreach workers and interrupters to all nonfatal gunshot victims from Camden that show up at Cooper University Hospital.

Other non–law enforcement efforts, such as the demolishing of abandoned and vacant buildings, have also likely contributed to crime declines. Research has made a connection between such dwellings serving as "stash" or "drop" houses used to store weapons and drugs, while serving as areas that increase criminal opportunity due to reduced guardianship. In a two-year assessment conducted by CamConnect and the Camden Community Development Association from 2012 to 2014, 3,417 (14.9%) of the city's 22,906 buildings were abandoned and vacant (Shelly, 2014a). The assessment also found that Camden had 8,142 empty lots that did not include parks or commercial parking lots. All told, Camden's aggregate percentage for vacant land and abandoned buildings was 37.1% of the entire city, which Alan Mallach—an expert on housing, land use, and urban affairs working for the Brookings Institution at the time—described as "up there with Detroit" (Shelly, 2014a).

From 2010 to 2014, 464 city buildings were razed (Adomaitis, 2015a). In 2015, then-Mayor Dana Redd announced a new initiative to continue knocking down abandoned houses. Redd stated, "These eyesores deteriorate our quality of life and create havens for unlawful activities" (Laday, 2015a). From 2015 to 2017, 600 vacant houses were torn down—marking the largest demolition project in state history. "We are eliminating places for prostitutes to go. We are eliminating the places for them to stash their drugs or sell their drugs," stated then-Deputy Chief Joseph Wysocki (6ABC, 2017). Those six hundred included a vacant home on the 1500 block of Louis Street where the CCPD previously discovered and removed a gun safe containing multiple firearms (Adomaitis, 2015a). In 2021, Mayor Vic Carstarphen announced another two-year "Camden Strong" initiative to tear down an additional three hundred blighted and abandoned structures (Vannozzi, 2021). During the mayor's press conference, the CCPD Chief Gabe Rodriguez weighed in: "I consider these abandoned homes to be incubators for criminal activity" (CBS News Philadelphia, 2021; Zucker, 2021).

Such efforts have not been empirically tested in Camden for their effect on crime; however, there is a substantial and growing body of work from across the country that has consistently found a link between demolishing abandoned buildings and reductions in crime and violence. They include Detroit (Larson et al., 2019), Philadelphia (Branas et al., 2016), and Rochester, NY (Jay et al., 2022). This is an important and necessary first step in Camden, but it requires a proper follow-up plan that includes what to do with those properties once they are taken down. Critics and media have reported that the city, since such demolitions have picked up, lacks a detailed and comprehensive approach (Gillette, 2013; Zucker, 2021). For select properties, investment and rebuilding may be suitable. Remediating vacant lots, particularly through greening and gardening, might also be a worthwhile option as research shows such efforts lead to reductions in crime and violence (Sadatsafavi et al., 2022). The city of Camden also recently announced in the late summer of 2022 an ongoing collaboration between the city, PSE&G (New Jersey's largest gas and electric utility company), and Hopeworks (a nonprofit based in Camden) to identify and replace dim streetlights with upgraded energy-efficient LED ones (Miller, 2023). From August 2022 through March 2023, approximately one hundred streetlights in the Whitman Park neighborhood were replaced and the city plans to implement the collaboration citywide. A systematic review and meta-analysis found that improved streetlighting and related interventions significantly reduce crime (Welsh, Farrington, & Douglas, 2022).

What all this should convey is that addressing crime and violence is a collaborative effort involving entities beyond law enforcement. The CCPD has received much credit—deservedly so—in making changes and bringing down violent crime from the record highs of around 2012. But we need to also acknowledge the CCPD's other law enforcement partners and must look beyond the narrow view of exclusively focusing on police to solve public safety problems. Nonprofits and other organizations looking to strengthen families, neighborhoods, and schools; community- and hospital-based violence intervention programs, including Cure4Camden; and interventions into addressing abandoned buildings, vacant lots, and poor-quality streetlighting have and will continue to influence the level of offending and victimization in Camden and beyond. The problems of crime and violence are complex and multifaceted—stemming from a host of factors both within the individual, such as one's biological influence over levels of self-control, and outside, such as peer influence. Crime is influenced at levels both micro (familial) and macro (neighborhood and community factors). It is naive to believe that law enforcement and the criminal legal system more broadly—alone—can fix them.

Stakeholders and politicians in Camden city and county also appear to rely heavily on law enforcement as the *sole* producers of public safety, depending on police-centric responses, whereas other places around the state and country have taken steps to empower community groups and businesses to become *co*-producers. For example, cities such as Newark and St. Louis, through Rutgers University–Newark and the Center for Policing Equity, respectively, have established formal collaborative efforts that actively engage in partnerships between police and non–law enforcement entities. The Newark Public Safety Collaborative and the Public Safety Collaborative in St. Louis alike bring police, city officials, and community as well as business stakeholders together through the democratization and dissemination of crime data and place-based analytics to mobilize local community groups and businesses to assist as actionable change agents. These efforts, which take the form of regularly scheduled meetings, have been characterized as data-informed community engagement or DICE. Camden and most places around the country that struggle with crime could benefit from incorporating similar models and making a better commitment to empowering non–law enforcement organizations to have a seat at the table, so to speak, and join in co-producing public safety. Failure to do so will make it difficult to effectively address both policing and crime.

Root Causes versus Proximal Solutions Debate

Part of the reason why little seems to get done in the realm of both police reform and addressing public safety is due to communities' and administrators' political and philosophical differences over a false choice between addressing (1) the underlying or root causes of crime and violence versus (2) employing police-related interventions. Often, politicians and the public view this as an either/or decision. Concentrated economic disadvantage and residential segregation, isolation, and overall inequality represent some of the strongest and most consistent correlates of crime and violence (see Pratt & Cullen, 2005). Addressing these broader societal ills should always be a policy goal; however, these long-term objectives take time and feature less evidence of "what works" (see MacDonald, 2023). On the other hand, there are proven strategies with a deep evidence base to address crime and violence in the nearer term that focus on some of the more proximal causes, particularly involving the police. Examples include increasing police presence in hot spot areas, affording police the opportunity to engage in problem-solving projects, and focusing on the prolific, high-rate offenders who are usually nested within broader criminal social networks.

Using law enforcement in these evidence-based ways is akin to "stopping the bleeding" as Thomas Abt (2019) has appropriately described it. Evidence-based policing offers short- and nearer-term policy solutions that produce an "uneasy peace"—that is, tenuous and potentially fleeting and temporary—according to Patrick Sharkey (2018). Such policing and justice system interventions cannot address, and are incapable of ever addressing, some of the underlying root causes of crime and violence as previously mentioned. The most they can do—aside from saving lives and preventing crime in the short and near term—is buy more time for communities to hopefully address root causes, which, unfortunately, happens less often than we would like to admit. Even such short-term policing and justice system interventions are unsustainable in the long run: grant funding and resources for more officers and overtime hours dries up. New leadership at either the police department, the prosecutor's office, or the political level decides to make changes and do away with those efforts. The creation of a temporary "uneasy peace" represents the best-case scenario for police departments and the broader justice system employing evidence-based strategies in a procedurally just, fair, and constitutional manner. Those departments that engage in overly aggressive and unconstitutional patterns of behavior while also failing to protect victims risk jeopardizing any long-term successes by alienating segments of the population and fostering perceptions of "legal cynicism" (Sampson & Bartusch, 1998) and "street code values" (Anderson, 2000), which encourage retaliatory violence and self-help to settle disputes in lieu of contacting the police and relying on the legal system.

Still, effective policing in the short term *is* capable of addressing one of the root causes of crime: opportunity. This is a point often missed by those who favor addressing the other root causes of crime, such as poverty, failing schools, income inequality, and the unequal access to employment, while largely dismissing shorter-term policing interventions. Criminologists over the past several decades, including Cohen and Felson (1979), Clarke (1980), and J. Wilson and Kelling (1982), in addition to many leading contemporary scholars such as Jerry Ratcliffe and Graham Farrell, among others, argue—correctly—that criminal opportunity can and should be viewed as a root cause of crime. And while policing and officers are not the sole authority in altering criminal opportunity structures, law enforcement and its footprint play a role in addressing opportunity through peoples' perceptions of risk and certainty of getting caught (see Bucci, 2023).

Policing or the lack thereof will always have the most impact on people and communities on the margins. Areas that are destabilized due to economic disadvantage tend to lack informal social control mechanisms and collective efficacy (Sampson & Groves, 1989; Sampson, Raudenbush, & Earls, 1997). The lion's share of the research examining the crime drop in the 1990s through the recent uptick in gun violence and homicide in the wake of the COVID-19 pandemic suggests that those with the most to gain from effective policing as well as the most to lose from police pullbacks and ineffectiveness are young minority men in the poorest neighborhoods (see Del Pozo et al., 2022; Johnson & Roman, 2022, MacDonald, Mohler, & Brantingham, 2022). Unfortunately, a large percentage of the residents and neighborhoods within the city of Camden are marginalized, given the city's high levels of poverty, inequality, and segregation from the rest of Camden County. In the past twelve years, the CCPD and its fellow law enforcement partners, community organizations, and other non–law enforcement efforts to address crime have been able to achieve some degree of an "uneasy peace"—a reprieve from the excessive and unacceptable levels of violence in 2011–2012. However, Camden's political officials and business interests are not doing the men and women of the CCPD nor the residents of Camden any favors by failing to vigorously address more of those root causes, find long-term solutions, or facilitate an equitable economic revival.

Unequal Economic Revival and the Failure to Address Many Root Causes

The entire experiment in police reform in Camden—dissolving an existing organization and creating an entirely new one—cannot be fully comprehended without an understanding of the broader attempts to economically revive the city. Camden needed to do something bold to address the exorbitant levels of violent crime that consistently gave the city the unwanted notoriety of a label like "murder capital" of the United States from the 1990s through the first decade of the twenty-first century. There were tremendous financial and business interests at work in making the changes that led to the creation of the CCPD, and this is an appropriate lens through which to couch the dissolve and rebuild effort.

Some of the most influential figures in the creation of the CCPD hold similar influence over Camden's business interests. For them, public safety has been and continues to be the foundation for economic growth. In an interview in *USA Today* back in 2014, George Norcross III—a successful businessman, Democratic party organizer, and chairman of Cooper University Hospital—stated that he knew years ago that public safety was the "No. 1 issue" when it came to attracting investment to the city: "Subaru would not have relocated here had there been no changes in policing," said Norcross (Shelly, 2014b). The nonprofit security firm CNA, in its final report after working with the CCPD, echoed a similar sentiment on the inextricable link between addressing violent crime and enticing more businesses to the city (CNA Analysis & Solutions, 2019, 16):

> The first stop for investors interested in economic opportunities in Camden is the mayor's office, and their second stop is the police headquarters. Chief Thomson stated that investors want to know that the progress in public safety is real and will continue. The chief assured them with great confidence that it will "because the people of Camden will not reverse course."

Economic revitalization efforts are nothing new in Camden and have been ongoing since the 1990s. Residents, community organizations, activists, and most scholars following the city's developments have generally agreed that the vast majority of all investment—predominantly in the form of tax breaks—has gone either to the waterfront area or to attracting new businesses and tourists to the city (Burney, 1992; Gillette, 2005, 2022). That is, little in the way of economic development ever trickles down to the majority of Camden residents and neighborhoods—resulting in an incredibly unequal revival plan. The size and scale of Camden's revitalization efforts grew exponentially in the past twelve years, starting under Governor Chris Christie's administration. In 2013, the New Jersey state legislature passed the Economic Opportunity Act with key amendments made the following year. The legislation massively expanded the state's tax break system, particularly in South Jersey and the Camden area, with the goal of jump-starting economic development in the wake of the 2008 Great Recession.

As a result, $1.6 billion in tax breaks were awarded to corporations and businesses who committed to either moving to or keeping their headquarters in the city of Camden. For many years, there was no independent data to verify how—if at all—the tax incentive program impacted the hiring prospects for Camden residents. A January 2019 audit by the NJ State Comptroller stated that the Economic Development Authority—the entity tasked with reviewing applications and making determinations about tax breaks—"lacks an adequate monitoring system" to assess whether promised jobs have been created (Solomon & Pillets, 2019). An investigation conducted by WNYC and ProPublica uncovered that $1.1 billion of the $1.6 billion in tax incentives—more than two-thirds (68.75%)—were awarded to George Norcross III and his associates: their own companies, business partners, political allies, and clients of George Norcross III's brother (Solomon & Pillets, 2019; see also Friedman & Landergan, 2019). However, measures of the number of Camden residents employed by the companies receiving such generous tax breaks remained elusive until early 2023.

In the summer of 2022, activists in Camden submitted a grassroots petition to the city clerk that sought a new ordinance to require companies with at least twenty-five employees to list how many of them come from the city itself (Friedman, 2022a). Camden initially fought this movement. The city clerk rejected the petition; the petitioners subsequently sued before the city eventually accepted the new petition and the City Council passed the ordinance (Friedman, 2022b). The new ordinance led to bombshell reporting after the first iteration of data was collected for the second half of 2022 and released in early March 2023. For many of the companies, some of which received hundreds of millions of dollars to either retain or relocate their offices to the city, they employ very few Camden residents (Solomon, 2023; see also Friedman, 2023):

- Subaru ($118 million in tax breaks): 10 Camden residents employed out of 786 total employees in the company's Camden office (1.3%)
- Philadelphia 76ers Corporate Office and practice facility ($82 million in tax breaks): 11 Camden residents employed out of 275 total employees in the team's Camden office (4%)
- Lockheed Martin ($107 million in tax breaks): 3 Camden residents employed
- American Water ($164 million in tax breaks): 7 Camden residents employed
- Conner Strong & Buckelew ($86 million in tax breaks): 6 Camden residents employed out of 402 total employees in the firm's Camden office (1.5%)
- NFI LP—a trucking and logistics firm ($79 million in tax breaks): 9 Camden residents employed out of 524 total employees in the company's Camden office (1.7%)
- Holtec International ($260 million in tax breaks): 37 Camden residents employed out of 1,623 total employees in the company's Camden office (2.3%)

Eastern Metal Recycling, by contrast, which received $132 million in tax breaks, employed 186 Camden residents out of its 648-employee total workforce (28.7%).

For the most part, the tax incentive program in Camden missed several opportunities, such as community benefit agreements to better guarantee that a certain number or percentage of jobs would go to locals, to truly address the root causes and provide long-term solutions in the form of employment to a significant portion of city residents. These dismal employment figures confirm and validate what most critics have been saying for decades: there is little trickle down and few tangible benefits to residents and neighborhoods from the city's corporate recruitment efforts (Burney, 1992; Gillette, 2005, 2022). Cynical observers may wonder whether Camden's developers are not continuing to benefit year after year from the city's continued levels of need in the form of state aid, and if such an incentive structure is ever likely to lead them to contribute to improving the city's well-being. In 2021, sixteen out of the city of Camden's nineteen census tracts (84.2%) continued to have poverty rates in excess of 25%—marking little progress from the mid-2010s, nearly a decade prior (NJ Department of Labor, n.d., 2023). The figures epitomize the hyper unequal nature of Camden's most recent revitalization efforts. The CCPD's job would be easier if a larger proportion of the city's population was lifted out of poverty and more of the city's children grew up seeing their parents working in stable jobs.

Summary

This chapter presented a critique of the police-centric approach to public safety as well as the near exclusive attention and coverage the CCPD received in the summer of 2020 as drivers of Camden's safety. It also provided a commentary on how we must start thinking about crime control and public safety more broadly: with factors and organizations beyond just law enforcement. There is much room for the collaborative efforts at work in places like Newark, NJ, that foster data-informed community engagement or DICE. Those interested in improving public safety—politicians, practitioners, researchers, and journalists—should work to avoid the false dichotomy of having to choose between root causes or more proximal policing and justice system interventions. Those two goals are not incompatible with one another and should instead be performed in concert. Effective evidence-based policing interventions should help communities buy more time to address those root causes like poverty, economic disadvantage, residential segregation, and overall inequality. If those root causes are not confronted in a meaningful way, then the CCPD—and all police departments for that matter—will have a difficult time maximizing their impact.

10

Conclusion

The previous nine chapters presented a full account of the experiment with police reform in Camden, New Jersey. The new CCPD that started on May 1, 2013, received an overwhelming amount of attention not only when then-President Obama visited the city two years into the new department's tenure but also following the murder of George Floyd in the summer of 2020. Protests during the summer of 2020 remained peaceful in Camden in contrast to the contentious clashes in two hundred other cities across the country (U.S. Crisis Monitor, 2020), and the viral photograph of then-Chief Wysocki and other CCPD officers marching in solidarity with protesters became an iconic image that provided hope to many communities. However, it was the Minneapolis City Council's vote to disband the Minneapolis Police Department and replace it with a Department of Community Safety and Violence Prevention—a plan that never came to fruition—that led to the massive media coverage of Camden and the CCPD, coverage that was largely positive. Perhaps the most relevant question posed during this time came from the *New York Times*: "Could this city [Camden] hold the key to the future of policing in America?" (Goldstein & Armstrong, 2020). This precise question led to the current endeavor. The purpose of this final chapter is to provide a summary and a brief synthesis of the most important lessons from Camden's experiment. Additionally, it presents a few points of departure to serve as a springboard for future debate on issues of policing and police reform as well as the best paths forward for ensuring public safety.

Similarities and Differences

One of the primary goals set out in the introductory chapter was to examine: (1) whether Camden is unique, in which case many of the factors at work there may not be necessarily applicable elsewhere, or (2) if there are, indeed, valuable lessons to be learned for other cities and their police departments that are grappling with accountability-related issues and overall reform efforts. The insights in these pages offer both similarities to other places and differences that do set Camden and the CCPD apart. Starting with the potential similarities to other cities around the United States, the old CPD struggled to make basic changes for decades. The CPD received five negative reviews from the state AG, over a twenty-year period from the 1980s through the early 2000s, that all, essentially, had the same conclusions and recommendations: the department was ineffective at combating crime because it failed to properly allocate and deploy cops on the street. Many troubled police departments across the country—including in Minneapolis (Phelps, 2024)—can relate to failed reform efforts despite changes in leadership and other accountability mechanisms that are introduced. Other places can also relate to problematic police unions and other interests that stymie any and all attempts at reform.

Yet, there were a multitude of factors in Camden that are not necessarily present in many other places, including Minneapolis. Camden was functionally bankrupt for years, relying on a tremendous amount of state aid—approximately 87% of its total budget in 2011—to function and even pay its first responders, teachers, and public works employees. In other words, the city's operating budget that year was $167 million, but it only collected $21 million in property taxes (Zernike, 2012). Camden's entire municipal government was under state control starting in 2002, and its police department had been "superceded"—the equivalent of a state-based consent decree—and placed under the control of the state AG's Office from 2003 through 2010, thanks, in part, to the powers afforded to the AG from the NJ state constitution. Camden's municipal government, therefore, had little-to-no bargaining power to fight the dissolve and rebuild efforts, which may explain why Mayor Redd and all city council members except one were in favor of handing control of the new department over to Camden County. Such dynamics, particularly Camden's dismal financial situation, are not at play in many municipalities.

If other cities are looking toward Camden as a model and are interested in the financial details and projected annual savings of dissolving one organization and starting anew, then they will not find a model of cost cutting. All of the public information regarding these details—namely, the lack thereof—left a lot to be desired. Throughout the entire process, there was a profound absence of transparency with very few financial disclosures. Look no further than both the quotes in Chapter 3 from Dr. Brendan O'Flaherty, who was asked about and unable to make sense of the one-page disclosure (Rudolf, 2012), and even the experience of Brian Coleman, a sitting Camden city councilman, who was provided little access to relevant financial information before needing to make a decision on the dissolve and rebuild (D. Simon & Vargas, 2012). That said, while the new department did not use fewer financial resources than the old department, there is reason to believe it operated more efficiently with the funds it used.

Lessons to Be Learned

There are a number of potential lessons to be learned from what the CCPD did well and the mistakes that it made early on. For one, the hope is that this book provides more details about how the actual transition from one department to the other was carried out, particularly during the months of January through April 2013, when there were essentially two police departments operating at the same time. The CCPD, now with adequate staffing, was finally able to make and sustain a host of operational changes to boost not only the officers' presence in the community but the officers' proactivity with lighter workloads. These changes include the creation of NRTs and the restructuring of the patrol division, the outsourcing and civilianization of office tasks, and investments in technology, such as the ability to conduct "virtual patrols" to surmise whether a particular call warrants a uniformed police officer as well as the use of GPS and other internal controls like color-coded maps in RT-TOIC to ensure that officers are—geographically—where they are supposed to be located. With more time at their disposal and no longer needing to travel from one dispatched call to another all shift long, NRTs at last had the capability to improve their visibility in the community, problem-solve, and engage the community in the form of positive nonenforcement contacts with residents and small businesses. Whether the officers actually did the latter tasks to the best of their ability during the first year and a half to two years of the new CCPD—compared to the high level of enforcement activity in the form of vehicle and pedestrian stops as well as citations for low-level violations that took place—is a different story. The point is that they now had both the time and the opportunity to police well as opposed to the circumstances plaguing officers in the old CPD.

On the other hand, the early years of the CCPD offer insight into what to be cognizant of in order to avoid problematic officer behavior that is harmful to public perceptions. When the CCPD added more officers and took steps to better free up their time, they also opened the door for officers to engage in overly aggressive tactics, particularly for low-level matters.

Departments should do their best to (1) rigorously collect information and properly manage measures on a wide range of officer outputs—e.g., stops made, tickets written—and (2) have a robust system whereby supervisors monitor those measures and try to correct the conduct of frontline staff falling under their span of control. Employing an Internal Affairs- or Professional Standards–type of unit to investigate the top ticket writers, offering innovative training and carefully selecting the right officers to facilitate said training, and creating stricter and clearer administrative policies that are reinforced by training and technology (e.g., VirTra V-300® simulator and other role-playing activities) are all ideas that can be applied elsewhere and beyond Camden.

Another salient theme showcases the vast differences in police union leadership between the CPD and the CCPD. The former union leadership actively fought against any attempts to challenge the status quo—even when the active chief and the state's AG were the ones trying to spur change. The latter worked collaboratively with the CCPD's executive leadership and other non–law enforcement organizations such as the Policing Project at NYU School of Law and the ACLU-NJ to facilitative positive changes that benefited both officers and community members. Other cities with union leadership resembling that of the old CPD must take steps to remedy such contentious and adversarial relationships. Unfortunately, in some places, union leadership actively feuds with select politicians and district attorneys. Changes in the police union leadership from one department to the other were a critical factor in addressing the divergent organizational cultures that have come to define both agencies.

Was It Worth It?

The dissolving of the CPD and the creation of a new law enforcement agency that is controlled by Camden County has always been controversial. The time period from 2011 through early 2013 saw a city, its residents, and the old police department divided across whether such a plan should move forward. Community organizers attempted and were ultimately blocked—by local and county politicians—in their effort to create a ballot measure that would have put the decision to abolish and start anew to a vote in the November 2012 election. The NJ Supreme Court ruled in 2015—two years after the CCPD began—that the City and County of Camden acted illegally in trying to thwart the voter referendum. The resistance to dissolving the old agency saw strange bedfellows in the form of the local chapter of the NAACP and the old police union in agreement with one another. The entire process, particularly regarding financial information, was shrouded in a certain degree of secrecy, including for voting members of the Camden City Council.

Many of the initial claims, including that the new police agency would result in cost savings, never came to fruition. All of these factors collectively have fueled debate as to whether the dissolve and rebuild was the right course of action.

A few things are clear. The status quo of the old city department in 2011–2012 was utterly unsustainable. The police budget under the previous system could only pay for approximately 250 officers, which made for a woefully understaffed department. The CPD had been dealing with mismanagement and a lack of accountability for decades. It was unable to effectively address crime and violence, which rose to a record high of sixty-seven homicides in 2012. Basic reforms to more appropriately deploy resources and staffing—proposed and favored by the chief of police and the state's AG—were stymied. Drastic changes needed to be made, and there were asymmetrical power dynamics between the city of Camden, Camden County, and the state of New Jersey.

Yet, there were also causes to be skeptical of the transfer of power. Policing in the city of Camden—a city that is racially quite minority-majority (95% Black and Hispanic) and overwhelmingly poor, economically disadvantaged, and segregated—would be controlled by Camden County, which is whiter and more affluent. That is, the residents of the city of Camden are disenfranchised with little input and ability to influence how they are policed. Even so, the preponderance of evidence suggests that the CCPD, especially post-2015, following its change of course after negative attention, provides better quality service relative to the dysfunctional lack of policing during the old CPD. Crime and violence are unequivocally down. But, perhaps, it is unfair and disingenuous to continuously compare current crime rates to the city's absolute worst year on record—2012 and the final year of CPD—for violent crime and homicides. Even after the transition, Camden is still one of the most violent cities in the state of New Jersey and the country. Radical transformation was necessary; however, it remains to be seen whether all of the correct decisions and actions were made and can contribute to a successful department. The true story of police reform in Camden is complex and nuanced. And it is still being written.

Summary

Much has changed from the final years of the old CPD especially in 2011–2013. Many of those changes are welcome: those regarding crime and violence and a better functioning police department that is capable of pivoting in response to intentional internal and external demands. There is little doubt that the creation of the CCPD has dramatically altered policing and segments of public life for many city residents, business owners, and visitors.

Moreover, CCPD itself has transformed and progressed over time—certainly from a few of the controversies that it experienced in the first two years from 2013–2015. The challenges continue, particularly in terms of turnover and officer retention and how to most effectively police a city that is among the poorest in the nation. Continuing on the current path and, perhaps, making further inroads into reducing crime, violence, and other problems will be difficult and require constant self-reflection and evaluation as a police organization. The CCPD may also hit a ceiling if it does not begin to share the burden and empower non–law enforcement groups to share in the coproduction of public safety. The city and county may themselves hit a ceiling if they do not broaden their economic revitalization efforts to translate into bettering the lives and communities of most city residents. What lies ahead recalls the quote about the people of Camden in the 2006 final report from the Camden Commission on Public Safety, "The future, is, for the most part, in their hands." The choices and actions are up to not only the CCPD but also the city and county leaders, representatives, businesses, and residents.

References

Abt, T. (2019). *Bleeding out: The devastating consequences of urban violence—and a bold new plan for peace in the streets.* Hachette, U.K.: Basic Books.
ACLU (American Civil Liberties Union). (2013, January 10). *Camden agrees to pay $3.5M to victims of police corruption.* Press Release. Available at https://www.aclu.org/press-releases/camden-agrees-pay-35m-victims-police.
ACLU-NJ (American Civil Liberties Union of New Jersey). (2015, May 18). *Policing in Camden has improved, but concerns remain.* Press Release. Available at https://www.aclu-nj.org/news/2015/05/18/policing-camden-has-improved-concerns-remain.
ACLU-NY (American Civil Liberties Union of New York). (2012, May 9). *NYPD stop-and-frisk activity in 2011.* Available at https://www.nyclu.org/en/publications/report-nypd-stop-and-frisk-activity-2011-2012.
ACLU-PA (American Civil Liberties Union of Pennsylvania). (2010, November 4). *ACLU-PA and civil rights firm file class action lawsuit against Philadelphia Police Department for racial profiling.* Available at https://www.aclu.org/press-releases/aclu-pa-and-civil-rights-firm-file-class-action-lawsuit-against-philadelphia-police.
Adams, I., Nix, J., & Mourtgos, S. M. (2023, February 7). Memphis police numbers dropped by nearly a quarter in recent years—were staffing shortages a factor in the killing of Tyre Nichols? *The Conversation.* Available at https://theconversation.com/memphis-police-numbers-dropped-by-nearly-a-quarter-in-recent-years-were-staffing-shortages-a-factor-in-the-killing-of-tyre-nichols-199078.
Adomaitis, G. (2015a, January 21). Camden eyes safety, crime in vacant home demolition effort while neighbors question future. NJ.com. Available at https://www.nj.com/camden/2015/01/demolition_of_abandoned_vacant_camden_houses.html.
———. (2015b, June 19). Body cameras, "ShotSpotter" expansion for Camden County Police Department. NJ.com. Available at https://www.nj.com/camden/2015/06/body_cameras_shotspotter_expansion_for_camden_coun.html.

———. (2015c, July 3). Community policing lesson for Camden County Police to come from retired U.S. Marine. NJ.com. Available at https://www.nj.com/camden/2015/07/retired_us_marine_to_teach_camden_county_police_de.html.

———. (2015d, November 2). Little love for gov outside Christie's Camden visit. NJ.com. Available at https://www.nj.com/camden/2015/11/little_love_for_gov_outside_christies_camden_polic.html.

———. (2016, August 31). Camden County police talk turnover during hiring push. NJ.com/NJ Advanced Media. Available at https://www.nj.com/camden/2016/08/camden_county_police_are_hiring.html#:~:text=%22Across%20the%20country%2C%20police%20departments,minorities%2C%22%20the%20chief%20said.

Alpert, G. P., McLean, K., & Wolfe, S. (2017). Consent decrees: An approach to police accountability and reform. *Police Quarterly, 20*(3), 239–249.

Anderson, E. (2000). *Code of the street: Decency, violence, and the moral life of the inner city*. New York: W. W. Norton.

Andrew, S. (2020, June 9). This city disbanded its police department 7 years ago. Here's what happened next. CNN. Available at https://www.cnn.com/2020/06/09/us/disband-police-camden-new-jersey-trnd/index.html.

Ang, D., Bencsik, P., Bruhn, J., & Derenoncourt, E. (2021). Police violence reduces civilian cooperation and engagement with law enforcement. Available at https://scholar.harvard.edu/files/ang/files/abbd_crimereporting.pdf.

Arco, M. (2015, February 22). Camden crime fighting: Christie touts success, but too early to claim victory. NJ.com. Available at https://www.nj.com/politics/2015/02/camden_county_police_department_metro_division.html.

Arietti, R. (2024). Do real-time crime centers improve case clearance? An examination of Chicago's strategic decision support centers. *Journal of Criminal Justice, 90*, 102145.

Asher, J. (2021, September 22). Murder rose by almost 30% in 2020. It's rising at a slower rate in 2021. *New York Times*. Available at https://www.nytimes.com/2021/09/22/upshot/murder-rise-2020.html.

Atherley, L. T., & Hickman, M. J. (2013). Officer decertification and the national decertification index. *Police Quarterly, 16*(4), 420–437.

Aziani, A. (2022). What happens when the police go on strike? Homicides increase. Evidence from Ceará, Brazil. *Global Crime, 23*(4), 365–391.

Bates, J., & Vick, K. (2020, August 6). America's policing system is broken. It's time to radically rethink public safety. *Time*. Available at https://time.com/5876318/police-reform-america/.

Bauman, A., & Chakrabarti, M. (2020, June 11). Portrait of police reform: How Camden, New Jersey rebuilt its police department. *WBUR's On Point*. Available at https://www.wbur.org/onpoint/2020/06/11/police-reform-camden-new-jersey-rebuilt-its-police-department.

Baxter, C., & Megerian, C. (2011, August 2). Camden County to form regional police department. NJ.com. Available at https://www.nj.com/news/2011/08/camden_county_to_form_regional.html.

BBC News. (2020, July 16). George Floyd: What happened in the final moments of his life. BBC News. Available at https://www.bbc.com/news/world-us-canada-52861726.

Beck, B., Holder, E., Novak, A., & Kaplan, J. (2023). The material of policing: Budgets, personnel and the United States' misdemeanour arrest decline. *British Journal of Criminology, 63*(2), 330–347.

Becker, M. G., Hall, J. S., Ursic, C. M., Jain, S., & Calhoun, D. (2004). Caught in the crossfire: The effects of a peer-based intervention program for violently injured youth. *Journal of Adolescent Health, 34*(3), 177–183.

Bender, W. (2020, November 29). Can Philadelphia transform its police force from "warriors" to "guardians"? This de-escalation training could help. *Philadelphia Inquirer*. Available at https://www.inquirer.com/news/philadelphia-police-icat-training-deescalation-cit-walter-wallace-20201129.html.

Bender, W., Gambacorta, D., & Laker, B. (2022, December 22). Number of Philly cops out injured drops 31% after *Inquirer* investigation uncovers abuse. *Philadelphia Inquirer*. Available at https://www.inquirer.com/news/philadelphia-police-injury-claims-heart-lung-abuse-reform-20221220.html.

Beym, J. (2015, May 17). Turnover at Camden County police force an issue, reports say day before Obama's visit. NJ.com. Available at https://www.nj.com/camden/2015/05/turnover_at_camden_county_police_force_an_issue_re.html.

Bierie, D. M. (2017). Assault of police. *Crime & Delinquency, 63*(8), 899–925.

Biryukov, N. (2022, May 18). N.J. moves to license cops in bid to increase public trust in policing. *New Jersey Monitor*. Available at https://newjerseymonitor.com/2022/05/18/n-j-moves-to-license-cops-in-bid-to-increase-public-trust-in-policing/.

Bishopp, S. A., Klinger, D. A., & Morris, R. G. (2015). An examination of the effect of a policy change on police use of TASERs. *Criminal Justice Policy Review, 26*(7), 727–746.

Blackburn, E., & Mares, D. (2019). The hidden costs of police technology: Evaluating acoustic gunshot detection systems. *Police Chief Magazine*. Available at https://www.policechiefmagazine.org/the-hidden-costs-of-police-technology/.

Blumgart, J. (2020, June 30). Camden, New Jersey, isn't really a model for police reform. *City Monitor*. Available at https://citymonitor.ai/government/camden-new-jersey-isnt-really-a-model-for-police-reform.

Boren, M. (2014, December 7). In Camden, police crackdown clogs court. *Philadelphia Inquirer*. Available at https://www.inquirer.com/philly/news/20141207_In_Camden__police_crackdown_clogs_court.html.

———. (2015, April 26). Complaints rise under Camden Police. *Philadelphia Inquirer*. Available at https://www.inquirer.com/news/inq/complaints-rise-under-camden-police-20150425.html.

Boren, M., & Steele, A. (2016, January 3). In Camden, fewer killings, but tougher to solve. *Philadelphia Inquirer*. Available at https://www.inquirer.com/philly/news/new_jersey/20160103_In_Camden__fewer_homicides__but_tougher_to_solve.html.

Boren, M., & Wood, S. (2015, May 17). Camden County Police Department struggling to keep officers. *Philadelphia Inquirer*. Available at https://www.inquirer.com/philly/news/new_jersey/20150517_Camden_County_Police_Department_struggling_to_keep_officers.html.

Borodkin, B. (2022). Officer-created jeopardy and reasonableness reform: Rebuttable presumption of unreasonableness within 42 U.S.C. § 1983 police use of force claims. *University of Michigan Journal of Law Reform, 55*(4), 919–957.

Borowski, N. (2023a, January 26). CCPD misses mark in recruiting all-Camden class of recruits. *TapIntoCamden*. Available at https://www.tapinto.net/towns/camden/sections/police-and-fire/articles/ccpd-misses-mark-in-recruiting-all-camden-class-of-recruits.

———. (2023b, May 1). Camden police, once flawed, now seen as an international best practice. *TapIntoCamden*. Available at https://www.tapinto.net/towns/camden/sections/police-and-fire/articles/camden-police-once-flawed-now-seen-as-an-international-best-practice.

———. (2024a, January 4). Camden's murder count in 2023 equaled 2022. *TapIntoCamden*. Available at https://www.tapinto.net/towns/camden/sections/police-and-fire/articles/camden-s-murder-count-in-2023-equaled-2022.

———. (2024b, May 8). New CCPD contract: Higher pay to enable recruitment, retention. *TapIntoCamden*. Available at https://www.tapinto.net/towns/camden/sections/police-and-fire/articles/new-ccpd-contract-higher-pay-to-enable-recruitment-retention.

Braga, A. A. (2021). Improving police clearance rates of shootings: A review of the evidence. Manhattan Institute. Available at https://manhattan.institute/article/improving-police-clearance-rates-of-shootings-a-review-of-the-evidence.

Braga, A. A., Turchan, B. S., Papachristos, A. V., & Hureau, D. M. (2019). Hot spots policing and crime reduction: An update of an ongoing systematic review and meta-analysis. *Journal of Experimental Criminology, 15*, 289–311.

Braga, A. A., & Weisburd, D. L. (2012). The effects of focused deterrence strategies on crime: A systematic review and meta-analysis of the empirical evidence. *Journal of Research in Crime and Delinquency, 49*(3), 323–358.

Branas, C. C., Kondo, M. C., Murphy, S. M., South, E. C., Polsky, D., & MacDonald, J. M. (2016). Urban blight remediation as a cost-beneficial solution to firearm violence. *American Journal of Public Health, 106*(12), 2158–2164.

Brenan, M. (2020, August 12). Amid pandemic, confidence in key U.S. institutions surges. Gallup. Available at https://news.gallup.com/poll/317135/amid-pandemic-confidence-key-institutions-surges.aspx?utm_source=twitterbutton&utm_medium=twitter&utm_campaign=sharing.

Breslauer, B., Ramgopal, K., Abou-Sabe, K., & Gosk, S. (2020, June 22). Camden, N.J. disbanded its police force. Here's what happened next. NBC News. Available at https://www.nbcnews.com/news/us-news/new-jersey-city-disbanded-its-police-force-here-s-what-n1231677.

Bucci, R. (2023). Addressing the "dirty little secret" in deterrence: Testing the effects of increased police presence on perceptions of arrest risk. *Journal of Quantitative Criminology*. Advanced online publication. https://doi.org/10.1007/s10940-023-09570-3.

Bureau of Labor Statistics. (2018). *There were 500 workplace homicides in the United States in 2016*. Washington, DC: U.S. Department of Labor. Available at https://www.bls.gov/opub/ted/2018/there-were-500-workplace-homicides-in-the-united-states-in-2016.htm.

Burke, M. (2017, August 2). Camden County police have yet to post promised data online. *The Philadelphia Inquirer*. Available at https://www.inquirer.com/philly/news/new_jersey/shore/camden-police-have-yet-to-post-promised-data-online-other-cities-have-20170802.html.

Burke, M., & Cohen, A. (2022, July 7). Ex-Cleveland officer who fatally shot Tamir Rice resigned from Pennsylvania department, attorney says. NBC News. Available at https://www.nbcnews.com/news/us-news/ex-cleveland-officer-fatally-shot-tamir-rice-hired-pennsylvania-boroug-rcna37074.

Burney, M. (1992, March 14). Hope on the waterfront. *Washington Post*. Available at https://www.washingtonpost.com/archive/realestate/1992/03/14/hope-on-the-waterfront/dedb7b7c-1873-4c69-acf2-a5f3a3441f22/.

———. (2007, March 20). 4 charged with theft from city schools: They are accused of stealing $40,000 from schools, parents in Camden. *Philadelphia Inquirer*. Available at https://www.inquirer.com/philly/news/new_jersey/20070320_4_charged_with_theft_from_Camden_schools.html.

Butts, J. A., & Delgado, S. A. (2017). *Repairing trust: Young men in neighborhoods with Cure Violence programs report growing confidence in police*. JohnJayREC Research Brief 2017-01. New York: John Jay College of Criminal Justice, Research and Evaluation Center.

Byrne, J., & Marx, G. (2011). Technological innovations in crime prevention and policing: A review of the research on implementation and impact. *Journal of Police Studies*, 20(3), 17-40.

Caffrey, M. (2015, May 24). "They have a choice": How Camden police are guarding teens from gang violence. NJ.com. Available at https://www.nj.com/camden/2015/05/they_have_a_choice_how_camden_police_are_guarding.html.

Callimachi, R. (2020, June 24). 9 departments and multiple infractions for one New Jersey police officer. *New York Times*. Available at https://www.nytimes.com/2020/06/24/nyregion/new-jersey-police.html.

Camden Food Access Work Group. (2020). *Healthy food access Camden: Recommendations*. Available at https://thefoodtrust.org/wp-content/uploads/2022/07/report_healthy-food-access-camden_october-2020.original.pdf.

Capuzzo, J. (2006, February 12). Camden's rankled ranks. *New York Times*. Available at https://www.nytimes.com/2006/02/12/nyregion/camdens-rankled-ranks.html.

CBS News Philadelphia. (2021, June 16). Camden begins demolition of dilapidated homes in effort to improve quality of life for city residents. Available at https://www.cbsnews.com/philadelphia/news/camden-begins-demolition-of-dilapidated-homes-in-effort-to-improve-quality-of-life-for-city-residents/.

CCPD (Camden County Police Department). (2022). *Statistical overview—Citywide crimes*. Available at https://www.camdencounty.com/wp-content/uploads/2022/01/YTD-CRIME-STATS_Graphs-1-1-22.pdf.

———. (2023). *CCPD Policies*. Available at https://camdencountypd.org/ccpd-policies/.

CCPO (Camden County Prosecutor's Office). (2021). *CCPO records highest homicide solve rate in office history*. Available at https://camdencountypros.kinsta.cloud/ccpo-records-highest-homicide-solve-rate-in-office-history/.

———. (2023). *Units page*. Available at https://camdencountypros.org/units.

Center for Family Services. (n.d.). Cure4Camden. Available at https://www.centerffs.org/our-services/trauma-victim-response/cure4camden.

Chalfin, A. (2022, January 27). How a focused approach to policing made New York safer. Niskanen Center. Available at https://www.niskanencenter.org/how-a-focused-approach-to-policing-made-new-york-safer/.

Chalfin, A., Hansen, B., Weisburst, E. K., & Williams Jr., M. C. (2021, May 18). When cities add cops, Black residents could have the most to gain—and the most to lose. Niskanen Center. Available at https://www.niskanencenter.org/when-cities-add-cops-black-residents-could-have-the-most-to-gain-and-the-most-to-lose/.

———. (2022). Police force size and civilian race. *American Economic Review: Insights*, 4(2), 139-158.

Chalfin, A., LaForest, M., & Kaplan, J. (2021). Can precision policing reduce gun violence? Evidence from "gang takedowns" in New York City. *Journal of Policy Analysis and Management*, 40(4), 1047-1082.

Chang, A. (2012, December 6). Crime-ridden Camden to dump city police force. NPR/WHYY. Available at https://www.npr.org/2012/12/06/166658788/crime-ridden-camden-to-dump-city-police-force#:~:text=As%20the%20New%20Jersey%20city,off%20the%20entire%20police%20department.

Chanin, J. M. (2015). Examining the sustainability of pattern or practice police misconduct reform. *Police Quarterly, 18*(2), 163–192.

Cheng, T. (2024). *The policing machine: Enforcement, endorsements, and the illusion of public input.* Chicago: University of Chicago Press.

Christie, C. (2010, February 11). Executive Order #14. Available at https://nj.gov/infobank/circular/eocc14.pdf.

Clarke, R. V. (1980). Situational crime prevention: Theory and practice. *British Journal of Criminology, 20*(2), 136–147.

CNA Analysis & Solutions. (2019). *Camden County (New Jersey) Police Department: Safer Neighborhoods through Precision Policing Initiative.* Arlington, VA: CNA.

CNN. (2011, January 18). Crime-ridden Camden, N.J., cuts police force nearly in half. Available at https://web.archive.org/web/20111123232055/http://articles.cnn.com/2011-01-18/us/new.jersey.layoffs_1_police-force-police-officers-public-safety?_s=PM:US.

Cohen, L. E., & Felson, M. (1979). Social change and crime rate trends: A routine activity approach. *American Sociological Review, 44*(4), 588–608.

Colligan, P. (2015, May 18). *Letter to President Barack Obama.* NJ State Policemen's Benevolent Association, Inc. Available at http://pbalocal382.org/?zone=/unionactive/view_article.cfm&HomeID=498847.

Cooper, C., Eslinger, D. M., & Stolley, P. D. (2006). Hospital-based violence intervention programs work. *Journal of Trauma and Acute Care Surgery, 61*(3), 534–540.

Council on Criminal Justice. (2021). *De-escalation policies and training.* Available at https://assets.foleon.com/eu-west-2/uploads-7e3kk3/41697/de-escalation_training.9f4b662e97c2.pdf.

Courier-Post. (1971, August 26). "You should have seen the people flying out of here. . . . There were moving trucks all over the place."

Crowd Counting Consortium (2020). *Study of 2020 protests shows difference between reality and perception.* Available at https://today.uconn.edu/2020/10/study-2020-protests-shows-difference-reality-perception/#.

C-SPAN. (2015, May 18). *President Obama touring Camden police center.* Available at https://www.c-span.org/video/?326110-2/president-obama-touring-camden-police-center.

Cuellar, D. (2019, August 22). Camden County Police Department revises the use of force policy. 6ABC Action News. Available at https://6abc.com/camden-co-police-department-revises-the-use-of-force-policy/5484117/.

Culnan, D. (1979, December). Focus on Camden. New Jersey Business 25.

Danley, S. (2020, June 16). Camden police reboot is being misused in the debate over police reform. *Washington Post.* Available at https://www.washingtonpost.com/outlook/2020/06/16/camden-nj-police-reboot-is-being-misused-debate-over-police-reform/.

Deblasio, V. (2019, July 14). Four years after joining Initiative, Camden County Police have not posted data online. *TapIntoCamden.* Available at https://www.tapinto.net/towns/camden/sections/police-and-fire/articles/four-years-after-joining-initiative-camden-county-police-have-not-posted-data-online.

Delgado, S. A., Alsabahi, L., & Butts, J. A. (2017). *Young men in neighborhoods with Cure Violence programs adopt attitudes less supportive of violence.* JohnJayREC DataBits, 2017-01. New York: Research and Evaluation Center, John Jay College of Criminal Justice, City University of New York.

Del Pozo, B., Knorre, A., Mello, M. J., & Chalfin, A. (2022). Comparing risks of firearm-related death and injury among young adult males in selected US cities with wartime service in Iraq and Afghanistan. *JAMA Network Open, 5*(12), e2248132.

den Heyer, G. (2016). *Delivering police services effectively.* Boca Raton: CRC.
Desmond, M., Papachristos, A. V., & Kirk, D. S. (2016). Police violence and citizen crime reporting in the black community. *American Sociological Review, 81*(5), 857–876.
Devi, T., & Fryer Jr., R. G. (2020). Policing the police: The impact of "pattern-or-practice" investigations on crime (No. w27324). National Bureau of Economic Research.
DiUlio, N. (2020, November 16). Behind the Camden comeback. *New Jersey Monthly.* Available at https://njmonthly.com/articles/jersey-living/camden-comeback/.
Division of Criminal Justice. (1987). *A management study the Camden Police Department: Executive summary.* NJ Attorney General's Office, Department of Law & Public Safety.
———. (1996). *Report on the Camden Police Department.* NJ Attorney General's Office, Department of Law & Public Safety.
———. (2002). *Report on the Camden Police Department.* NJ Attorney General's Office, Department of Law & Public Safety.
Doubek, J. (2020, June 8). Former chief of reformed Camden, N.J., force: Police need "consent of the people." NPR. Available at https://www.npr.org/sections/live-updates-protests-for-racial-justice/2020/06/08/872416644/former-chief-of-reformed-camden-n-j-force-police-need-consent-of-the-people.
Duhart, D. T. (2001). *Violence in the workplace, 1993–99.* Washington, DC: U.S. Department of Justice, Office of Justice Programs.
Economist, The. (2009, November 28). Ungovernable? Camden's crisis. Available at https://www.economist.com/united-states/2009/11/26/ungovernable.
Electronic Frontier Foundation. (2024). "Atlas of surveillance: Real-time crime center." Available at https://atlasofsurveillance.org/atlas.
Engel, R. S., Corsaro, N., Isaza, G. T., & McManus, H. D. (2022a). Assessing the impact of de-escalation training on police behavior: Reducing police use of force in the Louisville, KY Metro Police Department. *Criminology & Public Policy, 21*(2), 199–233.
Engel, R. S., Corsaro, N., Isaza, G. T., & Motz, R. T. (2021). *Examining the impact of integrating, communications, assessment, and tactics (ICAT) de-escalation training for the Louisville Metro police department: Supplemental findings.* IACP/UC Center for Police Research and Policy.
Engel, R. S., Isaza, G. T., Motz, R. T., McManus, H. D., & Corsaro, N. (2022b). De-escalation training receptivity and first-line police supervision: Findings from the Louisville Metro Police Study. *Police Quarterly, 25*(2), 201–227.
Engel, R. S., McManus, H. D., & Herold, T. D. (2020). Does de-escalation training work? A systematic review and call for evidence in police use-of-force reform. *Criminology & Public Policy, 19*(3), 721–759.
Evans, W. N., & Owens, E. G. (2007). COPS and Crime. *Journal of Public Economics, 91*(1–2), 181–201.
Everett, R. (2019, August 22). Camden police launch strict "last resort" use-of-force policy. County wants it to be national model. NJ.com. Available at https://www.nj.com/camden/2019/08/camden-police-launch-strict-last-resort-use-of-force-policy-chief-wants-it-to-be-national-model.html.
———. (2020a, October 6). Camden killings more than doubled in bloody 6-week span. What's being done about it. NJ.com. Available at https://www.nj.com/camden/2020/10/camden-killings-more-than-doubled-in-bloody-6-week-span-whats-being-done-about-it.html#:~:text=What's%20being%20done%20about%20it%3F,-Updated%20Oct%2006&text=We've%20had%2012%20homicides,have%20not%20seen%20since%202012.%E2%80%9D.

———. (2020b, December 20). Arrest video of armed man shows how cops can avoid police shootings, Camden says. NJ.com. Available at https://www.nj.com/camden/2020/12/arrest-video-of-armed-man-shows-how-cops-can-avoid-police-shootings-camden-says.html.

Fedarko, K. (1992, January 20). The other America. *Time*. Available at https://content.time.com/time/subscriber/article/0,33009,974708,00.html.

Federal Bureau of Investigation. (2010, October 14). *Two Camden police officers indicted for conspiracy to deprive others of civil rights*. Press Release. Available at https://archives.fbi.gov/archives/philadelphia/press-releases/2010/ph101410b.htm.

Ferdik, F. V., Kaminski, R. J., Cooney, M. D., & Sevigny, E. L. (2014). The influence of agency policies on conducted energy device use and police use of lethal force. *Police Quarterly, 17*(4), 328–358.

Ferguson, A. G. (2017). *The rise of big data policing: Surveillance, race, and the future of law enforcement*. New York: New York University Press.

Forman Jr., J. (2017). *Locking up our own: Crime and punishment in Black America*. New York: Farrar, Straus and Giroux.

Forrest v. Parry. (2019, July 10). United States Court of Appeals for the Third Circuit. No. 16-4351. Available at https://www2.ca3.uscourts.gov/opinarch/164351p.pdf.

Fridell, L., Faggiani, D., Taylor, B., Brito, C. S., & Kubu, B. (2009). The impact of agency context, policies, and practices on violence against police. *Journal of Criminal Justice, 37*(6), 542–552.

Friedersdorf, C. (2013, December 12). The Surveillance City of Camden, New Jersey. *The Atlantic*. Available at https://www.theatlantic.com/national/archive/2013/12/the-surveillance-city-of-camden-new-jersey/282286/.

Friedman, M. (2022a, June 22). Camden activists take the initiative. *Politico*. Available at https://www.politico.com/newsletters/new-jersey-playbook/2022/06/22/camden-activists-take-the-initiative-00041238.

———. (2022b, August 4). Some strange news out of Camden. *Politico*. Available at https://www.politico.com/newsletters/new-jersey-playbook/2022/08/04/some-strange-news-out-of-camden-00049744.

———. (2023, March 8). Camden Rising? *Politico*. Available at https://www.politico.com/newsletters/new-jersey-playbook/2023/03/08/camden-rising-00086019.

Friedman, M., & Landergan, K. (2019, May 2). Task force scrutinizes tax incentives in Camden—and Norcross. *Politico*. Available at https://www.politico.com/states/new-jersey/story/2019/05/02/task-force-scrutinizes-tax-credits-in-camden-and-norcross-1004222.

Fussell, S. (2020, July 1). What disbanding the police really meant in Camden, New Jersey. *Wired*. Available at https://www.wired.com/story/disbanding-police-really-meant-camden/#:~:text=In%202011%2C%20then%20governor%20Chris,saved%20almost%20%2490%2C000%20per%20officer.

Fyfe, J. J. (1978). Shots fired: An examination of New York City police firearms discharges. Unpublished doctoral dissertation, State University of New York at Albany. Ann Arbor, MI: University Microfilms International.

———. (1979). Administrative interventions on police shooting discretion: An empirical examination. *Journal of Criminal Justice, 7*(4), 309–323.

———. (1982). Blind justice: Police shootings in Memphis. *Journal of Criminal Law and Criminology, 73*(2), 707–722.

———. (1988). Police use of deadly force: Research and reform. *Justice Quarterly, 5*(2), 165–205.

———. (1996). Training to reduce police-civilian violence. In W. A. Geller & H. Toch (Eds.), *Police violence: Understanding and controlling police abuse of force* (pp. 165–179). New Haven, CT: Yale University Press.

Gagis, J. (2019, August 30). A look at Camden and the pros and cons of shared services. *NJ Spotlight News*. Available at https://www.njspotlightnews.org/video/a-look-at-camden-and-the-pros-and-cons-of-shared-services/.

Gambacorta, D., Laker, B., & Bender, W. (2022a, February 7). "Absolutely repulsive": Philly police commissioner slams cops who abuse injured-on-duty benefits. *Philadelphia Inquirer*. Available at https://www.inquirer.com/news/outlaw-philadelphia-police-heart-lung-abuse-krasner-kenney-20220207.html#:~:text=Police%20Commissioner%20Danielle%20Outlaw%20has,are%20too%20injured%20to%20work.

———. (2022b, October 18). Philly has spent $205 million on salaries for injured police since 2017. An audit found little is done to prevent fraud. *Philadelphia Inquirer*. Available at https://www.inquirer.com/news/philadelphia-audit-rhynhart-police-injured-heart-lung-disability-fop-20221018.html.

Gammage, J., Rushing, E., & Graham, K. A. (2020, June 1). National Guard troops deploy in Philly as confrontations continue between police and protesters. *Philadelphia Inquirer*. Available at https://www.inquirer.com/news/philadelphia-national-guard-protests-george-floyd-looting-fires-20200601.html.

Geller, W. A., & Scott, M. (1992). *Deadly force: What we know—A practitioner's desk reference on police-involved shootings*. Washington, DC: Police Executive Research Forum.

Gettleman, J. (2004, December 29). Camden's streets go from mean to meanest. *New York Times*. Available at https://www.nytimes.com/2004/12/29/nyregion/camdens-streets-go-from-mean-to-meanest.html.

Gibson, C. (1998). Population of the 100 largest cities and other urban places in the United States: 1790 to 1990. U.S. Census Bureau, Population Division (Working paper No. 27). Available at https://www.census.gov/library/working-papers/1998/demo/POP-twps0027.html.

Gibson, G., & Renshaw, J. (2011, July 1). Gov. Christie signs state budget after series of deep cuts. NJ.com. Available at https://www.nj.com/news/2011/07/christie_signs_state_budget_af.html.

Gillette, H. J. (2005). *Camden after the fall: Decline and renewal in a post-industrial city*. Philadelphia: University of Pennsylvania Press.

———. (2013, August 21). If demolition is the "price for progress," where's the larger vision? Rutgers University–Camden Blog. Available at https://gillette.camden.rutgers.edu/2013/08/21/if-demolition-is-the-price-for-progress-wheres-the-larger-vision/.

———. (2022). *The paradox of urban revitalization: Progress and poverty in America's postindustrial era*. Philadelphia: University of Pennsylvania Press.

Goh, L. S. (2020). Going local: Do consent decrees and other forms of federal intervention in municipal police departments reduce police killings? *Justice Quarterly*, 37(5), 900–929.

———. (2021). Did de-escalation successfully reduce serious use of force in Camden County, New Jersey? A synthetic control analysis of force outcomes. *Criminology & Public Policy*, 20(2), 207–241.

Goldenberg, A., Rattigan, D., Dalton, M., Gaughan, J. P., Thomson, J. S., Remick, K., . . . & Hazelton, J. P. (2019). Use of ShotSpotter detection technology decreases prehospital time for patients sustaining gunshot wounds. *Journal of Trauma and Acute Care Surgery*, 87(6), 1253–1259.

Goldman, H. (2020, June 10). Why "defund the police" is a chant with many meanings. *Washington Post.* Available at https://web.archive.org/web/20200616135237/https://www.washingtonpost.com/business/why-defund-the-police-is-a-chant-with-many-meanings/2020/06/09/40be444c-aa43-11ea-a43b-be9f6494a87d_story.html.

Goldstein, J. (2011, March 7). After deep police layoffs, Camden feels vulnerable. *New York Times.* Available at https://www.nytimes.com/2011/03/07/nyregion/07camden.html.

———. (2017, April 2). Changes in policing take hold in one of the nation's most dangerous cities. *New York Times.* Available at https://www.nytimes.com/2017/04/02/nyregion/camden-nj-police-shootings.html.

Goldstein, J., & Armstrong, K. (2020, July 12). Could this city hold the key to the future of policing in America? *New York Times.* Available at https://www.nytimes.com/2020/07/12/nyregion/camden-police.html.

Griffith, J. (2024, July 24). Deputy who killed Sonya Massey worked for 6 agencies in 4 years. *NBC News.* Available at https://www.nbcnews.com/news/us-news/deputy-killed-sonya-massey-worked-6-agencies-4-years-rcna163409.

Grunwald, B., & Rappaport, J. (2020). The wandering officer. *Yale Law Journal, 129,* 1676–1782.

Guerette, R. T., & Przeszlowski, K. (2023). Does the rapid deployment of information to police improve crime solvability? A quasi-experiment impact evaluation of Real-Time Crime Center (RTCC) technologies on violent crime incident outcomes. *Justice Quarterly, 40*(7), 950–974.

Hartman, T. (2024, August 8). Woodlynne Police Department in New Jersey will be disbanded; to be covered by Camden County PD. *6ABC.* Available at https://6abc.com/post/woodlynne-police-department-new-jersey-will-disbanded-covered-camden-county-pd/15160146/.

Heininger, C. (2009, February 4). Chris Christie promises change to a "broken" state in campaign kickoff. *The Star-Ledger.* Available at https://www.nj.com/news/2009/02/chris_christie_promises_change.html.

Hernandez, J. (2015, August 11). NJ Supreme Court rules in favor of Camden police petitioners. WHYY. Available at https://whyy.org/articles/nj-supreme-court-rules-in-favor-of-camden-police-petitioners/.

———. (2016, December 1). Project Guardian tries to nudge Camden kids away from a life of crime. WHYY/NPR. Available at https://whyy.org/articles/project-guardian-tries-to-nudge-camden-kids-away-from-a-life-of-crime/.

Hickey, B. (2017, November 30). A scared-straight program (without fear) in Camden. *PhillyVoice.* Available at https://www.phillyvoice.com/watch-scared-straight-program-without-fear-camden/.

Hoban, J. E., & Gourlie, B. J. (2019, April 4). Training Camden: 3 steps to creating a protector culture. *Police1.* Available at https://www.police1.com/police-training/articles/training-camden-3-steps-to-creating-a-protector-culture-bw3yHY1yoIksnJ2Y/.

Hollywood, J. S., Mckay, K. N., Woods, D., & Agniel, D. (2019). *Real-time crime centers in Chicago: Evaluation of the Chicago Police Department's Strategic Decision Support Centers.* Santa Monica, CA: RAND Corporation.

Isaza, G. T., McManus, H. D., Engel, R. S., & Corsaro, N. (2019). *Evaluation of police use of force de-escalation training: Assessing the impact of Integrating Communications, Assessment, and Tactics (ICAT) training program for the University of Cincinnati, OH Police Division (UCPD).* Available at https://www.theiacp.org/sites/default/files/Research%20Center/UCPD_ICAT%20Evaluation_Final.pdf.

Jacobs, J. (1961). *The death and life of great American cities*. New York: Vintage Books.

Jay, J., de Jong, J., Jimenez, M. P., Nguyen, Q., & Goldstick, J. (2022). Effects of demolishing abandoned buildings on firearm violence: A moderation analysis using aerial imagery and deep learning. *Injury Prevention, 28*(3), 249–255.

Jennings, J. T., & Rubado, M. E. (2017). Preventing the use of deadly force: The relationship between police agency policies and rates of officer-involved gun deaths. *Public Administration Review, 77*(2), 217–226.

Jewish Federation of Camden County. (1972). *With vision and compassion: A history of the Jewish Federation in Camden County*. Cherry Hill, NJ: Author.

John Jay College Research Advisory Group on Preventing and Reducing Community Violence (2020). *Reducing violence without police: A review of research evidence*. Available at https://johnjayrec.nyc/wp-content/uploads/2020/11/AV20201109_rev.pdf.

Johnson, N. J., & Roman, C. G. (2022). Community correlates of change: A mixed-effects assessment of shooting dynamics during COVID-19. *PLoS ONE, 17*(2): e0263777.

Jones, J. M. (2020, August 12). Black, white adults' confidence diverges most on police. Gallup. Available at https://news.gallup.com/poll/317114/black-white-adults-confidence-diverges-police.aspx.

Jordan, S. K. (1997, January). Automatic license plate reader: A solution to avoiding vehicle pursuit. In *Security Systems and Nonlethal Technologies for Law Enforcement* (Vol. 2934, pp. 44–48). International Society for Optics and Photonics. https://doi.org/10.1117/12.265419.

Joyce, N., & Pearson, J. (2019). *Comprehensive approaches to violent crime: The Camden County Crime Coalition*. Arlington, VA: CNA.

Juillard, C., Cooperman, L., Allen, I., Pirracchio, R., Henderson, T., Marquez, R., . . . & Dicker, R. A. (2016). A decade of hospital-based violence intervention: Benefits and shortcomings. *Journal of Trauma and Acute Care Surgery, 81*(6), 1156–1161.

Katz, M. (2008, July 20). Camden police chief quits: Succession unclear. *Philadelphia Inquirer*. Available at https://www.inquirer.com/philly/news/local/20080720_Camden_police_chief_quits__succession_unclear.html.

Kennedy, R. (1997). *Race, crime, and the law*. New York: Vintage Books.

Kernahan, R., & Valasik, M. (2019). *The impact of license plate readers on violent crime in Tigerland, LSU: A geospatial case study*. Crime and Policy Evaluation Research Group.

Koper, C. S., & Lum, C. (2019). The impacts of large-scale license plate reader deployment on criminal investigations. *Police Quarterly, 22*(3), 305–329.

Koper, C. S., Taylor, B. G., & Park, S. (2019). Optimizing the geographic deployment of hot spot patrols with license plate readers. *Journal of Experimental Criminology, 15*(4), 641–650.

Kurlander, D. (2020, June 18). The Camden policing model (with Anne Milgram and Scott Thomson). *Café*. Available at https://cafe.com/stay-tuned/the-camden-policing-model-with-anne-milgram-scott-thomson/.

Laday, J. (2013a, March 10). Camden County police officers tasked with building new department. NJ.com. Available at https://www.nj.com/camden/2013/03/camden_county_police_officers.html.

———. (2013b, March 19). Camden County police offer jobs to 120 prospective officers. NJ.com. Available at https://www.nj.com/camden/2013/03/camden_county_police_offer_job.html.

———. (2013c, April 8). New Camden County police take to streets in first day of field training. NJ.com. Available at https://www.nj.com/camden/2013/04/new_camden_county_officers_tak.html.

———. (2013d, April 20). New Camden police officers get to know their neighborhood. NJ.com. Available at https://www.nj.com/camden/2013/04/new_camden_police_officers_get.html.

———. (2013e, May 15). Camden County Metro Division boasts $4.5 million in surveillance equipment and other technologies. NJ.com. Available at https://www.nj.com/camden/2013/05/camden_county_metro_division_b.html.

———. (2015a, January 16). Camden to begin large-scale demolition of abandoned, vacant homes on Tuesday. NJ.com. Available at https://www.nj.com/camden/2015/01/camden_to_begin_large-scale_demolition_of_abandone.html.

———. (2015b, April 2). Camden reports 48 percent reduction in gunfire. NJ.com. Available at https://www.nj.com/camden/2015/04/camden_reports_48_percent_reduction_in_gunfire.html.

———. (2015c, April 13). Camden County police testing body cameras on officers. NJ.com. Available at https://www.nj.com/camden/2015/04/camden_county_police_testing_body_cameras_on_offic.html.

Landergan, K. (2020, June 12). The city that really did abolish the police. *Politico*. Available at https://www.politico.com/news/magazine/2020/06/12/camden-policing-reforms-313750.

Larson, M., Xu, Y., Ouellet, L., & Klahm IV, C. F. (2019). Exploring the impact of 9398 demolitions on neighborhood-level crime in Detroit, Michigan. *Journal of Criminal Justice, 60*, 57–63.

Law Enforcement Management and Administrative Statistics. (2016). *2016 LEMAS survey*. Bureau of Justice Statistics: Washington, DC.

Lowery, W. (2021, February 22). The most ambitious effort yet to reform policing may be happening in Ithaca, New York. *GQ*. Available at https://www.gq.com/story/ithaca-mayor-svante-myrick-police-reform.

Luhby, T. (2011, January 17). Camden, N.J. to lose nearly half its cops. CNN. Available at https://money.cnn.com/2011/01/17/news/economy/camden_police_layoffs/index.htm.

Lum, C., Hibdon, J., Cave, B., Koper, C. S., & Merola, L. (2011). License plate reader (LPR) police patrols in crime hot spots: An experimental evaluation in two adjacent jurisdictions. *Journal of Experimental Criminology, 7*(4), 321–345.

Lum, C., Koper, C. S., Willis, J., Happeny, S., Vovak, H., & Nichols, J. (2019). The rapid diffusion of license plate readers in US law enforcement agencies. *Policing: An International Journal, 42*(3), 376–393.

Lum, C., Merola, L. M., Willis, J. J., & Cave, B. (2010). *License plate recognition technologies for law enforcement: An outcome and legitimacy evaluation*. Final report to SPAWAR and National Institute of Justice, Washington, DC.

MacDonald, J. (2023, March 30). Social control works: Lessons for criminal justice reformers. *Vital City*. Available at https://www.vitalcitynyc.org/articles/lessons-for-criminal-justice-reformers.

MacDonald, J., Mohler, G., & Brantingham, P. J. (2022). Association between race, shooting hot spots, and the surge in gun violence during the COVID-19 pandemic in Philadelphia, New York and Los Angeles. *Preventive Medicine, 165*, 107241.

Maciag, M. (2014, May 21). Why Camden, N.J., the murder capital of the country disbanded its police force. *Governing: The Future of States and Localities*. Available at https://www.governing.com/archive/gov-camden-disbands-police-force-for-new-department.html.

Madden, D. (2017, November 30). Camden police try to guide young people away from crime with "Project Guardian." CBS News Philadelphia. Available at https://www.cbsnews.com/philadelphia/news/project-guardian/.

Maguire, E., & Gantley, M. (2009). Specialist and generalist models. In E. Maguire & W. Wells (Eds.), *Implementing community policing: Lessons from 12 agencies* (pp. 45–55). Washington, DC: Office of Community Oriented Policing Services.

Maguire, E. R., Oakley, M. T., & Corsaro, N. (2018). *Evaluating Cure Violence in Trinidad and Tobago.* Washington DC: Inter-American Development Bank.

Manhattan Institute. (2020, October 13). *Police reformers: On the ground in Camden and Baltimore.* Available at https://www.youtube.com/watch?v=uzZXeztIFvk.

Mares, D. (2022). *Gunshot detection: Reducing gunfire through acoustic technology* (Response Guide No. 14). ASU Center for Problem-Oriented Policing. Available at https://popcenter.asu.edu/content/gunshot-detection.

Mares, D., & Blackburn, E. (2021). Acoustic gunshot detection systems: A quasi-experimental evaluation in St. Louis, MO. *Journal of Experimental Criminology, 17,* 193–215.

Mastrofski, S. D. (2006). Community policing: A skeptical view. In D. Weisburd & A. A. Braga (Eds.), *Police innovation: Contrasting perspectives* (pp. 44–73). New York: Cambridge University Press.

Matthay, E. C., Farkas, K., Rudolph, K. E., Zimmerman, S., Barragan, M., Goin, D. E., & Ahern, J. (2019). Firearm and nonfirearm violence after operation peacemaker fellowship in Richmond, California, 1996–2016. *American Journal of Public Health, 109*(11), 1605–1611.

McCarthy, C., & Stirling, S. (2018, November 29). How we built the most comprehensive statewide database of police force in the United States. NJ.com. Available at https://www.nj.com/news/2018/11/how_we_built_the_most_comprehensive_statewide_database_of_police_force_in_the_us.html.

McCoy, C. (2010). *Holding police accountable.* Washington, DC: Urban Institute Press.

McLean, K., Wolfe, S. E., Rojek, J., Alpert, G. P., & Smith, M. R. (2020). Randomized controlled trial of social interaction police training. *Criminology & Public Policy, 19*(3), 805–832.

McQuade, B. (2019). *Pacifying the homeland: Intelligence fusion and mass supervision.* Berkeley: University of California Press.

———. (2020, June 12). The Camden Police Department is not a model for policing in the post–George Floyd era. *The Appeal.* Available at https://theappeal.org/camden-police-george-floyd/.

Megerian, C. (2020, June 10). Disband the police? Camden already did that. *Los Angeles Times.* Available at https://www.latimes.com/politics/story/2020-06-10/disband-the-police-camden-already-did-that.

Mello, S. (2019). More COPS, less crime. *Journal of Public Economics, 172,* 174–200.

Meyer, M. W. (1980). Police shootings at minorities: The case of Los Angeles. *Annals of the American Academy of Political and Social Science, 452*(1), 98–110.

Milam, A. J., Furr-Holden, C. D., Leaf, P., & Webster, D. (2018). Managing conflicts in urban communities: Youth attitudes regarding gun violence. *Journal of Interpersonal Violence, 33*(24), 3815–3828.

Milgram, A. (2020, June 13). How a new kind of policing saved America's most dangerous city. CNN. Available at https://www.cnn.com/2020/06/13/opinions/police-camden-minneapolis-george-floyd-milgram/index.html.

Miller, J. (2023, March 17). Shedding light: Working streetlights mean a safer city. *TapIntoCamden.* Available at https://www.tapinto.net/towns/camden/sections/government/articles/shedding-light-working-streetlights-mean-a-safer-city.

Miltimore, J. (2020, June 17). Camden's success was achieved by de-unionizing, not defunding. *Foundation for Economic Education.* Available at https://fee.org/articles/camden-s-success-was-achieved-by-de-unionizing-not-defunding/.

Morabito, E. V., & Doerner, W. G. (1997). Police use of less-than-lethal force: Oleoresin Capsicum (OC) spray. *Policing: An International Journal of Police Strategies & Management, 20*(4), 680–697.

Morgan, K. (2020, July). The chief: It's a pivotal moment in policing—Joe Wysocki is leading by example. *SJ Magazine.* Available at https://sjmagazine.net/july-2020/camden-police-chief-joe-wysocki.

Moselle, A. (2015, August 3). Armed with respect and compassion, Camden cops making transition to "ethical protectors." *WHYY.* Available at https://whyy.org/articles/armed-with-respect-and-compassion-camden-cops-making-transition-to-ethical-protectors-photos/.

Moyer, R. A. (2022). The effect of a death-in-police-custody incident on community reliance on the police. *Journal of Quantitative Criminology, 38,* 459–482.

Mummolo, J. (2018). Modern police tactics, police-citizen interactions, and the prospects for reform. *Journal of Politics, 80*(1), 1–15.

Napoliello, A. (2021, February 16). The secret to solving murders? How detectives in this N.J. county closed almost every killing in 2020. *NJ.com.* Available at https://www.nj.com/crime/2021/02/the-secret-to-solving-murders-how-detectives-in-this-nj-county-closed-almost-every-killing-in-2020.html.

National Academies of Sciences, Engineering, and Medicine. (2018). *Proactive policing: Effects on crime and communities.* Washington, DC: National Academies Press.

National Advisory Commission on Civil Disorders. (1968). *Report of the National Advisory Commission on Civil Disorders.* Washington, DC: Government Printing Office.

National Conference of State Legislatures. (2020). *Policing legislation database.* Available at https://www.ncsl.org/civil-and-criminal-justice/policing-legislation-database.

National Consensus Policy on Use of Force. (2020). *Policy.* Available at https://www.theiacp.org/sites/default/files/2020-07/National_Consensus_Policy_On_Use_Of_Force%2007102020%20v3.pdf.

National Policing Institute. (2019). *Analysis of 2018 use of deadly force by the Phoenix Police Department.* Washington, DC: Author.

NBC 10 Philadelphia. (2011, August 3). Timoney to advise Camden co. cops. Available at https://www.nbcphiladelphia.com/news/local/timoney-camden/1908614/.

Nelson, B. (2018, November 29). Frequently asked questions about *The Force Report.* *NJ.com.* Available at https://www.nj.com/news/2018/11/frequently_asked_questions_about_the_force_report.html.

Newton, C. (2020, June 10). Is Camden NJ a model for change in US police forces? Yes and no. *Aljazeera.* Available at https://www.aljazeera.com/news/2020/6/10/is-camden-nj-a-model-for-change-in-us-police-forces-yes-and-no.

New York Post. (2010, April 3). 185 Camden cases tossed, "corrupt" police work blamed. *New York Post.* Available at https://nypost.com/2010/04/03/185-camden-cases-tossed-corrupt-police-work-blamed/.

New York Shipbuilding Corporation. (n.d.). WWII: Ships for the allies. Available at https://newyorkship.org/history/wwii-ships-for-the-allies/.

New York Times. (1992, December 22). Camden murder toll reaches a record 49. *New York Times*. Available at https://www.nytimes.com/1992/12/22/nyregion/camden-murder-toll-reaches-a-record-49.html.

NJ Attorney General. (2006). *Advisory Commission on Camden's public safety—Final Report*. Available at https://www.state.nj.us/lps/com-report-camden.pdf.

———. (2020, December). *Use of force policy*. Available at https://www.nj.gov/oag/force/docs/UOF-2020-1221-Use-of-Force-Policy.pdf.

———. (2021, April 28). 2020 first annual report to the legislature on the New Jersey Violence Intervention Program Report (January 2020–December 2020). Available at https://www.nj.gov/oag/oag/Report-to-the-Legislature-on-the-New-Jersey-Violence-Intervention-Program-Final-April-28-2021.pdf.

NJ Department of Labor. (n.d.). New Jersey census tracts with a poverty rate of 25% or greater by county. Available at https://www.nj.gov/labor/wioa/documents/resources/high_poverty_areas.pdf.

———. (2023). Personal communication with Leonard Preston who supplied 2021 ACS S1701.

NJ State Police. *Uniform Crime Reports archive*. Available at https://www.njsp.org/ucr/uniform-crime-reports.shtml.

———. (2014). Crime in New Jersey—Section 3 (State and county arrest summary, p. 73). Available at https://nj.gov/njsp/ucr/2014/pdf/2014_sect_3.pdf.

Nordheimer, J. (1995, October 29). Murder a growth industry in pool, reeling Camden. *New York Times*. Available at https://www.nytimes.com/1995/10/29/nyregion/murder-a-growth-industry-in-poor-reeling-camden.html.

NPR. (2014, September 2). How a new police force in Camden helped turn the city around. Available at https://www.npr.org/2014/09/02/345296155/how-a-new-police-force-in-camden-helped-turn-the-city-around.

Obama, B. (2015, May 18). *Remarks by the President on community policing*. The White House. Available at https://obamawhitehouse.archives.gov/the-press-office/2015/05/18/remarks-president-community-policing.

Observer. (2011, December 12). Governor deploys more state police resources to aid Camden. Available at https://observer.com/2011/12/governor-deploys-more-state-police-resources-to-aid-camden/.

Officer Down Memorial Page (n.d.). Police Officer Rand J. Chandler. Available at https://www.odmp.org/officer/2968-police-officer-rand-j-chandler.

Oftelie, A. M. (2019). *"We want guardians, not warriors": The transformation of the Camden Police Department*. Leadership for Networked World. Available at https://lnwprogram.org/sites/default/files/Guardians-Not-Warriors.pdf.

Osborne, J. (2011a, February 2). N.J. FOP hits push for county forces. *Philadelphia Inquirer*.

———. (2011b, December 9). Camden agrees to regional police force. *Philadelphia Inquirer*.

———. (2012, October 4). N.J. civil service panel's ruling boosts new Camden police force. *Philadelphia Inquirer*.

Osborne, J., & Simon, D. (2012, March 20). Officials advertise for proposed Camden County police force applicants. *Philadelphia Inquirer*. Available at https://www.inquirer.com/philly/news/politics/20120320_Officials_advertise_for_proposed_Camden_County_police_force_applicants.html.

Ozer, M. M. (2010). *Assessing the effectiveness of the Cincinnati Police Department's automatic license plate reader system within the framework of intelligence-led policing and crime prevention theory* (Doctoral dissertation, University of Cincinnati).

Paoline III, E. A., & Terrill, W. (2014). *Police culture: Adapting to the strains of the job.* Durham, NC: Carolina Academic Press.

Pearce, J. (2003, March 23). As Camden struggles, help from the courts. *New York Times.*

PERF (Police Executive Research Forum). (1996). *Themes and variations in community policing.* Washington, DC: Author.

———. (2015). *Re-engineering training on police use of force.* Washington, DC: Author. Available at https://www.policeforum.org/assets/reengineeringtraining1.pdf.

———. (2016a). *ICAT Integrating Communications, Assessment, and Tactics: A training guide for defusing critical incidents.* Washington, DC: Author. Available at https://www.policeforum.org/icat-training-guide.

———. (2016b). *Critical issues in policing: Guiding principles on use of force.* Available at https://www.policeforum.org/assets/30%20guiding%20principles.pdf.

———. (2023). *New PERF survey shows police agencies are losing officers faster than they can hire new ones.* Available at https://www.policeforum.org/staffing2023.

Peterson, I. (2000a, March 31). In Camden, another mayor is indicted on corruption charges. *New York Times.* Available at https://www.nytimes.com/2000/03/31/nyregion/in-camden-another-mayor-is-indicted-on-corruption-charges.html.

———. (2000b, July 17). Stricken Camden is to become a ward of the state. *New York Times.* Available at https://www.nytimes.com/2000/07/17/nyregion/stricken-camden-is-to-become-a-ward-of-the-state.html.

———. (2000c, December 22). Camden's mayor is guilty of 14 corruption counts. *New York Times.* Available at https://www.nytimes.com/2000/12/22/nyregion/camden-s-mayor-is-guilty-of-14-corruption-counts.html.

———. (2001, June 16). Former mayor of Camden is sentenced for corruption. *New York Times.* Available at https://www.nytimes.com/2001/06/16/nyregion/former-mayor-of-camden-is-sentenced-for-corruption.html.

Peyton, K., Sierra-Arévalo, M., & Rand, D. G. (2019). A field experiment on community policing and police legitimacy. *Proceedings of the National Academy of Sciences, 116*(40), 19894–19898.

Phelps, M. (2024). *The Minneapolis reckoning: Race, violence, and the politics of policing in America.* Princeton, NJ: Princeton University Press.

Philadelphia Inquirer. (2012, March 7). Groups against Camden County Police Department to hold community meetings. Available at https://www.inquirer.com/philly/blogs/camden_flow/141828445.html.

Philadelphia Office of the Controller. (2022). *Review and analysis of the Philadelphia Police Department and other related police spending.* Available at https://controller.phila.gov/philadelphia-audits/ppd-review/.

Pierson, E., Simoiu, C., Overgoor, J., Corbett-Davies, S., Jenson, D., Shoemaker, A., . . . & Goel, S. (2020). A large-scale analysis of racial disparities in police stops across the United States. *Nature Human Behaviour, 4*(7), 736–745.

Piza, E. L., Arietti, R. A., Carter, J. G., & Mohler, G. O. (2023). The effect of gunshot detection technology on evidence collection and case clearance in Kansas City, Missouri. *Journal of Experimental Criminology.* Advanced online publication. https://doi.org/10.1007/s11292-023-09594-6.

Piza, E. L., & Chillar, V. F. (2021). The effect of police layoffs on crime: A natural experiment involving New Jersey's two largest cities. *Justice Evaluation Journal, 4*(2), 176–196.

Policing Project. (n.d.). *Camden County Police Department use of force policy.* Available at https://www.policingproject.org/camden.

———. (2020a, January 13). *Policing Project, Camden police meet with community leaders to discuss new use of force policy.* Available at https://www.policingproject.org/news-main/2020/1/13/policing-project-camden-police-meet-with-community-leaders-to-discuss-new-use-of-force-policy.

———. (2020b, June 1). *Our statement regarding policing in the United States.* Available at https://www.policingproject.org/news-main/2020/6/1/policing-project-statement-on-policing.

Potts, J. (2018). Research in brief: Assessing the effectiveness of automatic license plate readers. *Police Chief Magazine.* Available at https://www.theiacp.org/sites/default/files/2018-08/March%202018%20RIB.pdf.

Powell, Z. A., Meitl, M. B., & Worrall, J. L. (2017). Police consent decrees and section 1983 civil rights litigation. *Criminology & Public Policy, 16*(2), 575–605.

Pratt, T. C., & Cullen, F. T. (2005). Assessing macro-level predictors and theories of crime: A meta-analysis. *Crime and Justice, 32,* 373–450.

Przeszlowski, K., Guerette, R. T., Lee-Silcox, J., Rodriguez, J., Ramirez, J., & Gutierrez, A. (2023). The centralization and rapid deployment of police agency information technologies: An appraisal of real-time crime centers in the US. *Police Journal, 96*(4), 553–572.

Queally, J. (2013, December 5). New police force brings hope to Camden as crime drops after years of bloodshed. NJ.com. Available at https://www.nj.com/news/2013/12/new_police_force_brings_hope_to_camden_as_crime_drops_after_years_of_bloodshed.html.

Rao, A. (2020, June 25). These New Jersey cities reformed their police—What happened next? *The Guardian.* Available at https://www.theguardian.com/us-news/2020/jun/25/camden-newark-new-jersey-police-reform.

Ratcliffe, J. H., & Sorg, E. T. (2017). *Foot patrol: Rethinking the cornerstone of policing.* Springer.

Ratcliffe, J. H., Taniguchi, T., Groff, E. R., & Wood, J. D. (2011). The Philadelphia foot patrol experiment: A randomized controlled trial of police patrol effectiveness in violent crime hotspots. *Criminology, 49*(3), 795–831.

Reason, J. (1990). The contribution of latent human failures to the breakdown of complex systems. *Philosophical Transactions of the Royal Society of London. B, Biological Sciences, 327*(1241), 475–484.

Renshaw, J. (2011, July 2). Outrage boils over Christie's line-item veto cuts. NJ.com. Available at https://www.nj.com/sunbeam-news/2011/07/outrage_boils_over_christies_1.html.

Ridgeway, G., & MacDonald, J. (2010). Methods for assessing racially biased policing. In S. K. Rice & M. D. White (Eds.), *Race, ethnicity, & policing: New and essential readings* (pp. 180–204). New York: New York University Press.

Roberts, D. J., & Casanova, M. (2012). *Automated license plate recognition systems: Policy and operational guidance for law enforcement* (No. 239604). Available at https://www.ojp.gov/library/publications/automated-license-plate-recognition-systems-policy-and-operational-guidance.

Roman, C. G., Klein, H. J., & Wolff, K. T. (2018). Quasi-experimental designs for community-level public health violence reduction interventions: A case study in the challenges of selecting the counterfactual. *Journal of Experimental Criminology, 14*(2), 155–185.

Romo, V. (2020, June 26). Minneapolis council moves to defund police, establish "holistic" public safety force. NPR. Available at https://www.npr.org/sections/live-updates

-protests-for-racial-justice/2020/06/26/884149659/minneapolis-council-moves-to-defund-police-establish-holistic-public-safety-forc.

Rudolf, J. (2012, November 19). Chris Christie pushes Camden police force to disband, despite questions over new plan's finances. Huffington Post. Available at https://www.huffpost.com/entry/chris-christie-camden-police_n_2025372.

Rutgers Center for Security, Race and Rights. (2023). *Shining a light on New Jersey's secret state intelligence system.* Available at https://csrr.rutgers.edu/issues/fusion-center-report/.

Sadatsafavi, H., Sachs, N. A., Shepley, M. M., Kondo, M. C., & Barankevich, R. A. (2022). Vacant lot remediation and firearm violence—A meta-analysis and benefit-to-cost evaluation. *Landscape and Urban Planning, 218,* 104281.

Sainz, A., Mustian, J., & Condon, B. (2023, February 7). Amid soaring crime, Memphis cops lowered the bar for hiring. Associated Press. Available at https://apnews.com/article/law-enforcement-tyre-nichols-memphis-crime-93033874b99a4893c6c996fd56676795?utm_source=homepage&utm_medium=TopNews&utm_campaign=position_04.

Sampson, R. J., & Bartusch, D. J. (1998). Legal cynicism and (subcultural?) tolerance of deviance: The neighborhood context of racial differences. *Law and Society Review, 32*(4), 777–804.

Sampson, R. J., & Groves, W. B. (1989). Community structure and crime: Testing social-disorganization theory. *American Journal of Sociology, 94*(4), 774–802.

Sampson, R. J., Raudenbush, S. W., & Earls, F. (1997). Neighborhoods and violent crime: A multilevel study of collective efficacy. *Science, 277*(5328), 918–924.

Sanchez, C. (2006, August 11). Widespread fraud alleged in Camden, N.J. schools. NPR. Available at https://www.npr.org/templates/story/story.php?storyId=5637480.

Saul, A. (2020, June 16). Let's not forget the complicated history behind Camden's transformed police department. *NJ Spotlight News.* Available at https://www.njspotlightnews.org/2020/06/op-ed-lets-not-forget-the-complicated-history-behind-camdens-transformed-police-department/.

Schuppe, J., Schapiro, R., & Ali, S. S. (2023, January 26). Memphis police's vaunted Scorpion unit under scrutiny after Tyre Nichols' death. NBC News. Available at https://www.nbcnews.com/news/us-news/memphis-police-scorpion-unit-tyre-nichols-rcna67711.

Sharkey, P. (2018). *Uneasy peace: The great crime decline, the renewal of city life, and the next war on violence.* New York, NY: W. W. Norton.

Sharkey, P., Torrats-Espinosa, G., & Takyar, D. (2017). Community and the crime decline: The causal effect of local nonprofits on violent crime. *American Sociological Review, 82*(6), 1214–1240.

Shaw, J. (2020, December 22). N.J. unveils new statewide police use-of-force policy that emphasizes de-escalation. *Philadelphia Inquirer.* Available at https://www.inquirer.com/news/new-jersey-attorney-general-use-of-force-policy-web-portal-20201221.html.

Shearn, I. T. (2020, August 20). State supreme court limits powers of Newark's Civilian Review Board. *NJ Spotlight News.* Available at https://www.njspotlightnews.org/2020/08/civilian-review-board-newark-subpoena-power-nj-supreme-court-police-unions/#:~:text=State%20Supreme%20Court%20Limits%20Powers%20of%20Newark's%20Civilian%20Review%20Board&text=The%20court%20ruled%20the%20board,office%20is%20conducting%20its%20own.

Shelly, K. C. (2014a, August 15). Survey: About 15% of Camden properties abandoned. *Courier-Post.* Available at https://www.courierpostonline.com/story/news/local/south-jersey/2014/08/14/survey-nearly-percent-camden-properties-abandoned/14059361/.

———. (2014b, December 12). Camden resets relationship between cops, community. *USA Today*. Available at https://www.usatoday.com/story/news/nation/2014/12/12/camden-county-community-policing/20301967/.

Sherman, L. W. (1978). *Scandal and reform: Controlling police corruption*. Berkeley: University of California Press.

———. (1980). Perspectives on police and violence. *Annals of the American Academy of Political and Social Science, 452*, 1–12.

———. (2018). Reducing fatal police shootings as system crashes: Research, theory, and practice. *Annual Review of Criminology, 1*(1), 421–449.

Shjarback, J. A. (2015). Emerging early intervention systems: An agency-specific pre-post comparison of formal citizen complaints of use of force. *Policing: A Journal of Policy and Practice, 9*(4), 314–325.

———. (2020). Early intervention systems. In R. G. Dunham, G. P. Alpert, & K. McLean (Eds.), *Critical issues in policing: Contemporary readings* (8th ed.; pp. 655–667). Long Grove, IL: Waveland.

———. (2023). Racial/ethnic diversity in positions of power in US law enforcement: An examination of active representation and disparities in vehicle stops. *Race and Justice*. Advanced online publication. https://doi.org/10.1177/21533687231174555.

Shjarback, J., Decker, S., Rojek, J. J., & Brunson, R. K. (2017a). Minority representation in policing and racial profiling: A test of representative bureaucracy vs. community context. *Policing: An International Journal, 40*(4), 748–767.

Shjarback, J. A., Pyrooz, D. C., Wolfe, S. E., & Decker, S. H. (2017b). De-policing and crime in the wake of Ferguson: Racialized changes in the quantity and quality of policing among Missouri police departments. *Journal of Criminal Justice, 50*, 42–52.

Shjarback, J. A., & Sarkos, J. A. (2025). An evaluation of a major expansion in automated license plate reader (ALPR) technology. *Justice Evaluation Journal*. Advanced online publication. https://doi.org/10.1080/24751979.2025.2473363.

Shjarback, J. A., & Ward, J. A. (2025). Moving targets: An examination of departmental deadly force policies and police shootings at vehicles. Policing: A Journal of Policy and Practice. Advanced online publication. https://doi.org/10.1093/police/paaf004.

Shjarback, J. A., White, M. D., & Bishopp, S. A. (2021). Can police shootings be reduced by requiring officers to document when they point firearms at citizens? *Injury Prevention, 27*(6), 508–513.

Sierra-Arévalo, M. (2024). *The danger imperative: Violence, death, and the soul of policing*. New York: Columbia University Press.

Simon, D. (2011a, May 24). Document details forming Camden County-wide police force, ending Camden City's. *Philadelphia Inquirer*. Available at https://www.inquirer.com/philly/news/local/20110524_Document_details_forming_Camden_County-wide_police_force__ending_Camden_City_s.html.

———. (2011b, October 6). Camden County releases consultant's plan for county police force. *Philadelphia Inquirer*. Available at https://www.inquirer.com/philly/news/local/20111006_Camden_County_releases_consultant_s_plan_for_county_police_force.html.

———. (2012a, June 20). Jose Cordero may be brought back for new Camden County police force. *Philadelphia Inquirer*. Available at https://www.inquirer.com/philly/news/local/20120620_Jose_Cordero_may_be_brought_back_for_new_Camden_County_police_force.html.

———. (2012b, October 16). New police force is one step closer. *Philadelphia Inquirer*.

———. (2013, January 18). Freeholders OK terms for Camden County police force grant. *Philadelphia Inquirer.* Available at https://www.inquirer.com/philly/news/new_jersey/20130117_Freeholders_OK_terms_for_Camden_County_police_force_grant.html.

Simon, D., & Vargas, C. (2012, August 31). Financial details outlined for Camden regional police force. *Philadelphia Inquirer.* Available at https://www.inquirer.com/philly/news/new_jersey/20120831_Financial_details_outlined_for_Camden_regional_police_force.html.

Simon, S. J. (2023). Training for war: Academy socialization and warrior policing. *Social Problems, 70*(4), 1021–1043.

6ABC. (2017, June 2). Demolitions begin to rid Camden of vacant eyesores. Available at https://6abc.com/new-jersey-news-camden-demolition-of-vacant-and-abandoned-buildings/2062919/.

Skogan, W. G. (2022). *Stop & frisk and the politics of crime in Chicago.* New York: Oxford University Press.

Skogan, W. G., Hartnett, S. M., Bump, N., & Dubois, J. (2008). *Evaluation of CeaseFire-Chicago.* Evanston, IL: Institute for Policy Research, Northwestern University.

Skoufalos, M. (2022, January 18). Stories invincible: Food insecurity in Camden city, Part I. *NJ Pen.* Available at https://www.njpen.com/stories-invincible-food-insecurity-in-camden-city-part-i/.

Smothers, R. (1999, July 20). Camden seeks bankruptcy protection, angering state officials. *New York Times.* Available at https://www.nytimes.com/1999/07/20/nyregion/camden-seeks-bankruptcy-protection-angering-state-officials.html.

Solomon, N. (2023, March 7). Companies that got huge tax breaks in NJ's poorest city barely employ its residents. *Gothamist.* Available at https://gothamist.com/news/companies-that-got-huge-tax-breaks-in-njs-poorest-city-employ-barely-its-residents.

Solomon, N., & Pillets, J. (2019, May 1). How companies and allies of one powerful democrat got $1.1 billion in tax breaks. *ProPublica.* Available at https://www.propublica.org/article/george-norcross-democratic-donor-tax-breaks.

SoundThinking. (2023). *ShotSpotter FAQs.* Accessed June 30, 2023. Available at https://www.soundthinking.com/law-enforcement/gunshot-detection-technology/.

Stafford, M. C., & Warr, M. (1993). A reconceptualization of general and specific deterrence. *Journal of Research in Crime and Delinquency, 30*(2), 123–135.

Star-Ledger, The. (2011, January 30). Camden needs rescue from regional police. NJ.com. Available at https://www.nj.com/njv_editorial_page/2011/01/post_26.html.

State of New Jersey. (2021, June 25). *Revising ABLE and ICAT training requirements for 2021.* Available at https://www.nj.gov/oag/dcj/agguide/directives/ag-directive-2021-7_Revising-Law-Enforcement-Training-Requirements-for-2021.pdf.

———. (2022, July 21). *Governor Murphy signs police licensing program bill into law.* Available at https://www.nj.gov/governor/news/news/562022/20220721b.shtml.

Steele, A. (2016, June 14). After 11 months in jail, Camden man released after cop's cases tossed. *Philadelphia Inquirer.* Available at https://www.inquirer.com/philly/news/new_jersey/20160614_After_11_months_in_jail__Camden_man_released_after_cop_s_cases_tossed.html.

Stoughton, S. W., Noble, J. J., & Alpert, G. P. (2020, June 3). How to actually fix America's police. *The Atlantic.* Available at https://www.theatlantic.com/ideas/archive/2020/06/how-actually-fix-americas-police/612520/.

Swan, T. A., Harris, G. L., Clayton, S. T., & Tuthill, L. (2020). *Camden County Police Department: Crime analysis, technical assistance, and consultation.* Washington, DC: Office of Community Oriented Policing Services.

Tawa, S. (2013, January 4). Camden City Council rubberstamps layoff of city's entire police department. CBS News. Available at https://www.cbsnews.com/philadelphia/news/camden-city-council-rubberstamps-layoff-of-citys-entire-police-department/.

Taylor, B., Koper, C., & Woods, D. (2012). Combating vehicle theft in Arizona: A randomized experiment with license plate recognition technology. *Criminal Justice Review, 37*(1), 24–50.

Terrill, W., & Paoline III, E. A. (2017). Police use of less lethal force: Does administrative policy matter? *Justice Quarterly, 34*(2), 193–216.

Thomas, K. J., Collins, P. A., & Lovrich, N. P. (2010). Conducted energy device use in municipal policing: Results of a national survey on policy and effectiveness assessments. *Police Quarterly, 13*(3), 290–315.

Thomson, J. S. (2020, June 18). As Camden's police chief, I scrapped the force and started over—It worked. *Washington Post.* Available at https://www.washingtonpost.com/outlook/camden-police-chief-old-new-department/2020/06/18/37407536-b0b8-11ea-856d-5054296735e5_story.html.

Tomlinson, C. (1972). A study of the proposed Waterfront Industrial Highway, Camden, New Jersey. Drexel University master's thesis.

Trischitta, L. (2017, May 8). Wilton Manors officer fired and under criminal investigation, agency says. *South Florida Sun-Sentinel.* Available at https://www.sun-sentinel.com/local/broward/wilton-manors/fl-sb-wilton-manors-officer-fired-20170508-story.html.

United Shades of America. (2016, May 15). Protect and Serve—episode transcript. Available at https://web.archive.org/web/20170710030741/http://www.cnn.com/TRANSCRIPTS/1605/15/se.01.html.

U.S. Crisis Monitor. (2020). *Demonstrations and political violence in America: New data for summer 2020.* Available at https://acleddata.com/2020/09/03/demonstrations-political-violence-in-america-new-data-for-summer-2020/.

Vannozzi, B. (2021, July 6). Camden to demolish abandoned homes to improve quality of life for residents. *NJ Spotlight News.* Available at https://www.njspotlightnews.org/video/camden-to-demolish-abandoned-homes-to-improve-quality-of-life-for-residents/.

Vargas, C. (2011, August 3). Camden City Council views memo on regional police force. *Philadelphia Inquirer.* Available at https://www.inquirer.com/philly/news/new_jersey/20110803_Camden_City_Council_views_memo_on_regional_police_force.html.

Vargas, C., & Simon, D. (2013, April 21). Promotions, raises mark launch of new Camden police force. *Philadelphia Inquirer.* Available at https://www.inquirer.com/philly/news/new_jersey/20130421_Promotions__raises_mark_launch_of_new_Camden_police_force.html.

Verniero, P. G. (1998, November 12). Letter from the Attorney General to Lee A. Solomon, Camden County Prosecutor.

Vice. (2014, June 13). *Surveillance City* (Season 2, Episode 12). Available at https://www.youtube.com/watch?v=fVDvJCeCe54.

VirTra. (N.D.). *V-300® firearms training simulator.* Available at https://virtraultra.wpenginepowered.com/wp-content/uploads/V-300-LE.pdf.

Vogt, E. (2020, June 10). NJ cop—31 and on his 9th job—charged with unprovoked attack. *New Jersey 101.5.* Available at https://nj1015.com/nj-cop-31-and-on-his-9th-job-charged-in-unprovoked-attack/.

Walker, S. (1977). *A critical history of police reform: The emergence of professionalism.* Lexington, MA: D.C. Heath.

———. (1993). *Taming the system: The control of discretion in criminal justice, 1950–1990.* New York: Oxford University Press.

———. (2005). *The new world of police accountability*. Thousand Oaks, CA: Sage.

———. (2014). *What a good police department looks like: Professional, accountable, transparent, self-monitoring*. Available at https://www.smart-policing.com/resources/what-good-police-department-looks.

Walsh, E. (2007, March 5). Miami blue: The testing of a top cop. *New Yorker*. Available at https://www.newyorker.com/magazine/2007/03/05/miami-blue.

Walsh, J. (2018, June 26). Camden County OKs almost $200k for cop suits. *The Courier-Post*. Available at https://www.courierpostonline.com/story/news/local/south-jersey/2018/06/26/camden-county-police-douglas-dickinson-lawsuit/733461002/.

———. (2021, January 14). A positive for de-escalation. *The Courier-Post*.

Webster, D. W., Mendel Whitehill, J., Vernick, J. S., & Curriero, F. C. (2013). Effects of Baltimore's safe streets program on gun violence: A replication of Chicago's CeaseFire program. *Journal of Urban Health, 90*(1), 27–40.

Weisburd, D., Telep, C. W., Vovak, H., Zastrow, T., Braga, A. A., & Turchan, B. (2022). Reforming the police through procedural justice training: A multicity randomized trial at crime hot spots. *Proceedings of the National Academy of Sciences, 119*(14), e2118780119.

Welsh, B. C., Farrington, D. P., & Douglas, S. (2022). The impact and policy relevance of street lighting for crime prevention: A systematic review based on a half-century of evaluation research. *Criminology & Public Policy, 21*(3), 739–765.

Wheeler, A. P. (2020). Allocating police resources while limiting racial inequality. *Justice Quarterly, 37*(5), 842–868.

Wheeler, A. P., & Phillips, S. W. (2018). A quasi-experimental evaluation using roadblocks and automatic license plate readers to reduce crime in Buffalo, NY. *Security Journal, 31*(1), 190–207.

White, M. D. (2000). Assessing the impact of administrative policy on use of deadly force by on-and off-duty police. *Evaluation Review, 24*(3), 295–318.

———. (2001). Controlling police decisions to use deadly force: Reexamining the importance of administrative policy. *Crime & Delinquency, 47*(1), 131–151.

White, M. D., Mora, V. J., Orosco, C., & Hedberg, E. C. (2021a). Moving the needle: Can training alter officer perceptions and use of de-escalation? *Policing: An International Journal, 44*(3), 418–436.

White, M. D., Orosco, C., Pooley, M., & Sorensen, D. (2021b). *Testing the impact of de-escalation training on officer behavior: The Tempe (AZ) Smart Policing Initiative* (final report). Arizona State University's Center for Violence Prevention and Community Safety. Available at https://www.smart-policing.com/sites/default/files/inline-files/Tempe%20SPI%20Final%20Report%2012-21.pdf.

White, M. D., Orosco, C., & Watts, S. (2023a). Beyond force and injuries: Examining alternative (and important) outcomes for police de-escalation training. *Journal of Criminal Justice, 89*, 102129.

———. (2023b). Can police de-escalation training reduce use of force and citizen injury without compromising officer safety? *Journal of Experimental Criminology*, 1–26.

Wiig, A. (2018). Secure the city, revitalize the zone: Smart urbanization in Camden, New Jersey. *Environment and Planning C: Politics and Space, 36*(3), 403–422.

Willis, J. J., Koper, C., & Lum, C. (2018). The adaptation of license-plate readers for investigative purposes: Police technology and innovation re-invention. *Justice Quarterly, 35*(4), 614–638.

Wilson, J. Q. (1968). *Varieties of police behavior: The management of law and order in eight communities*. Cambridge, MA: Harvard University Press.

Wilson, J. Q., & Kelling, G. L. (1982). Broken windows: The police and neighborhood safety. *Atlantic Monthly, 249*(3), 29–38.

Wilson, W. J. (1987). *The truly disadvantaged: The inner city, the underclass, and public policy*. Chicago: University of Chicago Press.

———. (1997). *When work disappears: The world of the new urban poor*. New York: Vintage Books.

Wolfe, S. E., & Lawson, S. G. (2020). The organizational justice effect among criminal justice employees: A meta-analysis. *Criminology, 58*(4), 619–644.

Wolfe, S., McLean, K., Rojek, J., Alpert, G. P., & Smith, M. R. (2022). Advancing a theory of police officer training motivation and receptivity. *Justice Quarterly, 39*(1), 201–233.

Wolfe, S., Rojek, J., McLean, K., & Alpert, G. (2020). Social interaction training to reduce police use of force. *ANNALS of the American Academy of Political and Social Science, 687*(1), 124–145.

Wood, G., Tyler, T. R., & Papachristos, A. V. (2020). Procedural justice training reduces police use of force and complaints against officers. *Proceedings of the National Academy of Sciences, 117*(18), 9815–9821.

Wood, S., & Boren, M. (2015, October 21). Losing recruits, Camden County police billing towns that hired them. *Philadelphia Inquirer*. Available at https://www.inquirer.com/philly/news/20151022_Losing_recruits__Camden_police_bill_towns_that_hired_them.html.

YouTube. (2015a, May 18). *Obama in Camden, NJ—Full speech*. Available at https://www.youtube.com/watch?v=-3RqEZvAgXM.

———. (2015b, November 24). *Broadway & Mickle man with a knife incident*. Available at https://web.archive.org/web/20170405001745/https://www.youtube.com/watch?v=YtVUMT9P8iw.

———. (2016, January 19). Meet the unsung heroes of Camden, NJ tackling gun violence head-on. Available at https://www.youtube.com/watch?v=JgVJuPNrTa0.

———. (2019, January 23). *ShotSpotter and healthcare*. Available at https://www.youtube.com/watch?v=2IRJcFPhhKg.

———. (2020a, August 28). Camden's turn: A story of police reform in progress. Available at https://www.youtube.com/watch?v=arzTB4ji_Ig&t=1703s.

———. (2020b, December 17). *CCPD taser deployment 9-14-20*. Available at https://youtu.be/l6Q--LBETl0.

———. (2021, February 6). *Police reform in NJ: How more than 200 cameras changed policing and left residents wary*. Available at https://www.youtube.com/watch?v=jnY63HkLZD4.

Zaremba, J. (2015, March 21). $67K raise for Camden police chief is "obscene," NAACP says. NJ.com. Available at https://www.nj.com/camden/2015/03/67k_raise_for_camden_police_chief_is_obscene_naacp.html.

Zernike, K. (2012, September 29). To fight crime, Camden will trade in its police. *New York Times*. Available at https://www.nytimes.com/2012/09/29/nyregion/overrun-by-crime-camden-trades-in-its-police-force.html.

———. (2014, August 31). Camden turns around with new police force. *New York Times*. Available at https://www.nytimes.com/2014/09/01/nyregion/camden-turns-around-with-new-police-force.html.

Zucker, N. (2021, June 16). Camden begins demolition of 300 derelict buildings. TapIntoCamden. Available at https://www.tapinto.net/towns/camden/sections/government/articles/camden-begins-demolition-of-300-derelict-buildings.

Zun, L. S., Downey, L., & Rosen, J. (2006). The effectiveness of an ED-based violence prevention program. *American Journal of Emergency Medicine, 24*(1), 8–13.

Index

Absenteeism, 50, 60
Abt, Thomas, 125
Acoustic gunshot detection system (AGDS), 9, 55–58, 63, 69–72, 77
"Active Bystandership for Law Enforcement" (ABLE), 113, 118
Administrative policies: use of force, 4, 8–10, 83–85, 104, 112–113, 115, 119, 134
Advance Peace model, 122
Adventure Aquarium, 21
American Civil Liberties Union of New Jersey (ACLU-NJ): press releases, 5–6, 87; use of force policy, 9, 48, 90–91, 134; excessive tickets/citations, 75–76, 78, 94, 101, 104
American Water, 129
Appel, Sam, 17
Automated license plate readers (ALPR), 55–56, 58–59, 68

Bankruptcy, 3, 7, 10, 20, 132
Bell, W. Kamau, 102
Bethea, Quinzelle, 116
Black Lives Matter, 2
Black People's Unity Movement, 17
Body-worn cameras, 92–93, 103, 113–115
Bratton, William, 36
Brooks, Jean, 22

Brown, Michael, 1
Bucci, Rebecca, 99, 126

Camden after the Fall: Decline and Renewal in a Post-Industrial City, 13–15, 17–20, 22, 128–129
Camden Churches Organized for People, 23
Camden Commission on Public Safety, 27, 136
Camden County Crime Coalition, 66–67
Camden Forge, 14
Camden Teacher's Association, 8
Campbell Soup Company, 13–15
Cappelli, Louis, 35, 38, 40, 117
Carstarphen, Vic, 123
Center for Family Services, 121–122
Center for Policing Equity, 124
Chalfin, Aaron, 50, 99–100
Chandler, Rand, 17
Chauvin, Derek, 1–2
Cherry Hill, 15–16, 19, 66
Christie, Chris, 6, 33–38, 40, 42, 128
Citizens' Community Committee for Public Safety, 37, 40
Civilianization, 50, 52, 59, 72, 99, 133
Civilian oversight, 112, 114, 119
Civil Service Commission, 29, 41–42, 109–110, 119

Civil unrest (Camden), 15, 17–18
Clearance/solve rates, 7, 55, 59, 66–68
Colello, John, 66
Coleman, Brian, 40–42, 133
Collective bargaining, 47
Collective efficacy, 126
Colligan, Patrick, 6
Collingswood, 15–16
Community-based crime solutions, 3, 11, 120–125, 136
Community benefit agreements, 129
Community policing, 4–5, 37, 51, 53–54, 69, 77, 79, 133
Concerned Black Clergy, 23, 46
Concerned Citizens of North Camden, 22
Conner Strong & Buckelew, 129
Cooper University Hospital, 122–123, 127
Cordero, Jose, 40–41
Corruption: mayors indicted, 22, 25; public school system, 22–23; police department, 31–33, 98
Corzine, John, 33
Courier Post, 35, 37
COVID-19 pandemic, 63, 122, 126
Criminal opportunity, 123, 126
Crisis Intervention Team (CIT), 80, 118
Cure4Camden, 121–124
Cure Violence model, 121–122

Data-Informed Community Engagement (DICE), 125, 130
Deaver, Yolanda, 2
De-escalation training: broad, 4, 9–10, 48, 80, 88–94, 113, 118; "Ethical Protector" course, 79, 93, 104; Polis Solutions' T3, 81–82; Tempe, AZ, 81–82
Defund the police movement, 3, 6, 97
Demolishing abandoned/vacant buildings, 123–124
Dickinson, Douglass, 116
Directed patrol, 51, 98–99
Distressed City Act, 33
Dubiel, Ryan, 116–117

Early intervention systems, 112–114
Eastern Metal Recycling, 129
Economic Opportunity Act, 128
Economic revitalization, 11, 21, 120, 127–129, 136
Electronic Frontier Foundation, 55
Errichetti, Angelo, 18, 22

"Ethical Policing Is Courageous" (EPIC), 113
Excessive force complaints, 6–7, 10, 60, 66, 77–78, 87, 91, 104, 106

Farrell, Graham, 126
Faulk, Warren, 32, 40
Federal consent decrees, 27, 114, 118, 132
Financial Review Board, 20
Floyd, George, 1–3, 6–7, 11, 26, 63, 79, 94, 112, 116, 131
Food desert/insecurity, 54
Foot patrol, 52, 59, 61, 65, 72, 78, 98
Force Report, The, 76
Forman, James, Jr., 19
Francis, Colandus, 40, 108
Fraternal Order of Police, 9, 37, 39, 40, 42–43, 47, 90, 111
Freedom Mortgage Pavilion, 21
Friedman, Barry, 87
Fyfe, James, 9, 83–84

Galindez, Luis, 22
Gallup: polling for confidence in policing, 3
Gang takedowns, 65–66
Garner, Eric, 1
Gillette, Howard, 13–15, 17–20, 22, 124, 128–129
Gonzalez, Edward, 68
Governing, 49–50
Graham v. Connor, 87, 93
Grayson, Sean, 116
Grewal, Gurbir, 91, 117
Guardian zones, 51, 56

Hardwick, Darnell, 108
Hargis, Edward, 28–29
Harvey, Peter, 27
Hill, William, 27
Hoban, Jack, 79
Holtec International, 129
Hospital-based violence intervention programs, 122, 124
Hot spots, 51–52, 56, 59, 72, 98–99, 125
Huffington Post, 41–42
Hunsinger, John, 68

Integrating Communications, Assessment, and Tactics (ICAT), 79–82, 94–95, 104, 113, 118–119
Internal Affairs, 6, 32, 94, 96, 102, 113, 117, 134

Internal control mechanisms, 56, 59, 98, 103, 106, 108, 112–114, 133

Jacobs, Jane, 54, 100

Kelling, George, 27
King, Rodney, 1
Kueng, J. Alexander, 1

Lane, Thomas, 1
Lang, Michael, 22
Layoffs, 6, 33, 35, 39, 42
Legal cynicism, 126
Lockheed Martin, 129
Locking Up Our Own: Crime and Punishment in Black America, 19
Loehmann, Timothy, 115
Lutz, Kevin, 79, 82, 92–94
Lynch, Michael, 45–46

Madi, Ojii BaBa, 46
Mallach, Alan, 123
Mares, Dennis, 56–57
Massey, Sonya, 116
McCoy, Candace, 9
McGreevey, Jim, 23
Melleby, Harold, 17
Milan, Milton, 22
Milgram, Anne, 28–31, 33, 40, 47–49, 98
Minneapolis City Council, 3, 6, 131
Moran, Frank, 37, 40
Multijurisdictional task forces, 61, 65
Municipal Rehabilitation and Economic Revitalization Act, 23
Murphy, Patrick, 83

National Association for the Advancement of Colored People, 8, 38, 40, 42, 108, 134
National Decertification Index, 112, 114
National Policing Institute, 84, 105
Neighborhood Response Teams (NRT), 51–52, 59, 99, 133
Newark Public Safety Collaborative, 124
Newark Star-Ledger, 35
New Jersey Attorney General, 26–29, 31, 33, 37, 40, 44, 48–49, 85–87, 90–91, 98, 117, 122, 132, 134–135
New Jersey State Police Benevolent Association, 6, 40
New Jersey Superior Court, 39, 40
New Jersey Supreme Court, 40, 43, 134

New York Ship Company, 13–15
NFI LP, 129
NJ.com/NJ Advance Media, 6, 76
Nonprofit organizations, 8, 121, 124
Norcross III, George, 40, 127–128

Obama, Barack, 4–7, 55, 75, 105, 107, 131
"Officer-created jeopardy/danger," 93
Officer turnover, 6, 10, 107–109, 112, 119, 136
O'Flaherty, Brendan, 42, 133
"Old Camden," 14–15
Open-air drug markets, 5, 10, 25, 48, 60, 65, 74, 77, 99–100, 102
Open Public Records Act, 9, 72, 76–77, 109
Organizational justice, 82

Pacheco, Carlos, 116
Peace Officer Standards and Training, 118
Pedestrian stops, 72–75, 77, 83, 95, 100–101, 104, 114, 133
Pennsauken, 15–16
Pennsylvania Heart and Lung Act, 110–111
Philadelphia Inquirer, 6, 35, 37, 41, 107–111
Philadelphia 76ers, 129
Pierce, Al, 17
Point and report policies, 85
Police Executive Research Forum, 9, 79–81, 90, 94–95, 113, 118–119
Police licensing, 114, 116–117, 119
Policing Project at New York University School of Law: front versus back-end accountability, 9–10, 107, 112–115, 117, 119; use of force policy, 48, 87–90, 95, 104, 134
Primas, Melvin, 19–20, 23, 27
Problem-oriented policing, 52, 125, 133
Procedural justice, 113, 118, 126
Project Guardian, 54
Proximal causes, 125, 130
Public Safety Collaborative, 124
Punishment avoidance, 99, 101

Ramsey, Charles, 52, 111
Ratcliffe, Jerry, 126
RCA Victor, 13–15
Real-Time Crime Center (RTCC), 54–55
Real-Time Tactical Operations and Information Center (RT-TOIC), 37, 54–55, 103, 133
Redd, Dana, 33, 35, 37, 39–40, 123, 132

Remediating vacant lots/greening, 124
Replacing and upgrading street lighting, 124
Repsher, William, 17
Resolution Group International, 79
Response times, 6, 10, 48, 57, 60–61, 77–78, 98
Rice, Tamir, 115
Rodriguez, Gabe, 123
Root causes, 53, 125–127, 129–130

Sarubbi, Vincent, 27
Shalom, Alexander, 91, 94
Sharkey, Patrick, 121, 125
Sherman, Lawrence, 9
Skogan, Wesley, 100–101
SoundThinking/ShotSpotter, 57, 63, 69–70, 77
Staffing, 28, 32–33, 36, 46, 48–50, 59–61, 66, 72, 107, 110–112, 133, 135
Stanford Open Policing Project, 72, 94–95
State financial aid, 10, 20, 22–25, 31, 33, 35, 45, 129, 132
State takeover, 12, 20, 23–26, 31, 132
Street-code values, 126
Subaru, 127, 129
Supercession, 27–29, 40, 132
Surveillance, 8, 37, 55, 68, 100

Tax incentives, 19, 23, 128–129
Taylor, Breonna, 1
Temporary Operating Procedure 237, 83
Tennessee v. Garner, 87
Thao, Tou, 1

Thomson, J. Scott, 4, 28–32, 41–42, 46–49, 52, 54, 61, 66, 79, 82, 92, 94, 97–98, 102–105, 111, 116, 119, 127
Thorton, Ralph, 92
Tickets/citations, 75–78, 94–96, 100–101, 104, 133
Timoney, John, 36–37, 39, 45
Traffic Unit, 28–29, 31, 103
Trash incinerator, 20
Turnover, 66, 107–110, 119

Union: contract, 7; resistance, 28, 30–31, 47, 98, 103–104, 132, 134; new leadership, 47–48, 103–104, 134
Use of force: general, 76–78, 83–91, 104; "Broadway and Mickle," 92–93, 104; September 2020 incident, 93–94, 104
USS New Jersey, 21

Vehicle stops, 72–73, 77–78, 100, 114, 133
Violence interrupters, 121
VirTra V-300® simulator, 91–92, 104, 134
Virtual patrols, 37, 55–56, 133
Voter referendum, 37, 40, 43, 134

Walker, Samuel, 9, 84, 105
Walter Rand Institute, 61, 65, 77
Wandering officers, 115–117
Webster, Arnold, 22
Wheeler, Andrew, 100
White flight, 10, 17–18
Whitman, Walt, 12–13
Woodlynne, 3, 43, 116–117
Wysocki, Joseph, 2, 54, 123, 131

John Shjarback is Associate Professor in the Department of Law and Justice Studies at Rowan University.

www.ingramcontent.com/pod-product-compliance
Lightning Source LLC
Chambersburg PA
CBHW020948230426
43666CB00005B/231